The Strange Death of
Heinrich Himmler

The Strange Death of
Heinrich Himmler

A Forensic Investigation

Hugh Thomas

St. Martin's Press ♏ New York

www.stmartins.com

Picture Acknowledgements: *After the Battle* magazine; AKG London; Archiv, Mönchengladbach; Bundesarchiv, Koblenz; Hoover Institution Archives, Stanford University; Hugo Jaeger/TimePix/Katz Pictures; Hulton Getty; *Illustrated London News*; Imperial War Museum; Mirror Syndication International; Pathé News; Press Association; private collection.

ISBN 0-312-28923-5

First published in Great Britain by Fourth Estate, A Division of HarperCollins*Publishers*, under the title *SS-1: The Unlikely Death of Heinrich Himmler*

First U.S. Edition: March 2002

10 9 8 7 6 5 4 3 2 1

Contents

Acknowledgements

This book took over a quarter of a century to research. As a result the deceased now outnumber the living witnesses. My especial thanks to the only medical witness to the suicide, Captain Clement Wells, and his family, particularly Mrs Judy Crawford, for their generosity in affording me this key evidence in difficult circumstances. I am grateful to the consultant forensic surgeon who conducted the second post-mortem, Dr Ian Morris, and his wife Ann.

My thanks are also due to Colonel Browne for his expect guidance and testimony, including documents relating to the first post-mortem. I am grateful to Professor Keith Simpson, Professor Keith Mant, and Sir John Boyd for their forensic opinions; Professor Sognnaes for his unrivalled odontological forensic knowledge, and Frau Kathé Heusermann for her invaluable contribution. Colonel John McCowan revealed details of Himmler's dental records, and Corporal D.W. Williams, mortuary attendant at Hannover military hospital, recalled the second post-mortem in pithy detail. Major Norman Rimmer allowed me to tape his memories of the suicide, and I must also thank his fellow officer Colonel M.A.C. Osborne.

In the wider intelligence world, I owe thanks to Dr Carl Marcus for allowing Adrian Liddell Hart, British intelligence chief, and myself to take up so much of his time, and of course Adrian, who used his influence to open up several channels for me. Thanks also to James Angleton for his opinions about the significance of papers released by Swedish intelligence to the embryonic CIA after the war. French intelligence chief Pierre Villemarest, Sir William Stephenson, Sir Dick White, Sir Maurice Oldfield, Kenneth de Courcy, Dorothy Furse and Sir Stuart Hampshire all freely gave of their time.

Many thanks to my friend Peter Falk for his confidences, which in conjunction with information from Sir Peter Tennant, proved essential to the understanding of the dramatic events in Stockholm in May 1945. Peter's son Andrew Falk was also terribly helpful. Captain Henry Denham, Marcus Wallenberg, Baron Rolf von Otter, Sophie Unnie and the Bernadotte family also contributed information about this critical period.

I am grateful to Heinz Macher and Werner Grothmann, Himmler's adjutants, Albert Speer, Captain Peter Cremer, and Alan Nightingale for their testimony about the last days of the war, and to Alan Spence, formerly of the *Financial Times*, for his part in interviewing the family of Himmler's special representative, Karl-Heinz Krämer, about his activities during this period.

Anthony Marreco, Lord Elwyn Jones and Ralph Boursot provided a fascinating insight into events at Nuremberg. Professor Werner T. Angress of Stony Brook University, New York, generously provided a copy and translation of Himmler's diaries. Historian Heinrich Fraenkel and author Andrew Boyle offered useful comments, and Dr Scott Newton, Dean of History at Cardiff University, gave invaluable assistance and support.

I am also grateful to Mrs Attkins, wife of Major George, one of the dentists at the first post-mortem examination; Madame Baldet, who provided details of the Hotel Maison Rouge; Dr Richard Bogle for his advice on toxicology; Helmut C. H. Pless, editor of the *Lüneburger Heide* newspaper; Jeff Lindhurst, curator of Warnham War Museum, and Winston G. Ramsay, editor of the meticulously researched magazine, *After the Battle*, for his assistance with photographs.

In the course of my researches I interviewed a number of active intelligence officers, and even some who have retired, who understandably prefer to remain anonymous. The same is true of a few archivists. Thanks to all for their testimony and for obtaining crucial documentation through official and unofficial channels.

Lastly my thanks to Clive Priddle for his support and to Catherine Blyth for her expert and untiring editing, and to both for their sense of humour.

List of Illustrations

Preface

Reichsführer SS Heinrich Himmler's suicide by cyanide poisoning while in British custody on 23 May 1945 has never before been subject to scrutiny. As shocked Allied troops discovered the countless victims of Himmler's regime, none dissented from the unquestioning jubilation that met the demise of the architect of the Holocaust.

On 24 May 1945 the story of Himmler's death was broadcast to the world. Australian War Correspondent Chester Wilmot interviewed British Army Colour Sergeant-Major Edwin Austin, fresh from the scene of the suicide of Lüneburg. Austin was a confident, down-to-earth interviewee who said exactly what a bluff NCO might have been expected to say. He was apparently guileless:

> Before he arrived I didn't know it was Himmler; I was only told there was an important person whom I was to guard. As he came into the room – not the arrogant figure which we all knew, but dressed in an Army shirt, a pair of underpants, with a blanket wrapped around him – I immediately recognised him as Himmler. Speaking to him in German and pointing to an empty couch, I said, 'That's your bed. Get undressed.' He looked at me, then looked at an interpreter and said, 'He doesn't know who I am.' I said, 'Yes I do; you're Himmler, but that's still your bed. Get undressed.' He tried to stare me out, but I stared at him back, and eventually he dropped his eyes and sat down on the bed.

Austin relished his bit-part in history. His robust account was to become the official version of events. It has been repeated by historians ever since, in spite of the hundred-year ban imposed by the

xii THE STRANGE DEATH OF HEINRICH HIMMLER

British on documentation relating to the suicide, which one might have expected to inspire greater curiosity. Austin's version of events has remained unchallenged until now.

In order to understand events surrounding the death of the prisoner identified as Himmler it has been essential to obtain first-hand information from men who were there at the time. Other witnesses far more credible than Austin were present at the suicide. I was fortunate enough to start my investigation at a time when key people, including doctors and dentists, were still alive and able to pass me their recorded data. I discovered that Himmler was not just discreetly interred: in fact the British ordered a post-mortem. Then months after the body was buried on Lüneberg Heath, it was exhumed and a second post-mortem examination was conducted. Even after this second scrutiny, British inquiries into Himmler's death continued. None of this has been reported before.

It became evident that interest in Himmler's death was not just related to concerns about the suicide's identity. Surprisingly, Kim Philby had set up a costly secret operation 'to lay to rest the ghost of a live Himmler'. Other intelligence personnel and financiers revealed unsuspected intrigues and secret agreements, some seeming to suggest Himmler's post-war influence. Through investigation, the circumstances and the exact scientific facts about the death are now known. At long last we can savour the uncertainty that plagued Philby in 1946.

Critical documents relating to negotiations with Himmler in Stockholm at the end of the war have already vanished from the British Public Record Office. When the ban is eventually lifted, the file on Himmler's suicide is likely to be as empty as the grave on Lüneburg Heath. This book is for those who do not want to wait until 2045.

I

Reincarnation and Exorcism

'This whole case is regarded by the Allied Counterintelligence officers, and in particular by the British, as being the most important single case in the history of counterespionage.'

Unidentified officer, FBI files

In January 1946, in the fierce grip of winter, the defeated Reich had become a 143,200-square-mile frozen madhouse. At the height of the Nazis' power their empire stretched from the Atlantic coast of France to the outskirts of Moscow. Now Germany was half the size of France, with eight million refugees pouring in from the east to share the woes of 48 million citizens who were already confused, embittered and starving.

A proud empire lay dramatically humbled. Remnants of bridges were awash on her river banks. The stately Autobahns were pulverised by the treads of invading tanks. What little traffic there was picked its way laboriously along the smashed up roads, frequently stopping to let Allied convoys pass. Germany's great cities reeked of sewage. Workmen toiled in tattered clothes while women formed endless chains to pass them bricks, working all day and through the icy night. As they struggled to restore some kind of order their children collapsed at school from malnutrition and cold.

At the centre of this devastation was Nuremberg: the scene of Hitler's greatest triumphal rallies transformed into a grim stage for international retribution. The Albrecht Dürer Haus stood in glorious isolation amid the ruins. The bombed-out red shell, miraculously propped up by its central beam, presented a surreal landscape. As distinguished writer Rebecca West observed, Nuremberg in 1946 looked more like a woodcut by Dalí than by Dürer. SS prisoners of war rebuilt the nearby Justizpalast at frantic speed. They continued to work throughout the marathon proceedings of the International Military Tribunal, which sat from November 1945 until mid-1948, looking for all the world like plaster-covered, maudlin clowns, wordless witnesses to their former leaders' fates.

The Justizpalast had been adapted by the Nazis to achieve a level of efficiency that makes Henry Ford look prodigal. It housed twenty courtrooms; a penitentiary of meagre cells, each with a fifteen-inch window that denied any privacy; a prison yard, and a scaffold. In the glory days of the Third Reich, a man could be hauled in, charged, tried, convicted and hanged, all under one roof, before he had time to grow a six o'clock shadow.

In 1946 the Justizpalast was the showcase for a unique collection of Nazi nabobs. If it were possible to ignore the macabre nature of the proceedings, Nuremberg offered a great spectacle for the discerning viewer. British prosecuting counsel Lord Elwyn-Jones likened it to 'a larger than life butterfly collection'.[1] An imaginative court ruling that prisoners could choose their own clothing displayed the Third Reich's 'Superbia Germanorum' in their finest colours. Every morning, fascinated American white-cap guards would assemble by the pear tree in the prison yard to watch the prisoners' daily metamorphosis, emerging from their brown army-blankets to take their first hesitant steps along the 60-metre catwalk that led to the court. The blue admiral's coat of Hitler's chosen successor, Karl Dönitz, led the way, closely followed by former Minister-President Hermann Göring in dull cabbage-white leather. Then came Foreign Minister Konstantin von Neurath draped in full hunting furs, and Reich Youth Leader Baldur von Schirach in an expensive fur coat with a fetching sable collar. Grand Admiral Erich Räder swept behind them in a black, tightly-fitting, swallow-tailed Russian riding coat that his boy-friend had given him as he awaited trial in a Moscow dacha. Little wonder that a modestly dressed Albert Speer, who brought up the rear, hid under the hood of his anorak and was later to record his embarrassment.[2] Each procession would climax in a flutter of activity as they hovered over individually named seats, before settling to bask under blazing lights on the squat rostrum in the middle of the court.

Anthony Marreco was to witness this ritual countless times.[3] One of the British counsel for the prosecution, he was there to bring to justice members of allegedly criminal organisations, such as the Schutzstaffel (SS), the Sicherheitsdienst (SD), the Kriminalpolizei or Kripo, and the Geheime Staatspolizei (Secret State Police), unpopularly known as the Gestapo. Less openly, Marreco was also responsible for liaising between the Allied Secret Services and the judiciary. As the English and American intelligence agencies dominated proceedings to the exclusion of Russia and France, in effect he belonged to an exclusive Anglo-American club.

Marreco sensed the irony of seeing these men in the marble courtroom that had hosted the savage parodies of justice under National Socialism. How many helpless defendants had been condemned without pause by dour men in judicial robes tainted by swastika armbands? Now the Nuremberg trial judges sat before him, craning forward to avoid the freezing cold leather of their high-backed chairs. The emaciated figure of Chief Justice Robert H. Jackson, with his long, hairless head, hooded eyes and wrinkled neck, looked like a desiccated bald eagle perched in front of the stars and stripes of the American flag. In contrast stood German defending counsel Otto Kranzenbühler, an imposing man bolstered by self-importance and the ski suits under his robes.

Nobody had thought to restore the heating system; Nuremberg was a court sitting in refrigeration. People traipsed the aisles in ski boots. It looked as if everyone was talking animatedly; closer inspection revealed their soundless chatter resulted from the cold. Bulbs on the witness stand kept flashing yellow and red. Yellow meant 'the interpreter is behind you, please slow down', and red meant 'stop'. As prisoners gave their evidence through clenched teeth, the constant interruptions led to the nickname 'The Traffic Light Trial'.[4]

Marreco had taken the precaution of wearing not one, but two pairs of tights, as well as mittens. He clutched two files, each marked with red tabs that denoted 'hands off – British interest', as he sidled over to the window and pulled the brown curtain over his legs for extra warmth. He did not want to be distracted from the incredible impact that the subject of one of his files was making in the witness stand, a sight that would haunt him in later years.[5] The high-ranking SS Brigadeführer spoke calmly and quietly, oozing a self-assurance that was as repelling as it was fascinating. He leant forward with straightened arms in a manner that transformed the forbidding rostrum into a pulpit of light and reason. Marreco later recalled how 'the spectre of bestiality and the aura of evil that was my especial responsibility at Nuremberg seemed, in his hands, to become a frank talk by a guest speaker at a Women's Institute'.[6]

The Brigadeführer's perplexing confidence brought gasps from hardened newsmen. Lord Elwyn-Jones described this gentlemanly display as 'obscene legal pat-a-cake'.[7] Marreco's first reaction was to open his thin file, which he searched in vain for an explanation. Surely this Brigadeführer knew his words condemned him as much as they did his former colleagues, however much he sought to exonerate himself. If a deal had been struck, the documents that identified this man to be of 'British Special Interest' gave no hint of it. Anthony Marreco was not alone in wondering whether the Brigadeführer had come to some secret arrangement with the Allies. In the closing days of December 1945 the same thought had seared the tortured mind of the huge figure that peered out of his Nuremberg cell through eyes that were filled with hatred.

Himmler's deputy, Obergruppenführer Ernst Kaltenbrunner, had become a convenient focus of loathing for the world's media. It was as if the evil of Nazism had been made flesh. When he sat in the dock he dwarfed his co-defendants. Kaltenbrunner's disproportionately small hands were deeply nicotine-stained and armed with claw-like black finger nails that had made even Himmler cringe. A livid scar scored the left side of his white, pitted face, curling every attempted smile into a snarl. But the fear Kaltenbrunner's appearance induced in others was nothing in comparison with the encroaching terror he felt as the trial proceeded.

When the Brigadeführer made his initial appearance at court in November 1945 he had expertly explained the structure and role of the SS, and his status within it, in a way that minimised their role in the holocaust and other atrocities. Impressed, initially Kaltenbrunner asked for him to be a witness for his defence. It was a grave error. For all the Brigadeführer's fine words, it soon became apparent that he was no better than a covert witness for the prosecution, each delicate phrase another nail in Kaltenbrunner's coffin. By the first week of January 1946 Kaltenbrunner suffered a fine tremor in his hands. We can only imagine how painfully they were clenched as he watched the Brigadeführer being inexplicably cosseted by the Allies. He was so depressed by the performance that he complained to Albert Speer that he would 'only have needed a few seconds to wring the man's scrawny neck'.[8]

A clue to the Brigadeführer's special status was soon to come. It was still dark when Ralph Boursot, temporary legal clerk to the trial, began what he liked to call his early morning 'paper round'. Every day he would check the details of new prisoners in the penitentiary.[9] Boursot was up in time to watch two Queen Alexandra nurses tuck the Brigadeführer into a wheelchair and cover him with blankets. If that was not enough, he was wearing a black silk scarf and a long black Crombie coat bought at Savile Row in London before he came to Nuremberg. The legal clerk was not the only one watching this well-dressed man enjoy the touching solicitude of the British and Americans. Few prisoners truly slept at Nuremberg. Imagine how many suspicious eyes bored into the Brigadeführer's back, wondering where he was going at such an early hour with the British Intelligence officer who never left his side. A groan of envy came from somewhere on the first floor as a large stone hot-water bottle wrapped in blankets was delicately placed in his lap.

The small party was ushered out of the penitentiary in style by Fielding, the noisy American white cap guard from the first division who amused himself by stomping around the echoing building in jack-booted fashion.[10] Their departure did not even elicit comment from Göring in the cell opposite, who was known for his ready supply of sarcastic remarks.[11] As several of the more perceptive Nazi leaders imprisoned at Nuremberg recognised, the 'British Interest' card was being brazenly played in the middle of an international tribunal that was supposed to be dispensing justice.[12] Envy kept them silent.

★　　★　　★

In the early hours of that same morning Major Norman Whittaker was greeted by darkness and fine snow when he landed at Bückeburg airport. He arrived at a Hannover mess before the kitchens were opened and was driven off before breakfast by two corporals. Now he was waiting in the slanting light of Lüneburg forest. His meticulously neat moustache was half-frozen to give him a stiff upper lip that hardly reflected his earthy Lancastrian sentiments, as later related to a fellow intelligence officer at Monty's select 'C mess' (the 'Crouilly Club', named after the site where the intelligence group landed in France).[13] When a civilian finally appeared in his jeep, an hour late, Whittaker's feet were numb. Such a predicament would normally guarantee an outburst. But Whittaker was unusually quiet – because he was unusually and acutely embarrassed.

He had felt smug when he left the War Ministry in London. After all, the details he had given on the map denoting Himmler's grave 'were perfectly adequate for a moron, let alone the Ministry' to see at a glance exactly where the body was buried.[14] Whittaker, who had been demobbed in August 1945, was secretly delighted to be involved in this hush-hush Himmler business again, but the cold made him regret his presence, unnecessary as it was. Not that his self-confidence was dented. Before the jeep arrived he had been lecturing his companions on the exact use of map co-ordinates and descriptions. As soon as he had led its occupants up the track he had found so easily, he realised just how misplaced his confidence had been. It should have been easy. Only seven months earlier he had been driving in a similar jeep, squashed against his bulky chain-smoking Colour Sergeant Major Edwin Austin, followed by a Bedford truck driven by Sergeant Ray Weston, with poor Sergeant Bill Ottery stuck in the back, gagging over a corpse.

Back in May they too had set off before sunrise on their secret mission to dispose of the body of Reichsführer SS Heinrich Himmler. With their lights dipped, they left the car park behind 31a Ülzenerstrasse, drove down the rear of the street, and turned right back into Ülzenerstrasse, passing the house they had just left. What was supposed to have been a quick, efficient disposal mission soon descended into farce. As Whittaker put it, 'It was a hell of a job to find a lonely spot'.[15] They drove south out of Lüneburg and into the heath along the main Ülzen road, but although it was strewn with abandoned vehicles and it was still early in the morning, there were too many people around for comfort. The convoy turned off on to a quieter road leading to the north-east. This was too exposed, so they continued until they reached another main road, which they followed for some time without finding the cover necessary for their task. It did not help matters that it was so dark they could not see beyond the side of the road. Worse still, they did not possess an accurate, large-scale map. Whoever had drawn the one they had appeared to have marked Lüneburg after a particularly heavy drinking session. They stopped twice to reconnoitre possible sites, but neither seemed safe from scrutiny. It was so frustrating that they had driven a good part of the way back to Lüneburg before they finally discovered a spot where an old farm track joined the road obliquely from a slight incline. At least here was an opportunity to park their vehicles out of sight. Whittaker and Ottery jumped out to see where the track led.

Back in May it had seemed the perfect spot. There was a copse of trees that would screen them from prying eyes and the ground there was uneven enough to mask the digging. They carried the body forty yards from the truck into the copse, stopping just before the trees thinned into a glade. However, as dawn broke they discovered it was not so sheltered after all. A bunch of inebriated Polish soldiers had to be shooed away. Nevertheless, at the time Whittaker thought it was good enough. Once Ottery and Weston had dug, with some difficulty, a trench four feet deep, Whittaker took the jeep and drove back to the mess for some beers; despite the cold, it was hot and thirsty work. By the time he returned the body was buried and they were obscuring the grave with leaves and sticks. Sergeant Weston drove his motorcycle back to the copse twice in the following week to check it had not been disturbed. That, thought Whittaker, should have been that.[16]

But now, seven months down the line, it was obvious to Whittaker, after half an hour's search before 'I found where I'd buried the damn thing', that although covered by a thick layer of snow that drifted up against the trees, the site of the grave was distinctly vulnerable.[17] His discomfort was not helped by the acid comments of the 'bloody civilian' and the smirks of the corporals who had endured his lecture on accuracy in map-reading. The unnamed civilian immediately took charge. He ordered Whittaker and his men to exhume the body, stipulating that the top surface should be kept separate, so they could slot it back in without it being obvious that the ground had been disturbed. Whittaker thought this was futile, and struggled to contain his scorn. It took a good hour's digging through the frozen soil before they recovered the corpse.

When they were half-way through, a well-dressed German couple out walking their dog became curious, hovering in the nearby glade until one of the corporals was 'nasty to the dog' which 'retired for a recount'.[18] Perhaps fearing similar treatment, the couple hurried away. Just before midday another car pulled up. The civilian had obviously been expecting it and went with Whittaker to greet the newcomers. A languid man with a cut-glass accent got out and leant against the mud-spattered car to help himself from a hip flask, pointedly ignoring Whittaker and everybody else who was there for the military. This compounded Whittaker's discomfiture. A Mancunian who only tolerated southerners at the best of times, he later recalled that this man 'got on my nerves from 40 yards'.[19]

Matters did not improve for Whittaker when the body was uncovered and he was rudely dismissed. One of the corporals who had accompanied him from Hannover stood guard, while the other was asked to assist the party in the car. Whittaker could not understand why such a sensitive task was entrusted to a mere corporal, particularly this strangely silent one who 'had less to say than any other corporal' he had ever met.[20] It would not be out of character for the British to have planted an intelligence officer to keep an eye on Whittaker. Whatever the truth, he was deeply offended that, although he had been considered trustworthy enough to bury the body, he was excluded from all discussion over the remains of what Whittaker considered his corpse.

The second man to emerge from the car had to be propped up with each shaky step. He was 'bony, grey and ill looking and kept straightening his back as if in pain'.[21] He wore a long, black Crombie coat and his cadaverous face was muffled by a black silk scarf. Whittaker wandered over to the car, hoping to 'cadge a coffee' as he had not eaten breakfast, and was surprised to find two Queen Alexandra nurses sitting there.[22] Pretending he knew more than he did, it took no time to glean that the party had come from the British Military Headquarters at Bad Oeynhausen. The wraith-like creature they were nursing was a Nuremberg trial prisoner, the notorious Brigadeführer SS Walter Schellenberg, Himmler's right-hand man. This strangely vulnerable man bore no resemblance to the bull-headed Prussian warrior of Whittaker's imagination. There was a touch of vanity in the way his dark-brown quiff was carefully sculpted, a soft-focus frame for his liquid eyes. Set deep into his face, they were surrounded by dark circles that indicated the gravity of his illness. To many women at Nuremberg they seemed irresistibly careworn. There was a bluish tint to the edge of his lips, a hint of incipient decay that tinged every smile with a certain pathos.

Whittaker immediately realised that Schellenberg had been summoned to identify what remained of his master's corpse. It was impossible for him to hear what was being said at the graveside, but he noted with grim satisfaction that the glum looks of the group suggested that the answers Schellenberg had given were not what they had hoped for. With his usual trenchant turn of phrase, Whittaker recorded, 'at least somebody else wasn't happy'.[23] This thought consoled him as, once the other party had departed, he grudgingly tidied up 'his' site. He helped the corporals load the corpse on to sacking in the back of the truck for the return journey to Hannover British Military Hospital, where it was to undergo its second post-mortem. Back at the mess Whittaker watched in fascination as, a hand grenade's throw away, an SS uniform, cut off at the knee, danced amid the dustbins. Its new owner, a young girl pop-eyed with hunger, was scavenging for food.[24] It was strange how the costume of Aryan superiority could now inspire his pity.

Bomb damage had given the city a voice to lament its suffering. Wind tore through the creaking remains of its buildings with eerie reverberations that could wake the dead. Whittaker's mess was no exception; he barely slept for the two nights he stayed there as capricious gusts turned the empty rooms into howling echo chambers. Preparing for his mid-morning flight back to England, he reflected bitterly on the injustice of it all. The powers that be had informed him that his evidence would not be required at the secret Board of Inquiry to be held on Himmler's death. Still, he had done his duty. The body was recovered and he was assured that it was indeed Himmler. They could not take that away from him. Loyal silence on the subject would bring its own reward. He looked forward with some satisfaction to his new job with the War Crimes Commission, and the inevitable MBE.[25] In January 1946 these benefits seemed sufficient compensation for his exclusion from the graveside and the Board of Inquiry; even for his annoyance at an earlier slight.

Back in May 1945 Whittaker had been the senior officer in charge of the secret burial. Yet his commanding officer, Colonel L. M. Murphy, chose another spokesman to announce Himmler's demise. As popular belief has it, if you want something done, a sergeant major can always be trusted. So it came to pass that Colour Sergeant Major Edwin Austin was to give the only official statement on the burial of Heinrich Himmler, arguably the most powerful Nazi leader. The short BBC broadcast, 'The Death of Himmler', went out at 8 p.m. on 24 May. Later augmented by his testimony of historian Willi Frischauer, Austin's version of events became the accepted story of the Reichsführer's death, a story that would endure for the rest of the twentieth century. CSM Austin became an instant celebrity thanks to his account:

> I wrapped him in a couple of blankets, I put two of our army camouflage nets around him and tied him up with telephone wires. I put the parcel on the back of the lorry and drove off. I had to dig the grave myself. No one will ever know where he is buried.[26]

CSM Austin, a dustman's mate, could not even drive.

2

SS 1

The young boy's eyes were wide with fear. Naked, he stared into the smiling face of the balding man who bent towards him, holding out a red balloon. As the boy reached up for it the hand that had been gently ruffling his hair grabbed his scrawny shoulder. The hefty metal syringe hit his chest, thrusting him into the arms of Stefan Baretzki, who tossed the twitching boy on to the growing pile of bodies that lay behind the green wooden screen with its cheery red dragons.[1] Twenty-three agonising seconds later his suffering was over. A tiny speck of blood just below the left nipple was the only trace this casual murder had left.

This was just another ordinary day's work under the regime controlled by Reichsführer SS Heinrich Himmler. Oswald 'Papa' Kaduk was merely better at his job than most. As the Third Reich's foremost *Abspritzer* ('blow-away expert') he had received a special commendation from Himmler for his contribution to cost-effective killing.[2] He earned his nickname at the 1964 Auschwitz trial for his exceptional love of children. He certainly was an exceptional Papa – his work rate averaged at ten children per minute. Things were going well for Kaduk. Popular belief among his admirers held that the children 'looked as if they had died in their sleep'.[3] It is hard to imagine what nightmares could cause such tortured, gasping expressions as those worn by Kaduk's children after a 5cc dose of concentrated phenol had been injected directly into their hearts. As far as Kaduk was concerned, with his red balloons and dragons, this work was fun. The festive atmosphere of his office was full of expectation as he awaited the promised consignment from Łódź.

Meanwhile, Chaim Rumkowski felt anything but excitement.

Head of more than 320,000 Jews herded into the ghetto of Łódź, Rumkowski represented a people whose lives were soon to be exhausted by their forced labour at the new clothing factory. He was faced with the most brutal moral choice imaginable. Sadly, he was only one of many whose lives would be touched by the influence of Himmler, in his case directly, with such grave consequences. The chairman of the Council of Elders was waiting to hand over the sick, the elderly and the 24,000 children of the ghetto who were taking up family time that could be more profitably used in service to the Reich. He had agreed with his elders, mostly tailors from Jacuba Street, that they should entrust their weaker kin to the care of the Nazis, voluntarily consigning them to Auschwitz. Nobody was under any illusions about what their fate there would be. He stood alone in the square awaiting the visiting dignitary whose slightest displeasure would spell death for all. Rumkowski's entire being strained to make the right impression. He clutched a thin folder tightly at his side, full of data that would show the hard-won increase in their factory output, proof that those Jews still living were helping free up German workers to go to the Front.

Despair was something the inmates of Łódź were by now accustomed to. The previous winter they had been so cold that they had dismantled their own homes, stripping them of wood to burn. A contemporary observer described the destruction: 'Like crows on a cadaver, like jackals on a carcass, they demolished, they axed, they sawed. Walls collapsed, beams flew, plaster buried people alive. But no one yielded his position.'[4] This episode gives some measure of how the Jews at Łódź were progressively dehumanised by their deprivation. Viewed in this context, it becomes easier to understand how they could co-operate in the bizarre pretence of freely handing over their dependants to Heinrich Himmler.

Austrian photographer Walter Genewein recorded the visit on slides that came to light in 1987. It began on 5 June 1941 and was to last several days.[5] These images of the day Heinrich Himmler came to town show with brutal clarity how the spirit of these people was extinguished. Starving children were frozen in time tiptoeing about in search of elusive scraps of food. Women look up from their workbenches and gaze vacantly into the camera; their pinched faces are almost hidden behind the huge mounds of clothing from their own dead. There is panic behind their eyes, uncertain of how to please this unwelcome guest. Then we see the Reichsführer's dull-green BMW. It pulls into the square, dirty from the journey, and its pointed bonnet noses towards the assembled Jews like a dog scenting flesh. There is a shocking absence of ceremony, and few attendant guards. Heinrich Himmler does not need security. The man's reputation inspired a fear that guaranteed his safety.

The waiting crowds have tensed visibly. The slides show senior SS officers pontificating over the correct way to present Himmler with their facts and figures. Gauleiter Greiser, the man in charge, spreads the blueprints of a future German city, Litzmannstadt, across the car's bonnet. These documents set out to transform one of Poland's proudest university towns into a power house to fuel the National Socialist dream, packed with Jews and Polish POWs to labour for the cause.[6] Greiser proudly displays an array of due and necessary papers to show how this new Łódź has been cudgelled into a legal possibility. Himmler was always keen to have the paperwork to show proper Nazi respect for the law.

Finally Chaim Rumkowski is summoned to meet the Reichsführer. He is politely amazed at how well informed the Reichsführer is about the ghetto economy, and the hunger that is so damaging to their output. The day after Himmler's visit ended the ghetto authorities announced that more food would be available – at least, for those that remained.[7] The slides cannot adequately convey the horror inherent in such benevolence. Rations were not increased; there were simply fewer mouths to feed. The ignominy of the ghetto leaders' choice is glossed over by the rational generosity that Himmler prided himself on.

Scenes such as those in the Łódź ghetto took place time and again in the Third Reich. The stark truth is that Heinrich Himmler inculcated such fear that, in this instance alone, 320,000 Jews voluntarily agreed to sacrifice their children, their elderly and their infirm. Far from recognising the inhumanity of his demands, Himmler positively relished engaging victims such as Rumkowski in discussions about the morality and the spurious legality of the obscene decisions that were forced upon them. This pseudo-civilised veneer on inhuman savagery is totally in keeping with the character of the man. Ever concerned with the niceties of procedure and bureaucracy, Himmler's meticulous appointments book reveals how the visit to Łódź is recorded with equal gravity as a visit from his secretary Erika Lorenz to discuss appropriate Christmas presents for Italian diplomats.[8] Equal weight is given to mass murder and politic gifts. This man's personality and his power to terrify is key to understanding some of the greatest excesses of the Nazi regime.

Even Himmler's colleagues shared the awed horror felt by his victims. Walter Dornberger, who headed the Luftwaffe research station at Peenemünde that produced V2s, the most feared killing machines of the time, wrote of his fear and intense disquiet on meeting the Reichsführer SS in 1943, when Himmler's power was at its zenith. He vividly records the sinister undertones of Himmler's superficially innocuous appearance:

> He looked to me like an intelligent elementary schoolteacher, certainly not a man of violence . . . Under a brow of average height, two grey-blue eyes looked at me, behind glittering pince-nez, with an air of peaceful interrogation. The trimmed moustache below the straight, well-shaped nose traced a dark line on his unhealthy, pale features. The lips were colourless and very thin. Only the conspicuous receding chin surprised me. The skin of his neck was flaccid and wrinkled. With a broadening of his constant set smile, faintly mocking and sometimes contemptuous about the corners of the mouth, two rows of excellent white teeth appeared between the thin lips. His slender, pale, almost girlishly soft hands, covered with veins, lay motionless on the table throughout our conversation.[9]

Two months later, on 29 June, they met again when Himmler came to talk with senior researchers at Peenemünde. Dornberger wrestled with the contradictions between Himmler's manner and his policy:

Himmler possessed the rare gift of attentive listening. Sitting back with legs crossed, he wore throughout the same amiable expression. His questions showed that he unerringly grasped what the technicians told him out of the wealth of their knowledge. The talk turned to war and the important questions in all our minds. He answered calmly and candidly. It was only at rare moments that, sitting with his elbows resting on the arms of the chair, he emphasised his words by tapping the tips of his fingers together. He was a man of quiet unemotional gestures. A man without words.

Dornberger was as revolted as he was fascinated by the way Himmler expressed his aims, 'so concisely, simply and naturally'. He extolled the methods of Genghis Khan, explaining why it was essential that they update Genghis' approach to reduce the populations of Russia and Poland by some 30 million to enable German settlement (the key Nazi policy of *Lebensraum*). 'I shuddered at the everyday manner in which the stuff was related,' he recalled. 'But even as I did so I admired Himmler's gift for simplifying difficult problems in a few words that could be understood by anyone and went straight to the heart of the matter.'

It was this strange, logical reduction of evil into righteous legality that inspired Panzer General Heinz Guderian to call Himmler 'a man from another planet'.[10] What is most disturbing about the way Himmler and everyone surrounding him went about their business is their insistence on observing the niceties of bureaucracy. They routinely spent hours deliberating on the minutiae of their horrendous acts, creating endless forms, lists and files to impose civilised order on the business of mass murder. Polite and rigorous in their attention to detail, they exhibited a macabre obsession with procedure. Himmler consistently presented himself as a nice man. His efficiency and rectitude were key to the terror he could inspire. 'Except for Hitler,' wrote Goebbels' assistant Rudolf Semmler, 'no one is entirely without fear of Himmler. Goebbels considers that Himmler has built up the greatest power organisation imaginable.'[11] However, because he was thoughtful and remarkably ordinary in his appearance, Himmler successfully deceived even those who should have known him best. When Head of the Abwehr Admiral Wilhelm Canaris was arrested for his part in the failed plot to assassinate Hitler of July 1944, he asked Walter Schellenberg to promise to arrange an interview with Himmler because 'all the others are filthy butchers'.[12]

As the reasoned, responsible leader of the Nazi state, Himmler embodied the organised evil they propagated. The staff car that took him to Łódź proudly bore his personalised number plate, 'SS 1'. The runic script that rendered the Schutzstaffel's acronym as a double lightning flash is a telling example of the terrifying symbolism that he held so dear. Such attention to detail, coupled with the skill with which Himmler built up his power base, present us with a puzzle when we come to consider the manner of his death. The exhumation of his body at Lüneburg, and the subsequent actions of Kim Philby, arguably Britain's most effective, if treacherous, secret agent ever, pose a number of questions that this book will attempt to answer.

3

The Vengeful Chameleon

'Nations as well as men almost always betray the most prominent features of their future destiny in their earliest years.'

De Tocqueville

A short account of Heinrich Himmler's early years helps make sense
of how he came to be one of the most feared men in Europe. He
came into the world on 7 October 1900, the second of three sons
born to Anna and Dr Gebhard Himmler. He grew up in a drab
apartment block at 86 Amalienstrasse in Munich until 1913, when his
father was appointed joint head teacher at the *Gymnasium* (grammar
school) of Landshut, fifty miles north-east of Munich. Dominated
by an ancient castle, this small town was at the heart of Bavaria, a
conservative, Catholic region in southern Germany.

In Munich, the Himmler family lived in a modest second-floor
flat, but this modesty did not extend to its inhabitants. Dr Himmler
had once been tutor to Prince Heinrich of Bavaria, a member of
the royal household of Wittelsbach. He named his second son after
the Prince, who agreed to be the boy's godfather, and lost no
opportunity to impress on his children the importance of this royal
connection, tenuous though it was. At bedtimes the children were
told endless stories from German history that emphasised the distinction of the local royal family and the Himmler family's status by
association. (By contrast, his mother's obscure origins, and suspiciously heavy features, were later to cause the Reichsführer some
anxiety.) The children would say their prayers in front of an ivory
figurine of Christ, in an *Ahnenzimmer* – literally, ancestors' room –
an extraordinary luxury in a two-bedroomed flat. Night after night,

sitting on his father's knee in a living room lined with heraldic plaques, young 'Heini' would soak up this well-intentioned propaganda; its long-term effect might have been to invest him with an entirely false sense of his own significance, a dangerous *folie de grandeur*.

Heinrich soon became convinced that he was born and bred to lead. Later in life he occasionally claimed that his actions were based on those of Heinrich I, King of Saxony and conqueror of the Slavs AD 876–936, who first united the lands that became the Reich. Although he was the middle child, he quickly assumed authority over his brothers. A tense, righteous ambience also governed the Himmler household. Something can be gleaned of how it must have been to grow up in that family from his wife's observation about what must have been an intimidating duo, 'I always have to take a deep breath when I think of your parents.'[1]

In his autobiographical novel, *The Father of a Murderer*, Alfred Andersch records his distressing experiences at the hands of Himmler's father.[2] The narrator, a young boy, is sitting in his Greek lesson:

> Unexpectedly the headmaster Dr Himmler entered. A corpulent man, he wore a light grey suit with the jacket unbuttoned displaying a well-rounded paunch, a white shirt and an immaculate blue tie. His hair was smooth and white, his face surprisingly unlined for a man of sixty-three and lightly flushed. As the boys stood, his blue eyes inspected them benevolently from behind spectacles with a thin gold frame – the blue and the gold together gave somewhat of a twinkling lively appearance.

Dr Himmler calls the narrator to the blackboard and cruelly belittles him in front of his classmates. Following this humiliation, he brings out all the narrator's and his younger brother's grades. The real reason for Dr Himmler's visit was to discuss, publicly, the boys' father's inability to pay their school fees. These would normally be waived when illness struck the family. In spite of Andersch's father's record as a highly decorated officer, and the support of other masters, both boys were summarily dismissed. Young Andersch and his brother learnt another lesson in the cruelty of human nature that day: Dr Himmler instructed their fellow pupils not to associate with such people, so after what was their final day at the *Gymnasium* they were forced to walk home alone. This episode illustrates the pettiness and tyranny propagated by Himmler senior, and the hidebound conservatism of a society that was not inclined to question authority.

Historian Georg Hallgarten records how Dr Himmler had become an embarrassing joke in Munich, where his fawning towards the upper classes was notorious. On one occasion, caught in the steam room at the Munich municipal baths by Hallgarten's father, Dr Himmler grabbed a small flannel and, holding it in front of him with both hands, formally presented himself with a deep bow. Hallgarten senior laughingly recounted, 'There the man stood as nature made him and he introduced himself to me with all his titles.'[3] One can imagine how often this anecdote was recounted to the laughter of the men Dr Himmler craved to impress.

Hallgarten went to school with the future Reichsführer. For many years he failed to realise that the boy he knew as Himmler was the same man, so insignificant had he considered young Heini. It was not until 1949, when visiting Munich for the first time after the war, that he discovered it really was his old schoolmate who had become so infamous. He remembered him as

> Of scarcely average height but downright podgy – with an uncommonly milk-white complexion, fairly short hair and already wearing gold-rimmed spectacles on his rather sharp nose; not infrequently he showed a half embarrassed, half sardonic smile – either to excuse his shortsightedness or to emphasise a certain superiority.[4]

Young Himmler's conviction of his exalted station wrestled for many years with his physical deficiencies. He was weak, plump and short-sighted – no Aryan superman. School gym lessons were a terrifying ordeal; the rest of the class would hoot their mirth as he struggled with the horizontal bar. One can have some sympathy for him. At that time German society was aggressively masculine, and the Prussian ideals of the warrior-like male who lived in spartan simplicity, untrammelled by materialism, ruled over the imaginations of youth.

He soon began to develop ways to compensate for his corporeal shortcomings. Potential bullies were deflected by the fact that his father was headmaster. Popularity was never within his reach, but he began to defend himself with guile and insinuation. Probably for protection, he befriended the biggest boy in the class, Franz Müller, the son of a major-general, with whom he used to satisfy his sweet tooth, sitting by the river eating sandwiches and drinking chocolate. Few of his contemporaries from these early years can have been aware of what we now, with the benefit of hindsight, recognise as Himmler's key trait – a fastidiousness verging on the obsessional. In 1910 he started keeping a diary. This incredibly detailed record echoes the pompous self-regard his father had down to a fine art; the pages pedantically note the correct title of every adult referred to, and solemnly document each occasion their author had a bath or even combed his hair. Such attention to detail would seem odd enough in any young boy. Yet among the mundane minutiae of his daily life a darker strain appears. A series of entries document Himmler's growing contempt for the lower classes, people of lower intelligence, foreigners and Jews – all popular prejudices of the day.

Despite the inherent advantage of his father being headmaster, Himmler never achieved much academically, even though his father employed a personal tutor. His phenomenal memory served him well in history and geography. However, he failed to get in the top third of his graduation class, and passed his much-deferred *Abitur* examination with just two days to spare before taking up his place at technical college. Nor did he shine in music. He started learning to play the piano, but had no real talent for it, and was eventually persuaded to give it up. When war broke out in 1914, Himmler became inflamed with the patriotic zeal of the times and two years later his father unsuccessfully attempted to get him a commission. His diaries are drenched in the sentiments of the Kaiser's Intellectual Brigade of Guards, who believed in the intellectual superiority of the martial elite, and fervently expounded the concepts of the Pan-Germanic League that believed Germany should encompass all

German-speaking nations. He also wanted a colonial navy, desiring to expand the empire.

Himmler was by no means alone in some of his more extreme beliefs. Romanticism was the dominant cultural trend and distortions of its most striking ideas permeated society. One of the most influential figures was nineteenth-century German philosopher Friedrich Nietzsche, who championed the notion of the 'superman'. Young Himmler appropriated this concept for his own ends, incorporating it into his creed of Aryan racial superiority; such usage was popular at the time. Albert Ploetz published his arguments for selective breeding in *The Fitness of Our Race*, featuring the obligatory quotation from Nietzsche: 'Upwards leads our way from the Species into the Superspecies.' The adolescent avidly absorbed this work, as he did Hans Günther's *The Knight, Death and the Devil*, which he devoured in less than a week. Günther eulogises the 'most beautiful and talented Nordic race' with lip-smacking relish. His pages are populated with broad-shouldered, narrow-hipped men and their softer, charmingly slender female counterparts, aglow with 'shining skin flushed with blood, clear, conquering eyes with the perfect movements of a perfect body – truly a royal species among men'.

Ten years after Himmler was steeping himself in such fantasy, a secret society called the *Germanenorden*, formed to foster the myth of German superiority, came to his attention. It was created in Berlin in 1912 and Masonic-style lodges convened throughout the country. Himmler was also impressed by the Thule Society, an offshoot of the *Germanenorden*. It took its name from 'Ultima Thule', the supposed birthplace of the Germanic race. (This concept overlooked the fact that at least 40 per cent of Berliners originated from Slavic races, as indeed did the majority of the population of the Brandenburg region.)

The Bavarian branch of the Thule was to shape the course of history. Most of its members derived from the aristocracy, the judiciary and the professions, and they would meet regularly in Munich's Hotel Vierjahreszeiten. Himmler's father was often to be seen hanging about their meetings. It supported its own secret army, the *Freikorps Oberland*, ran the Munich newspaper *Völkischer Beobachter*, and built up a sophisticated intelligence network that spanned Bavaria. This group spawned radical intellectual Anton Drexier, who was to draw an unemployed ex-soldier, Adolf Hitler, into politics. In the late nineteenth century Heinrich von Treitschke attracted thousands to rallies in Berlin. He whipped his audience into a frenzy of excitement about the glory of the 'State at war'. Himmler's diaries regurgitate Treitschke's writings, undigested: war was the civilising factor that allowed the fit to rule over the unfit; it was the German's god-given duty to purify other races.

Another frequently quoted source in Himmler's early diaries was an Englishman, Houston Stewart Chamberlain. His writings were based on the simple but highly marketable premise that the Germans had been the unique creative force in European civilisation for the past 1500 years. More pernicious was his rabid anti-semitism. Chamberlain's pamphlet, *Race and Nation*, excited Himmler to condemn 'this atrocious Jewry' in 1924. Such anti-semitism permeated the Bavaria of Himmler's youth. He avidly read Theodor Fritsch's *Handbook of the Jewish Question* – the 28th edition of a book that was published only four years earlier. Himmler's diary recorded his reaction: 'Even an initiate shudders when he reads all this with understanding.'[5] Fritsch's *The False God* engendered the view that 'This frightful Jewish scourge is a danger which will throttle us'.[6]

At the same time he was reading with indignation *Bolshevism from Moses to Lenin* by Dietrich Eckhart. Himmler now knew with a dreadful certainty that the Germans needed a war, needed to rule and needed to weed out Bolsheviks and Jews. His further reading included the works of Admiral Alfred von Tirpitz, which complained about dismissive British attitudes to Germans, and the biography of the politician von Bülow; books filled with avenging fury against the non-Germanic races who humiliated Germany in the post-war Treaty of Versailles. These books gave no space to Germany's responsibility for defeat and going to war in the first place. The stage was already set. Heinrich Himmler was one of the *Halbgebildeten* – the semi-educated – convinced of violently simplistic solutions for their world's ills.

Himmler was a disappointment to his father, who was disturbed by early academic failures and then watched his son's political fervour overtake his ambitions for a career. Yet by sheer force of character Heinrich established a dominant position within the family. His attitude to his younger brother Ernst, for instance, was as high-handed as if he had been the boy's uncle. 'Little Ernst,' he wrote from college on 14 November 1920, 'I am very pleased with your good report, but do not rest on your laurels. Moreover I expect you to do well in history. Do not become unbalanced, be a good brave boy and do not vex Daddy and Mummy.'[7]

Himmler was no less patronising to his elder brother Gebhard. In 1923 Gebhard became engaged to Paula Stölzle, daughter of a local banker. She was an attractive young woman with pretty legs. Unfortunately these qualities brought her a reputation for flirtatiousness. Heinrich was quick to disapprove. He wrote to her, unprompted, on 18 April that year with this advice:

> If your union is to be a happy one for the two of you, and salutary for our people, the very foundation of which must be healthy, clean-living families, you will have to be ridden on a tight rein, and with the utmost severity. Since your own code of behaviour is not a strict one, and your future husband is too kind-hearted, someone else must perform this function. I feel it my duty to do so.[8]

His easygoing elder brother took a back seat. Paula was incensed. She took ten weeks to answer the letter, and mockingly, over-effusively thanked him for his concern. Not satisfied with her answer, nor her subsequent behaviour, Heinrich went to see his parents, demanding that they cut out Paula from their family and confront Gebhard about her unsuitability. Paula, who was visiting the Himmler family at the time, was sent to the next room to await her fate. She could clearly hear Heinrich inveighing against her.

Believing that in response Paula had had the temerity to complain to friends about the way he had treated her, Himmler wrote another, this time threatening letter. He would not rest until she had been 'socially and morally deleted from the ranks of society'.[9] He did not stop there. Max Blüml, a private detective from Munich, was appointed to confirm his suspicions that Paula had other boyfriends, including a teacher called Rieger. These investigations became so troublesome that Paula's father wrote disapprovingly to the Himmlers. On 14 March 1924 Blüml reported back her innocence, but not before Heinrich had asked a civil servant colleague of Paula's, Rössner, to verify that the warmth he had felt in her embrace was indeed unnatural. It was a typically naïve interpretation of what constituted sexual licence. Himmler got carried away with investigative zeal, pressing Rössner to turn agent: 'May I request you to inform me by return, of all you know about Paula Stölzle and particularly about her relationship with your colleague Daffner?'[10] Paula reproved Gebhard for allowing his younger brother to 'educate me on your behalf according to his experience of life.'[11] The situation had become intolerable: Gebhard broke off the engagement. Himmler's priggish moral righteousness and prurience had won a memorable first battle.

The pattern of a lifetime was established. He was a man of no outstanding intellectual gifts other than his memory, and no physical attraction, who set out to dominate the lives and minds of others. He was goaded by an unpleasant combination of ambition and officiousness that he disguised as high moral purpose. That he succeeded so well, then in a modest way, but later on a scale which brought disaster to mankind, must be attributed partly to hereditary make-up, and partly to the indoctrination of his father, which left him with exaggerated ideas of his own importance. This episode shows an outstandingly pompous man, middle-aged at 24.

Heinrich's primary career ambitions reflected his love for the martial ethos. He attempted to join the Eleventh Bavarian Infantry Regiment, something he assumed he would manage as a matter of course. He boasted in his diary on 17 June 1919, 'Since I am transferring to the Reichswehr in a few days' time.'[12] The Reichswehr thought otherwise: they took one look and rejected him outright. On 13 October 1919 Himmler eventually graduated from Landshut *Gymnasium*, two years later than his father had anticipated. Two days later he took up a place to study agricultural chemistry, specialising in fertilisers, at the University of Munich Technical High School.

Working on a farm near Ingolstadt for his practical qualification, on 4 December 1919 he fell ill with paratyphoid, and was advised by Doctor Grünstadt at the local hospital to give up farm work because his frail physique was not up to it.

It was not all gloom. Life became a frenetic whirl of social activity. Himmler was dazzled by the prospect of social success and determined that he should be in the first rank. In this he was hindered by shyness. Another person might have settled down to study hard. Himmler craved acceptance and went out of his way to achieve it. First he joined the Apollo Club, a hard-drinking set who reluctantly accepted his membership. It did not last. Himmler was ejected at the first opportunity, when they realised that he was only prepared to burp peppermint water during their sing-alongs, as alcohol was against his Catholic ideals. To their horror, their new member came to the first meeting asking for a special dispensation from the club, absolving himself from the necessity of getting drunk on medical grounds.

Then he realised the immense social kudos of duelling, an activity as ritualised as the Apollo Club's drunken singsongs – no pistols at dawn or fights to the death, but a gentlemanly fencing match. This decision cost him another struggle with his beliefs, but pragmatic ambition beat conscience hands down. The Church had recently called for duelling to be banned, and Himmler recorded in his diary: 'I believe that I have come into conflict with my religion, but come what may, I shall always love God and pray to him, and shall remain faithful to the Catholic Church and defend it, even if I am expelled from it.'[13] His courage paid off. A scribbled diary entry detailed how, after thirteen rounds of fencing, he received a cut to his left cheek that bled enough to soak three tierce cloths.[14] His best friend, Dietl, held his head while he was stitched up without anaesthetic by a Mr A. H. Reichl of Passau, the surgical apprentice on duty. Afterwards Himmler returned to the benches of the sports room for the plaudits, and watched the match of a fellow student, Brunner, before going home, his head aching. At one o'clock he had a celebratory lunch with another student, Hottner, and his brother Gebhard, and spent the afternoon discussing the bravery of others who shared the distinguishing mark of masculine honour, the cherished duelling scar.

Unfortunately, there was no easy badge of success when it came to girls and sex. Heinrich's natural shyness and prudish behaviour, as shown in his treatment of Paula Stölzle, got in the way of easy relations with women, just as these characteristics excluded him from the Apollo Club. At twenty-two he became friendly with a distant relation, Maja Loritz, who lived in her mother's Munich boarding house. It was never more than a platonic relationship. Himmler's diaries give an insight into his inability to take things further, revealing him as an exceptionally prim man who was shocked to the core by any overt display of what he considered to be sexuality. Even the sight of a naked three-year-old girl elicited the comment that her mother had 'absolutely no sense of shame'.[15] Nowhere is his naivety better illustrated than in the passage which describes his Aryan ideal:

> A real man will love a woman in three ways − first as a dear child who must be admonished, perhaps even punished when she is foolish [. . .] secondly he will love her as a wife and a dear comrade who helps him fight in the struggle of life, always at his side but never dampening the spirit [. . .] thirdly he will love her as the wife whose feet he longs to kiss and who gives him the strength never to falter, even in the worst strife, in the strength that she gives thanks to her child-like purity.[16]

This was pure Wagnerian fantasy, very different from his own faltering practice. His journal is full of mild sexual rebuffs, all of which are rationalised away. In 1921 he wrote, 'Accompanied Fräulein Buck home, she did not take my arm, which, in a way, I appreciated.'[17]

Maja soon tired of sitting eating chocolate and went off with Hans Knipp, who became a leather merchant. Short of conquests, Heinrich fell back on his own innate moral superiority: he felt certain that he was very impressive and that he had a hypnotic effect on women, who were overawed by his intellect and presence. He probably bored them to death. He recorded in his diary a chance meeting on a train: 'She was very sweet and obviously very interested in Bavaria and King Ludwig.'[18]

Discovery that women did not automatically succumb to his charms led him to some bizarre conclusions. For instance, someone excessively beautiful, and therefore unobtainable, was in his view automatically doomed to moral degradation and downfall. But once a woman had fallen and become stained, he could regard her with a certain amount of condescending pity, even if she were a Jewess. By his early twenties he was vehemently anti-semitic, calling his former classmate Wolfgang Hallgarten (a relation of the historian) a 'Jewboy', and 'Jewish louse'.[19] Similarly, he decried the Russians who were 'multiplying like vermin'. However, he generously referred to an attractive Jewish cabaret artist, who was turned out of her room after an affair with a fellow-student, as 'a girl who deserves respect'.[20] In short, Himmler's ideas about women were irredeemably abstract. The simple truth was that despite the moral bluster of the diaries, he lacked confidence. His timidity was probably largely based on his awareness of his looks. However, any potential sense of inadequacy was translated into contempt for those who did not share his limitations. When his friend Ludwig, who had lost his virginity, started encouraging Heinrich to be more adventurous and less inhibited, he remarked in his diary, 'Ludwig seems to me to be more and more incomprehensible, I now have doubts about his character.'[21]

Rather than consider his want of sexual success as undermining his masculinity, he grandly assumed the role of heroic defender of both men's and women's purity:

> I have experienced what it is like to lie closely together body to body, hot – one gets all fired up, must summon all one's reasoning. The girls are so far gone they no longer know what they are doing. It is the hot unconscious longing for the whole individual, for the satisfaction of a really powerful natural urge. For this reason it is also dangerous for the man, and involves so much responsibility. Deprived as they are of their will power, one could do anything with these girls and, at the same time one has to struggle with oneself.[22]

It is hardly surprising that his purity remained intact until he found a 'dear child' to admonish. He was twenty-six when he swept off his snow-covered Tyrolean hat in the lobby of a Berchtesgaden hotel and soaked the dress of Margarete Concerzowo. This blonde nurse of Polish origin was seven years older than Himmler, ran a nursing home and kept a herbal garden. He sheepishly admitted to Otto Strasser that he lost his virginity only just before their marriage in 1928 – a fact that met with much hilarity. The ecstatic couple bought a house and smallholding where they kept 50 chickens at Waltruding, ten miles from Munich, and had one child, Gudrun, who was known as 'Puppi'. Later, when in a position of power, Himmler plucked up the courage to keep a mistress in Berlin, choosing his secretary Hedwig Potthast. But these two are the only women known to have enjoyed intimate relations with Himmler.

Throughout Himmler's life the sight of flaunted femininity would throw him off balance. The mistress of his dreaded deputy Reinhard Heydrich, Lina von Osten, took advantage of this bashfulness to further her future husband's and especially her own affairs. She would cross her legs provocatively at just the right moment of a tricky situation and the Reichsführer would be lost for words.

4

The SS State

It is easy to understand why it took Georg Hallgarten so long to realise that his old schoolmate had risen to become Reichsführer SS. There was little in his early life to suggest that he would achieve a commanding position in the Nazi empire, let alone an iron grip over the hearts and minds of a nation committed to manliness and physical prowess. The secret of his success lay in a strange mixture of unobtrusive qualities. His exceptional memory, itself a powerful weapon, was sharpened by a vindictive nature. These traits were all the more dangerous because they were masked by such an innocuous appearance.

After graduating from technical college in August 1922, Himmler worked as a laboratory assistant in a fertiliser firm, Stickstoff-Land GmbH. He became friendly with Captain Ernst Röhm, military leader of the burgeoning Nationalist Socialist movement, and was his ensign at the failed Munich beer hall putsch of November 1924. While leaders Hitler, Erich Ludendorff and Hermann Göring were in the vanguard, Himmler characteristically lurked in the background. However, a photograph of him in action beside Röhm gives us a memorable glimpse of how he caught the scent of power. There he stands at the wire barricade, open-mouthed, clutching his gun and flag, part of the vanguard of a defiant mob facing down the police. It is not surprising that after this heady experience he never went back to work in the conventional sense, but devoted all his time to political activity.

Naivety and a mild manner, combined with an eagerness to please, suggested that he posed no threat. This in turn rendered his ambition, which at first he did not try to conceal, both ridiculous and inoffensive. What flights of fancy could unite a laboratory assistant in a fertiliser firm with high-risk politics? He was immensely industrious, working tirelessly day and night. At first his ambition seemed amateurish, but Himmler had a trump card – a Swedish motorcycle. This asset made him indispensable at a time when Nazi Party funds were low and it was difficult to find transport. He gained many contacts, much gratitude and kudos by simply running Party errands for Otto and Gregor Strasser, two founder members of the Party. The brothers found their new recruit doubly useful: Himmler was 'full of frustrated ambition and he's got a motor bike!' They took a dimmer view of his talents. Gregor told fellow National Socialists, 'He's devoted to me and I use him as a secretary [. . .] He's very ambitious but I won't take him along North [to Berlin], he's no world-beater, you know.'[1]

Just as Himmler began to suspect that the Strassers were exploiting him he found new inspiration in a strange, magnetic German, Walter Darré. Born in Argentina, Darré had been educated at King's College, Wimbledon, and was an official in the Department of Agriculture in Berlin. Himmler was transfixed by his theories of the Nordic peasant: tall, blond, beautiful and martial and an archetype of essential nobility. Darré was obsessed with stopping the drift from country to town, promoting settlement schemes to strengthen the peasantry, who were 'the only truly reliable basis for purity in our race'.[2] Darré even suggested farming out non-Aryans to other areas. Himmler seized on this policy with ultimately horrifying results.

In an early masterstroke, Himmler recognised how much Darré's idyllic theories of blood and soil would appeal to Hitler and how they could translate into reality the high-flown ideas expounded by the Party's chief ideologue, Alfred Rosenberg. Rosenberg promulgated notions of Germanic racial superiority, and it was a brilliant piece of sycophantic opportunism on Himmler's part to show the Führer that Darré's schemes furnished an excellent means to their end. Years later, Himmler described his practical approach to achieving Rosenberg's racial ideal in a wartime speech that shows he did not forget his agricultural roots: 'We went about it like a nursery gardener trying to reproduce a good old strain which had been adulterated and debased. We started from the principles of plant selection and then quite unashamedly proceeded to weed out the men we did not think we could use.'[3]

Himmler joined the embryonic Schutzstaffel in 1925, one of two hundred 'shock troops' that were dedicated to the defence of their Führer, a separate force from the Party's military wing, the SA (Sturmabteilung) mob of brownshirts. Wielding his mystic new dogma with considerable skill, Himmler was appointed Deputy Gauleiter of Upper Bavaria and Swabia, and in 1926 he was promoted to Deputy Reich Propaganda Chief and Deputy Commander of the SS. (It was common for Party nomenclature to anticipate their future rule of the Reich.) The turning point came in February 1929 when Hitler exalted the 28-year-old Bavarian to the newly created position of Reichsführer SS.

Himmler was barely into his new uniform when he had an outstanding piece of good fortune. Ferreting through files in SS headquarters, he came across a forgotten report that might have been composed especially for him. Written by Ludolf Haase, the local Nazi leader for Hannover South, it was a brilliantly concise as well as detailed and articulate account of the 'difficult times' that lay ahead for the party after the failure of the Munich putsch.[4] Haase argued that the Party had disintegrated because it had no corps of leaders, and that the leaders themselves had no instrument of power. 'What was needed', claimed Haase, was a 'National Socialist order within the Party', a secret body that would keep the Party in trim. The men of this select group would 'cleanse the organisation, including, if necessary, affiliated formations and authorities'. The new organisation's first task was to 'obtain indispensable knowledge concerning the enemy's plans'. Such researches would enable the new élite corps to be 'the instrument which a senior leader must have if he is successfully to pursue any popular policy of power'.[5]

Himmler was impressed. The report was retyped to pass as his own and submitted to the Party hierarchy. Their response was more condescending than enthusiastic, but he did not let this discourage him. Haase's report was the template of Himmler's future actions. The messianic saviour of the Party was on his way to leading his own order of Teutonic knights. The young Reichsführer yoked together Haase's practical recommendations with Darré's vague theories of racial superiority. He let loose a force that, in its distinctive black uniform, with its insignia of double silver flashes and shiny black boots, proved irresistible to a nation deprived of its military pride. The best description of their role was that 'the SS will be the Imperial Guard of the new Germany'.[6] Himmler's ambition to create a self-regulating SS state within the Reich was cloaked by the motive of defending Führer and Party. It is impossible to say which aim was uppermost in his mind. Anyone who criticised the autonomy that he sought could be construed as not caring about the Party. He was back where he liked it best, securely ensconced on the moral high ground.

Himmler's SS men were a cut above, and deliberately kept separate from, the much larger SA rabble. Order number one, issued by SS headquarters on 13 September 1927, states: 'The SS man and SS commander shall remain silent and shall never become involved in matters concerning the political leadership and SA which do not concern him.'[7] He used the aura of exclusivity to attract the sort of men he had failed to impress at the Apollo Club; the upper classes came in droves, adding their money and their influence to the Reichsführer's rapidly expanding power base. The Grand Duke of Mecklenburg; the Prince of Waldeck and Pyrmont; Prince Kristoff and Prince Wilhelm of Hesse; Count Bassewitz-Behn; Prince Hohenzollern-Emden; Count Friedrich Werner von Schulenburg, and many other famous names from Prussian military history were entered on the roll. Close behind came a wave of intellectuals, university professors and lawyers. Finally, most important of all, bankers and economists gravitated to the new SS empire that seemed to offer them economic stability and to have retained the hierarchical structure of the old republic, a status quo that had always served them well.

Himmler instinctively understood how to capture the heart of German conservatism. There were two key strategies. Honorary SS commanderships were bestowed on influential officials, party functionaries and members of the diplomatic corps, and secondly, élite societies such as the Equestrian Association were given SS membership, dramatically increasing numbers and achieving social acceptability for the SS in one fell swoop. The SS became the antithesis of the SA, a fanatically disciplined force that was, according to an anti-Nazi contemporary, 'super efficient but certainly arrogant'.[8] Its motto was, 'The aristocracy keeps its mouth shut'. The iron discipline that evolved in the SS was such that they were commanded to 'never take part in discussions at members' meetings [. . .] no SS man shall smoke during the address and no one will leave the room'. Suspension resulted from the slightest neglect of duty.

Himmler completed the architecture to ensure absolute autonomy with another brilliant move. He decreed that because SS men were in a class of their own, those that committed a misdemeanour were above normal justice and could be tried only by an SS court – in effect, German law no longer applied to them. The implications were monstrous, yet nobody complained vigorously enough to prevent it from becoming fact. In a quaint echo of his college days, Himmler resurrected the right of the accused to defend his honour by force of arms, so the duel became an SS prerogative.

By the time Germany was at war Himmler's power base was so daunting that everybody apart from Hitler was scared of him. This reflects the extraordinary feat that Himmler achieved in the ten years that followed the Nazi takeover in 1933, through assiduous manoeuvring and manipulation, playing one rival off against another while always staying in the background. Himmler started by progressively taking over the police. He wanted to create a unified Reich police force out of the sixteen *Länder*, 'for a nationwide police force is the strongest linch-pin a State can have'.[9] Since Hermann Göring already controlled some under his role as deputy Führer, Himmler could not avoid clashing with him. So he began a covert operation of double-dealing against his formidable adversary. One by one, each provincial police force succumbed until only Berlin remained outside his control. Göring held his own for a time, although he could not match the ruthlessness of the sordid intrigues that Himmler specialised in. Then the Reichsführer realised that fate had dealt him the ace that, as time went by, he played again and again.

Hitler was pathologically afraid of being assassinated. Himmler manipulated this phobia to earn his leader's undying gratitude and, more importantly, his backing on almost every issue. Early in March 1933 Himmler had arrested Count Arco-Valley, the man who had murdered the Socialist President of Bavaria Kurt Eisner in 1919. Although sentenced to life imprisonment in an era when life meant exactly that, Himmler had him released, then arrested and questioned again. Unsurprisingly, the count confessed to an irresistible urge to repeat the trick on the Führer. Hitler responded to this news with weekly lectures on the ghastly implications of a coup. 'The effects on the public of a successful attack on me would be fearful', declared the Führer on 7 March.[10] Observing the tremendous dread that seized Hitler when he heard about Arco-Valley, Himmler quickly discovered another plot. This time he found three Soviet agents who had been planning to blow up the Führer in his car at a most appropriate spot – outside the Wagner Memorial.

In order to ensure Hitler's safety, Himmler created a new Praetorian Guard, the Leibstandarte-SS Adolf Hitler, with 150 select men under SS Obergruppenführer Joseph 'Sepp' Dietrich. The original concept of the SS as Hitler's personal protection squad was realised, and it seemed logical that Himmler should provide similar squads for the protection of other Nazi leaders. Wasn't Göring, for example, even allowing for his control of the Berlin Gestapo, almost equally at risk? Göring's protestations could not prevent a special squad from being quickly and deviously forced upon him. Himmler's favourite, SS Obergruppenführer Reinhard Heydrich, sent Hitler a report that his department had unearthed a Communist plot to kill the Deputy Führer. Contacting Hitler rather than Göring ensured that the Führer would immediately take action and that Göring would be faced with a *fait accompli*; it was impossible for Göring to refuse Hitler's generosity. As Göring formally handed over control of the Gestapo on 10 April 1934 he was reported to have remarked drily, 'No point in tripping over every corpse' – perhaps thinking he was fortunate not to be one himself.[11]

By surrounding his colleagues with men who had taken an oath of allegiance to Hitler and, of course, to himself, the Reichsführer ensured that he could take care of them in every sense. This simple ploy was a significant advance towards absolute power. Potential rivals were surrounded by SS chauffeurs, secretaries and valets. Hitler was effusively grateful; in his eyes, Himmler could do no wrong. The Berlin police force was the last part of the jigsaw. All the police, including the Kripo and the Gestapo, were under Himmler's control. He even gained permission for the SS to form its own armoured units, a formidable military force termed the *Verfügungstruppe* (renamed Waffen SS in 1940) that was formally constituted as an independent force on 20 July 1934. The repressive forces Himmler commanded – including the concentration camps inherited from Göring, such as Dachau, where political dissidents were incarcerated from 1933 – were self-evident. However, the financial and economic empires that he went on to construct, from 1938 onwards, were far less well known.

In the early 1940s Albert Speer realised, too late, the insidious competition that he faced for his control of the Economic Section of the Reich. By straightforward threats, by mixing half-truths with deliberate lies about production figures in the factories he acquired, and by denigrating the performance of his colleagues, Himmler ousted everyone unable to compete with such tactics. He assumed responsibility for the rocket establishments on the Baltic where the V rockets were being developed, and eventually took control of the Luftwaffe Research Station. Wherever Himmler cast his shadow a climate of fear instantly developed. 'Even today', wrote Speer after the war, 'the files reveal the panicky need for action unleashed by any query of Himmler's.'[12] Before the Second World War, Himmler already commanded a 'monolithic state within a state', as historian Gerald Reitlinger described it.[13] It was a distinctly separate power organisation, cosseted by its own laws and justly feared by all his adversaries. Himmler's web of financial intrigue was in itself a work of art.

All this had been achieved at remarkably little cost in terms of Himmler's personal standing. In the eyes of the Nazi Party, Himmler's record was faultless. He ran this sinister empire with consummate skill. Part of his success derived from his attention to detail, part from his understanding of the German love of mysticism and martial pomp, and the rest from the structure of the SS that had been carefully designed to ensure Himmler's self-preservation. Perhaps the greatest paradox of the man was the way he combined calculated manipulation of others with a fanatical belief in those mystical concepts that he adapted to his own ends. It was a winning combination.

Analysts are often baffled by the varying and duplicate functions of many departments of Himmler's hydra-headed organisation, the inanity of some of which beggars the imagination. For example, the Department of Ancestral Heritage (recalling the Himmler family's *Ahnenzimmer*) had a section devoted to the research of ancient Teutonic and Nordic runes. The major problem confronting analysts is the absence of any clear hierarchical order. Each department head seemed to think that he was directly answerable to the Reichsführer and tolerated no interference by other departments or department heads. The picture that emerges is one of organised chaos, and indeed that was close to the truth. Yet outsiders remarked on the structure's brutal efficiency.

Buchenwald survivor and historian Eugen Kogon described the SS as 'A monolithic organisation directed by the demoniac will of one man [. . .] a super organised master and slave system, every part at all times controllable [. . .] pursuing a plan consistently, step by step, at any cost, each small step sought out with a degree of ruthlessness completely transcending ordinary concepts.'[14] Doubtless this was a view Himmler encouraged, but it would be wrong to assume that the design of this monolith was original to him. In fact the whole structure, which encouraged each section leader to act independently, was typical not only of the SS, but of Hitler's control of his minions, the economy and administration of the Third Reich in general, and fairly typical of Germany both before and after Bismarck. Each individual *Land* (district authority) vied with others for supremacy and had a high degree of autonomy. This created division and discord but also encouraged competition. The fight for power between its integral parts soon found a balance that allowed the whole machine to operate with dynamic drive, albeit in an atmosphere of creative tension.

It was a structure that Czech Foreign Minister Jan Masaryk called the hallmark of the Stalinist regime in Soviet Russia: 'the absence of system'. Moreover, the absence of devolved power to the lower levels shored up the importance of those at the highest level. Himmler's system may not have been unique to him, but the scope of his ambition and his capacity to realise it meant that more and more power accrued to the Reichsführer; his underlings were far too busy sniping at each other to even think about toppling their leader.

In the SS, ruthless competition and unquestioning obedience to the prescribed SS ideals were the norm. This fostered an atmosphere of jealousy in which commanders were encouraged to tell tales on each other for their own advantage. Rumour and intrigue were rife. In this maelstrom several unsavoury characters rose fast. SS Gruppenführer Artur Nebe, SS Gruppenführer Heinrich Müller and SS Obergruppenführer Kurt Daluege all had one thing in common: their personnel files all commented on their unscrupulousness and opportunism, qualities that were far from a hindrance to promotion. Although Himmler paid a great deal of attention to some of the bizarre subjects to which whole departments were devoted, he paid less attention to their internal structures. Four major departmental heads and Himmler's headquarters staff provided scapegoats to shoulder responsibility for decisions. It was structurally impossible for anyone other than Himmler to have a clear overview of SS activities.

The SS was effectively divided into two main parts. The first was the non-essential departments that were incapable of rapidly or effectively altering the balance of power, or even perceived power. This half of the SS comprised, for example, the Department of Resettlement, initially led by Obergruppenführer Ulrich Greifelt; the Department of Political Education under Gruppenführer August Heissmeyer; the Department of Ideological Research, run by Obersturmbannführer Dittel; the Legal Department, under Obergruppenführer Franz Breithaupt; the Officers Section, led by Gruppenführer

Maximilian von Herff, and the Department of Budget Administration under Standartenführer Josef Spacil.

Departments more essential to Himmler's needs were those where
men carried arms or wielded influence. Obergruppenführer Oswald
Pohl ran the Administrative Department, which was, among other
things, responsible for SS military supplies and the detailed planning
of concentration camps. Himmler also built up four massive concerns
– an equipment company, an experimental nutrition company, a
textile and leather company, and a building and construction company – that were incorporated into a firm called *Deutsche Gewerbliche
Unternehmen* (German Industrial Undertakings). Through this a large
part of Germany's economy was under his control without many
people being aware that it was run by the SS.

The massive police forces and the Waffen SS were Himmler's
most obvious assets. As ever, real power lay in the hands of only a
few of his subordinates. The Kripo was the thought police, the unit
for suppression of crime, or more accurately, the suppression of the
people. It was run by Artur Nebe until 1943 and then by Obergruppenführer Panzinger. The opportunist Heinrich Müller ran the
Gestapo (he had previously been a criminal police inspector and
espoused violently anti-Nazi views). It had been devised for 'active
investigation of the opposition'; Müller card-indexed and colour-
coded the nation. His 'A' file was divided into three categories of
urgency and listed all known or suspected enemies of the State
who were to be arrested at times of national crisis. Targets were
colour-coded on the corner of their cards: dark red for a Communist,
light red for a Marxist, brown for an assassin, and violet for a grum-
bler. Such administrative niceties applied throughout the SS state.
Local police and State Police arrest warrants were organised into
colour-coded categories, as were all concentration camp internees.
The whole nation was distilled into a vast card index. Even nowadays,
with all the advantages of computerisation, no police force has come
anywhere close to the omnipotent power of the combined SS and
State Police forces.

It was not Hitler, not the Nazi Party, nor local government that
exercised effective and immediate disciplinary control over the Ger-

man nation, but Himmler and the SS State. Both police forces, the Kripo and the Gestapo, were run by the 'blond beast' Reinhard Heydrich, until Ernst Kaltenbrunner took over after his assassination. Between them they enjoyed a reign of terror. The slightest examination of the role of uniformed police in Nazi Germany shows how much trust Himmler placed in his subordinate commanders, especially Obergruppenführer Kurt Daluege of the *Hauptamtordnungspolizei*, whom he had inherited from Göring. There were thirty senior SS Police Kommandants, each controlling his own district, and each directly subordinate to Himmler. This simple administrative step made it difficult to organise or co-ordinate any effective coup, as relations between Kommandants were more competitive than co-operative.

The SS's military arm, the Waffen SS, with its 1944 strength of 560,000 including 30,000 men of the SS Totenkopf Sturmbanne (concentration camp guards), was in practice under army control, but pledged its allegiance to Himmler. Although nominally run by General Hans Jüttner, Head of the Operational Department, it shared the same constraints as the police; divisional commanders reported directly to Himmler. Furthermore, Waffen SS General Karl Wolff created another bureaucratic layer of officers, a buffer system that provided an essential barrier against dissatisfaction amongst the rank and file, deflecting criticism from Himmler. Wolff went on to play a special role in the Reichsführer's affairs apart from his nominal responsibility for the Ancestral Heritage Department.

The most influential SS department was the Sicherheitsdienst (Security Department), which was originally devised to be the sole intelligence service to the Nazi Party. It was divided into two sections. Otto Ohlendorf's Inland Section produced *Reports from the Reich*, a nasty Nazi gossip magazine. Its truthfulness infuriated many and delighted several, not least the Reichsführer. It became known as the BBC of the SD and some, such as Dr Carl Marcus, deputy to Wilhelm Jahnke in a separate intelligence service, the Jahnke Büro, thought 'It was deliberately deployed to denigrate the Party to the glorification of the elitism of the SS State'.[15] The other, *Ausland* SD, was Walter Schellenberg's highly regarded Foreign

Intelligence Section. Schellenberg had earned a special place in Himmler's heart after saving his life.

Walter Schellenberg was one of Himmler's closest allies, assuming the place left by the death of Reinhard Heydrich. Heydrich had been the incarnation of Himmler's Aryan ideal. The tall, blond son of an opera singer and an actress, he shared their talent for histrionics; Heydrich played the violin so sensitively that he openly wept, inconsolable at the sheer beauty of his own performance. He matched this performance in his role as Himmler's assiduously brutal yet servile second in command. They made a formidable duo until his assassination in May 1942.

SS *Hauptamt* (headquarters) housed another of Himmler's most trusted associates, Gottlob Berger, a watchdog who would arrange murders for the Reichsführer. He completed the essential structure of the buffer zone in the SS machinery that allowed Himmler to control the unwieldy monster he had created. SS *Hauptamt's* functions were more than administrative. Berger's minions recorded and collated gossip about SS leaders as they vied for power. Officers from the Inland Section that worked as gossip columnists and spies planted in subordinate departments quickly discovered that there were no illusions about the *Hauptamt's* main function. The fiercest opposition to Berger emanated from the Waffen SS, which was immersed in the savage reality of the war. Many of its members failed to co-operate or even to report when ordered. The Kripo and Gestapo resisted to a lesser extent.

Himmler became so vexed by this failure to keep tabs on his Commanders that he appointed a personal representative to check all the reports coming in from the various head offices. Dr Richard Korherr was a devout Catholic and a brilliant statistician. Shy and obsessive, he was an irritable man with an inflated ego that could have been modelled on his master. He swiftly established that every department of the SS was falsifying its results, minimising problems and openly lying about insubordination, all to please the Reichsführer. Korherr's niggling reports so irritated the new head of the Race and Resettlement Section, Obergruppenführer Richard Hildebrandt, that, on 12 August 1943, he finally resorted to physical violence. Having been 'followed to the door', Korherr reported to his beloved Reichsführer, 'he gave me two resounding smacks one on each cheek! And as far as I can remember he said "Now get out", though I couldn't swear to it. I departed without a word or any attempt to retaliate.'[16] After waiting weeks for justice and retribution, Korherr found that all Himmler could extract from Hildebrandt was a half-hearted apology:

> Honoured Reichsführer,
> I respectfully request you to express my regret to Ober-regierungsrat Doctor Korherr for the physical assault I made on him.
> Heil Hitler,
> Yours,
> Hildebrandt[17]

Soon afterwards Dr Korherr retired to a new post at Regensburg whence he only emerged after much persuasion and great reluctance. Despite the internecine squabbling, carping and criticism of subordinates – a chaos Himmler did not discourage – he maintained complete control of the whole of his SS State until the end of the war. This was in itself a remarkable feat. But how did the master of organisation and self-preservation behave when wartime defeat, the ultimate disorder, threatened to overturn his ordered Reich?

In fact, it was when the war began to go disastrously wrong for Germany that Himmler's organisational skills proved most valuable. They ensured that he had unrivalled access to information and, once covert peace negotiations began, Himmler was able to show just how imaginatively he could use his position to strive for ultimate power.

5

Peace

I am the British Foreign Secretary.
> Montagu Norman, Governor of the Bank of England,
> New York, 1939

Imagine poor Schellenberg ever thinking that Himmler would
be party to plotting against the Führer.
> Hugh Trevor-Roper

The British are accustomed to believe that the Nazis were defeated
because of stalwart opposition to appeasement after Winston Churchill
became Prime Minister. The truth, as so often, is somewhat different.
A plethora of peace negotiations was undertaken throughout the
course of the war, motivated for the most part by financial interests
or individuals' thirst for power. It comes as no surprise to discover
that most negotiations involved men operating in the nebulous zone
where politics, industry and finance met. Given Heinrich Himmler's
appetite and aptitude for plotting, it is even less surprising to find
that his influence can be traced throughout.

Until now accounts of wartime peace negotiations have concentrated on rare overt diplomatic contacts and the activities of various
German resistance groups.[1] To document the hundreds of significant
covert meetings that went on would fill a book on its own. According
to Peter Tennant, banker and SIS (now known as MI6) agent who
was Press Attaché at the British Legation in Stockholm during the
war, such meetings seemed to occur at the exhausting rate of at least
one a week. I have therefore focused on key power groupings in
order to convey the inherent pattern of determined, ruthless ambition

displayed by Himmler's attempts to secure both peace and power.

It is not always possible to locate an order that can pin direct responsibility on the Reichsführer SS, yet the persistent appearance of his key henchmen is more than suggestive. After all, this was a man who commanded absolute loyalty, through fear if nothing else, and who was known for his consistency – if an opportunity appeared lost, an alternative would always be found. More significantly, the pattern of demands shifts in tandem with Germany's declining hopes of winning the war and Himmler's dawning realisation that the excesses of the SS regime made him unacceptable to the Allies as Hitler's successor. Thus, bold proposals for Himmler to take over Germany and unite with the Allies against Russia's Bolshevik threat give way to desperate measures to ensure his immunity from post-war prosecution. If Himmler was not the agency behind these secret negotiations, then their spirit so closely matches his interests that those involved must have had a window to the man's soul. In light of his strategy to retain absolute command of all departments of the SS, with every deputy reporting directly to him, I believe that he approached secret negotiations similarly, making it more difficult to detect his influence. The men who acted in German interests in the negotiations that follow were all employed as personal agents, working directly for Himmler, and tended to be bankers, financiers or lawyers. There were also several ineffectual peace factions within Germany that Himmler would, from time to time, exploit to achieve his own ends.

During the Second World War the Soviet threat to capitalism added to the desire of wealthy individuals for a peaceful solution that would keep Stalin at bay. British financiers were terrified that war might make them totally dependent on money from the United States, as Britain would be forced to borrow US money to prosecute war with any hope of success. During the phoney war, while Neville Chamberlain was still British Prime Minister, Treasury officials and City of London financiers, industrialists and members of the political hierarchy, including the royal family with their heavy investments in Europe, were united in their purpose. They wanted to end war quickly with Germany at all costs rather than enter a suffocating relationship of financial dependence upon the United States.[2] After Winston Churchill succeeded Chamberlain on 12 May 1940, interested parties in Britain and Germany focused on this intractable new Prime Minister as the main obstacle to peace.

In 1939 the British were faced with official peace offers emanating from Foreign Minister Joachim von Ribbentrop, and a plethora of separate offers which seemed to guarantee Hitler's removal. Sweden became the key site for unofficial overtures to peace because of its neutrality, wealth, geographic centrality, with a royal family closely related to Britain's through marriage with the Mountbattens. Numerous well-connected bankers were more than willing to become active agents. A key figure was Swedish Baron Knut Bonde. He had been married to Lord Rennal's niece for more than twenty years, and consequently had many friends in the English aristocracy. In the winter of 1939 Bonde was approached by German diplomat von Cramm, a tennis partner of King Gustav of Sweden and a great friend of Göring, with a proposal to achieve peace with Göring as leader. In the winter of 1939 Bonde met with the then British Foreign Minister Lord Halifax in great secrecy in the Dorchester Hotel. (Halifax reluctantly became the focus for the machinations of those who were discontented with Churchill and wanted peace.) Bonde handed over a memorandum from Göring that stated, according to Göring's brother-in-law who saw it beforehand, 'Göring is absolutely loyal to Hitler until the time comes to lock him up'[3] With his laudable if misplaced sense of decency, Lord Halifax declined the offer on the grounds that he preferred to deal with Hitler, not assassinate him.

Instead, later that winter Halifax used Colonel Christie, a shadowy adviser to the British Secret Service, to approach Himmler's agent No. 144/7957, the immensely wealthy Count Max von Hohenlohe-Langenburg. Christie asked von Hohenlohe-Langenburg to help soften Göring's approach while Halifax attempted to win over Hitler with flattery.[4] This bore no fruit. Christie's papers contain tantalising evidence that a senior member of the British royal family, probably the King, was actively involved in a very specific offer to Hitler. This was automatically doomed to failure because Hitler was too fired up by his victories to consider ending war by any other means than defeat of his enemies.

The Sweden–Germany–Allies connection spawned numerous other points of contact. On 18 January 1940 SOE agent Peter Tennant met with Dr Walter Jacobsen. Jacobsen was an old friend of Leipzig Mayor Carl Gördeler, a prominent opponent of Hitler and war who represented Himmler's financial interests in Sweden, for example, brokering Bosch shares. Gördeler had visited Jacobsen when he came to Stockholm on business for Himmler in the early months of war. Subsequent to Gördeler's visits, Jacobsen brought Tennant German peace proposals similar to those Göring had previously offered the British, including the removal of Hitler.[5] According to Canadian millionaire Sir William Stephenson, Churchill's confidant, the American Secretary of State, John Foster Dulles, intervened. Dulles prompted Roosevelt to urge the British to take the peace proposals seriously because they emanated not from the German resistance but from both Himmler and generals of the Wehrmacht. Gördeler had contacted Dulles directly and kept the American informed about every move in the Third Reich. This was not an altruistic relationship between strangers – Gördeler was exploiting a longstanding bond with Dulles that had been forged in fraud.

It may come as a surprise to learn that corporate lawyers John Foster Dulles and his brother Allen Dulles, who became head of the CIA after the war, were two of the most opportunistic financiers of the twentieth century. John Foster Dulles was attorney to the Wallenberg Holding Company that owned America Bosch, a subsidiary of the giant German concern. This brought him together with Jacob and Marcus Wallenberg, the powerful Swedish bankers who ran the Enskilda Bank, dealt in armaments shares and enjoyed global influence. Dulles was empowered to seize control of America Bosch should it be discovered that it had not severed links with its parent company in Stuttgart. Gördeler, a financial genius, had created, during the interwar period, a vast network of Bosch companies and intermediaries that masked the parent company's continued ownership of its international subsidiaries. (Himmler would go on to exploit Gördeler's talents for similar purposes.) The trail of concealed ownership led from Amsterdam to New York. This network was the reason for Gördeler's extensive foreign travel, during which he had made the connections he would exploit to further peace negotiations. This mucky scheme shows how the alliance of profitable self-interest wedded America to the Reich in a way that allowed Nazi leaders to influence Allied policy at the highest level.

Due to Roosevelt's interest, another acquaintance of Gördeler, Lord Vansittart, the hugely influential chief diplomatic adviser to the British government, gave cautious approval to the negotiations that had been conducted through Tennant and Jacobsen.[6] Michael Balfour of the Ministry of Information (which controlled SOE) prepared to go and see his old friend Helmut von Moltke, leader of the Kreisau Circle, a leading German resistance group. However, Churchill intervened and managed, with great difficulty, as Tennant understood it, to block this move. A compromise visit to Stockholm was arranged to sound out how serious the Germans' intentions were. Walter Monckton, who ran Churchill's private intelligence service, went on a lecture tour to Stockholm, and was introduced to von Moltke, who spelled out the terms of the agreement. According to Swedish intelligence sources, the British understood that the Gördeler/von Moltke group was backed by Himmler, who was being proposed to succeed Hitler.[7]

There were many links between Himmler and the group: Gördeler was his financial representative, and the SS provided transport and visas for von Moltke and Gördeler to travel from Germany. Monckton realised the Germans were entirely serious. Churchill had only played along until this point because he thought it was unlikely that there was sufficient German will to pose a real prospect of peace, and duly overrode the increasingly powerful peace party within the British cabinet. Dulles and others were left quietly fuming.

Matters did not rest here. A leading member of the peace faction within the British establishment, Sir Charles Hambro, was also connected with both Allen and John Foster Dulles through the international banking house of Schröder. It is likely, but cannot be proved, that the Wallenbergs brokered deals in Germany for Schröder,

Hambro and the Dulles brothers.[8] Probably working in conjunction
with Hambro, Lord Halifax engineered more meetings between
Montagu Norman, the Governor of the Bank of England, and German representatives, including officials of the Dresdner Bank, in
both New York and San Francisco.[9] These discussions were of great
interest to the FBI; the financial implications alone to any Anglo-
Nazi accord were immense. They bugged several meetings at the
Waldorf in New York and the Mark Hopkins Hotel in San Francisco.
Their records, for the most part, have still not been released. However, FBI sources say that the discussions were based on the premise
that Hitler would be removed as part of a peace plan. A record exists
of one meeting held on 27 November 1940 at the Mark Hopkins
Hotel. Only three people attended: Halifax supporter Sir William
Wiseman, who represented the American Kuhn Loeb bank, Hitler's
former aide Captain Fritz Wiedemann, who sat on the board of IG
Farben, a powerful German industrial group filled with SS leaders,
and a fascinating newcomer, Princess Stefanie von Hohenlohe-
Waldenburg. It lasted from 7.30 p.m. until 1.00 a.m.[10] The discussion
emphasised that Hitler had to go, the emphasis coming from the
Germans. Princess Stefanie suggested there was an alternative to the
return of the Crown Prince, 'Little Willie', to lead Germany, an
alternative she thought would prove far more practical: Reichsführer
SS Heinrich Himmler, who, she said, was a monarchist.[11]

Princess Stefanie was a fully-fledged Himmler agent with a
remarkable background. The attractive young Hungarian had
entered Vienna's Imperial Opera ballet school in 1906, and then
started an affair with the elderly Archduke Leopold Salvator, through
whom she became friendly with the wealthiest leaders of the upper
echelons of the European military. She married Prince Hohenlohe-
Schillingsfürst, and immediately embarked on a career as one of the
world's most successful courtesans. Her conquests included John
Warden, who ran American Standard Oil, and international banker
Donald Malcolm. Numerous members of the Anglo–German
Fellowship in London fell under Princess Stefanie's spell, including
loudmouth newspaper magnate Lord Rothermere, whom she indis-
creetly blackmailed about the fifty messages she had carried to Hitler

on his behalf expressing his rabid support for Nazi ideals. Supposedly an intimate friend of Hitler, she certainly became Captain Fritz Wiedemann's lover. Prior to this American adventure, Princess Stefanie had been having regular secret meetings with Sir Alexander Cadogan, permanent undersecretary to the Foreign Office and an adviser to Churchill, in her London apartment at 70 Brook Street.[12]

Small, dark and buxom, she was an aggressively confident woman of considerable presence. The FBI report shows that this Himmler-sponsored negotiator dominated the discussion.[13] Sir William Wiseman made no bones about representing the anti-Churchill faction. This is how he opened the meeting:

> What we talk about tonight [. . .] I will send straight to Lord Halifax, because I know he knows you. He is sympathetic and I will send it direct to him so that it is not circulated around the Foreign Office. Not even our Ambassador in Washington will know anything about it.[14]

The FBI furiously pressed for the extradition of all parties, particularly the Princess, who was only over from London on a temporary visa to visit her son. She resisted their efforts by the simple expedient of sleeping with the Director of the Bureau of Immigration and Naturalisation, Major Lemuel B. Schofield, an event also witnessed by the FBI.

The new Head of Covert Operations in North America, Sir William Stephenson, acted swiftly to prevent the extradition of Sir William Wiseman, which would have caused Britain grave embarrassment.[15] Stephenson told the FBI that Wiseman had been acting officially for the Secret Service in an attempt to draw out information from the Germans. In fact, Wiseman, who had run British Intelligence in the First World War, was an invaluable point of contact between the leadership of the American and British Secret Services, through secret clubs such as the ROOM and the WALRUS.[16] Fellow member Vincent Astor was Roosevelt's chief personal intelligence source until 1941. It was understandable that the British were reluctant to lose such a key link with the Americans, however hostile the FBI might have been to him, as Wiseman's continued presence was essential to the British war effort.

Subsequent statements from Wiseman and letters he received from Princess Stefanie make it clear that neither realised their conversations had been bugged, and so did not fully understand that concrete evidence was available to back the attempts to extradite them.[17] When questioned by the FBI Wiseman feigned ignorance of other meetings he had held in San Francisco and Chicago with Bank of England Deputy Governor Cyril F. Tiarks, who also ran the British branch of Schröder, and Herr Volkers. Volkers had previously worked for Abwehr Chief Admiral Wilhelm Canaris and had married into the Swedish Bofors family, who made armaments and were later heavily involved in the post-war cloaking of Bosch shares.[18]

The extent of the Halifax faction's activities in North America was exposed by the FBI.[19] Other bugged meetings took place in the Palace Hotel in San Francisco between Tiarks and Schacht, who governed the Bank of Germany until Hitler forced him to resign when war started, yet retained enormous influence. Bank of England Governor Montagu Norman and Tiarks were deeply implicated in the Halifax faction's alternative peace moves that aimed at the removal of Churchill and Hitler. The differences between the peace faction and Churchill were in danger of becoming public, and threatened to implicate the British royal family in political meddling. Canadian Prime Minister Mackenzie King and media magnate Lord Beaverbrook used their considerable influence in America to per-suade two defectors from the Halifax faction to inform on the continuing Anglo-Nazi negotiations. Lord Wigram, royal equerry, terrified of the consequences of the exposure of royal involvement, was the first to approach Churchill. Due to his close friendship with Mackenzie King, wealthy landowner Lord Willingdon also joined the Churchill camp. A furious Churchill asked Foreign Secretary Anthony Eden to see Montagu Norman in person to question him about American allegations that Norman's deputy Tiarks was plotting with the Germans. Eden did not want to rock the boat. He reported back meekly, claiming Tiarks had not seen German banker Schacht for over a year and that he did not believe that Tiarks' firm, Schröder, was doing business with the Germans at that particular time. This half-truth in answer to what amounted to a question of treason brought forth a resigned comment from Churchill: 'My dear Anthony the war has been going on not for ONE, but for a couple of years.'[20]

The beleaguered British Prime Minister turned to his friend Mackenzie King. Could he lend him the Governor of the Bank of Canada to replace Norman until the end of the war? But such was the power of the Halifax faction that this request was refused, and Norman refused even to contemplate resignation. Churchill had no choice but to tolerate Norman; if Churchill had sacked him it would have precipitated a political and financial crisis that might have made his already precarious position untenable.

While negotiators such as Princess Stefanie claimed to be sponsored by Himmler, others even claimed to represent specific proposals from him. Spain, neutral like Sweden, was another locus of many covert wartime peace negotiations. The British Ambassador in Madrid, Sir Samuel Hoare, was a key figure in the Halifax peace faction and hoped to wrench power from Churchill. In March 1941 Spanish General Aranda told the British Military Attaché, Colonel Torr, that Himmler wished for a settlement, implying his intention to finish the war and eliminate Hitler. Torr reported back to London that Sir Samuel Hoare was to meet with Himmler's agent Count Max von Hohenlohe-Langenburg. In response to alarmed Foreign Office queries, Hoare claimed he had repudiated all advances.

The Italian Ambassador in Madrid, whose intelligence agents gleaned inside knowledge, reported to his Foreign Office an entirely different version of these talks, which is so detailed that it is almost certainly correct. Hoare was quoted saying, 'The position of the British Government is insecure, Churchill can no longer count on a majority, sooner or later I will be called back to London with the precise task of making a compromise peace [. . .] I will only take this mission on condition I have full powers.'[21] SIS gave Churchill an almost identical version of Hoare's statement. Others in the Halifax faction shared Hoare's opinion. Indiscreet landowner Lord Londonderry's correspondence with the Duke of Windsor's friend,

Kenneth de Courcy, Duke of Grantmesnil, confirms the knife-edge on which Churchill balanced.[22] Had Churchill's adversaries been better organised, Churchill might well have fallen.

In the early years of war all peace talks emphasised the need to get rid of Hitler and Churchill. Himmler was perceived to back the German peace party and be prepared to remove Hitler, and consequently Himmler became the focus of the shadowy international financiers' efforts to negotiate with the Germans. At this time Himmler was still considered by Allied peace negotiators to be an acceptable interim leader who could keep Germany under control until a more amenable candidate could be found to replace him. The United States and Sweden were certainly keener on Himmler than the UK. Nevertheless, such confidence demonstrates just how powerful was the Reichsführer's grasp on Germany. Negotiators on the British side were told that if they precipitated Churchill's downfall because of his refusal to accept generous peace terms, this would give those with power in the Reich a legitimate and popular reason for acting against the Führer. Himmler was prepared to use the army as well as bankers, to further his personal ambition to rule Germany. His desire to find a popular, moral basis for Hitler's removal was truly in character, part of his constant search for legitimacy.

The Japanese attack on Pearl Harbor on 7 December 1941 came to Churchill's aid and brought the United States into the war, apparently putting everything on ice. Yet the negotiations continued their inexorable progress. They culminated on 15 January 1943, when Allen Dulles, the US Special Representative in Bern (his cover for his work with the OSS), met with Himmler's agent Count Max von Hohenlohe-Langenburg and a Nazi SD officer called Bauer. Von Hohenlohe-Langenburg took a somewhat naive view of Allen Dulles: 'A tall burly sporting type of about 45, healthy looking, with good teeth and a simple, fresh open-hearted manner.'[23] Another SD report stated, 'It may be assumed with certainty, and has been confirmed by investigation, that if faced with serious negotiators Mr Bull [the SD code name for Dulles] would never do anything underhand.' This solemn statement of confidence is designed to sound as if they had never met the simple American before, and previous authors have taken these statements at face value. In fact, von Hohenlohe-Langenburg had known Dulles for many years since they were introduced in Vienna, and had been a frequent visitor to the Dulles brothers' Long Island households.

Allen Dulles had spent many years cultivating important social and business contacts in Germany. As a young lawyer after the First World War he had joined his brother John Foster at Versailles, where they advised on war reparations while spinning a web of business connections through Gerhard Westrick and influential German banking colossus Kurt von Schröder. Dulles had secretly conspired with the huge conglomerate Du Pont to ship munitions to Germany in violation of the sanctions against German rearmament. As he was in charge of determining how much Germany should pay the Allies, Dulles was an expert on sanctions. Consequently, he was in the best possible position to help Du Pont evade sanctions; he knew every loophole and how to present the paperwork to ensure that imports escaped scrutiny. Working from his office in Berne for the OSS, most members of which were conservative right-wing corporate lawyers, attorneys and international bankers, his assistant was Gero Schulz von Gävernitz, a vertiginously tall, aristocratic, naturalised American banker, who had married into the German Stinnes family, personal friends of Schröder. Von Gävernitz lent his support to von Moltke's resistance group, the Kreisau Circle, having known von Moltke's father.

The encoded messages Dulles sent back to Washington in 1943 about his multiple negotiations with the German resistance groups who opposed Hitler show that at this time the resistance still emphasised the need for Germany to have a free hand for expansion in the East to defeat Bolshevism. Dulles laconically noted that the SS and resistance objectives were indistinguishable – as, of course, he had always known.

In 1943 Churchill remained under political pressure from the United States to reach a settlement that would keep Bolshevism at bay. MI5 chief Sir Stewart Menzies was seconded by Churchill to make an approach. He proposed some stringent preconditions to any discussion. Firstly, Hitler had to be put under house arrest in

Berchtesgaden. Then a de facto government should be set up in Germany, comprising a 'Council of Twelve' under Himmler's control. Only then could serious discussions begin. Such difficult objectives should have meant an end to further negotiations as, without any promise that peace would result from these actions, there was no immediate justification for taking them. However, according to Walter Schellenberg, lawyer Dr Carl Langbehn, acting as emissary for his neighbour Himmler, started meeting with the British in Stockholm in March and April 1943, as well as liaising with the American von Gävernitz in Switzerland.[24]

These meetings caused Langbehn to fall foul of the Gestapo. That September Heinrich Müller, the Gestapo Chief, came across a British radio message in an easily decipherable form (it is quite possible that the unenthusiastic British did this deliberately). It was clear proof of treason. Müller hastened to send it, not to Himmler, but direct to Hitler. Langbehn was imprisoned and charged with being a British agent.

Schellenberg took over the talks immediately. He asked Brandin and Møller, Directors of the Swedish Match Company, who had arranged talks with the Allies, to come to Berlin to meet Himmler. Then in October Schellenberg saw Jacob Wallenberg in Berlin. The Swedish financier had previously had talks with Langbehn. After this meeting Schellenberg rushed to Stockholm to continue negotiations with Wallenberg and others under the guise of visiting Brandin to present him with an inscribed porcelain plaque in recognition of his work for the Third Reich.[25] The groundwork for this Stockholm meeting had been laid by SS Colonel Carl Rasche, director of Dresdner Bank and yet another friend of Allen Dulles. Rasche pushed for what the Swedish intelligence agents who took part now openly termed 'the SS solution': peace in the West and Himmler to take over as Führer. In liaison with another Himmler agent, Legationsrat Pratski, von Hohenlohe-Langenburg's secretary Spitzi contacted the American Military Attaché in Lisbon and paved the way for another American visitor. The ever-shifting tableau of peace negotiators welcomed another newcomer, OSS agent Abraham Stevens Hewitt, a special envoy of Roosevelt's. Senior CIA officer James Angleton's laconic description of Hewitt was 'he was exceedingly well bred and possessed quite extraordinary equine intelligence'.[26] Angleton had a low opinion of horses' intellectual abilities.

Abraham Stevens Hewitt was the president of Campaign Contributors Associates, which American Intelligence agents gave the motto, 'bent arms – greasy palms'. This was a fairly accurate description of their activities representing the biggest names in American industry, all bent on placing a President in the White House. Hewitt had also helped the Dulles brothers to mask Bosch's interests in the Wallenbergs' Enskilda Bank. His visit to Stockholm combined self-interest with political business; the President's special envoy was also representing the US Commercial Company, who wanted him to persuade the Swedish firm of SKF to slow down the supply of ballbearings that were critical to German industry. Angleton was also doing business for the law firm of Lee Higginson. As ever, the peace agenda was entangled with the demands of corporate profit.

Hewitt arrived in Stockholm that autumn armed with a seven-point peace plan that made provision for the transfer of Wehrmacht troops to fend off the Russians in the East and some additional clauses to placate the British.[27] At their initial meeting at the Grand Hotel, Schellenberg and Hewitt quickly agreed that it was essential to move all German forces to the East as soon as peace had been established in the West. They met again some three days later at Abwehr Intelligence Officer Finke's house in Stockholm. It was agreed that if Roosevelt favoured Himmler's counterproposals an advert would appear several months later, for eight consecutive days, in the *Svenska Dagbladet* or the *Stockholm Tidningen* newspapers that would read, 'For sale – valuable goldfish aquarium 1524 Krona'.[28] If they needed to contact each other urgently, they were to go through the German Embassy at Lisbon. Hewitt was to approach Pratski or Schröder at the German Embassy in Lisbon using the code name 'Siegel'; Schellenberg was to use the code name 'Braun'.

All this secrecy was necessary because of Churchill's hostility. At the British Legation in Stockholm, Sir Peter Tennant reported back to his anxious SIS bosses that the American Legation assured him the talks were entirely private, Hewitt having 'No authority from the American Government'.[29] Fearing a premature settlement would disadvantage them, the British started a veritable flood of mischievous disinformation throughout Europe. An informant to the SD in Lisbon reported that the British now considered 'that a change of regime in Germany could only be brought about by the SS and not by the Wehrmacht'. The same agent went on to say, 'Reports that there is a possible or potential or even acute difference of opinion between the Führer and the SS can be clearly traced back to English sources.'[30] The British disinformation campaign killed off the prospect of any deal. Himmler, who had been due to visit Stockholm and finalise negotiations with Hewitt, called Schellenberg to the Munich Hotel Vierjahreszeiten, where they decided that the risk of a visit to Stockholm was too great because Gestapo Chief Müller and Ernst Kaltenbrunner were plotting to denounce them. The advert for the goldfish aquarium never appeared.

Throughout the war, Churchill was consistently well informed about unauthorised peace talks. Although he acted ruthlessly to counter each threat, he did so without forcing the treacherous majority within the British establishment to declare their hand, openly oppose him, and precipitate a political crisis that would have made his position untenable. It was a considerable exercise in self-control and diplomacy. Hitler, by comparison, was cocooned by a clique led by his secretary, Martin Bormann, that operated in an atmosphere of paranoia, self-delusion and savage reprisals. As a result Hitler did not see genuine intelligence reports and seemed to know nothing about Himmler's connection to plots against him. Albert Speer believed that the men cosseting Hitler were terrified of how Hitler might react to any attempt to expose Himmler, whom he completely trusted. There was also the small worry of crossing Himmler himself.

An attempt to reactivate the peace process came in February 1944. Two SS men asked Raoul Nordling, the Swedish consul in Paris and managing director of SKF, to approach King Gustav of Sweden on the Reichsführer's behalf. However, when Pierre Laval, the wily head of France's Vichy government, heard that Himmler was behind this peace initiative he refused Nordling permission to travel to Sweden. In March Nordling managed to get to Sweden and see the

King, reporting back at his SD debriefing that 'The King of Sweden would be honoured to act as intermediary for Himmler'.[31] Later actions suggest that the Swedish government and royal family did not pledge such support lightly.

Meanwhile, alarmed by Soviet military successes, behind the scenes the Americans continued to press for the Abraham Stevens Hewitt seven-point plan. Out of these negotiations arose one of the most bizarre plans hatched during the war, a mission so reckless that it is hard to credit Himmler's involvement, despite the documentation available. According to Spanish sources, 'Operation Kidnap' came about because the Americans insisted that Hitler should be handed over to them alive because they wanted to expose the man rather than create a myth.[32] A consortium of secret services led by the Vatican planned the abduction in intricate detail. Talks with the Americans were conducted by Paul Winzer, the German police attaché in Madrid, and a liaison officer from the Vatican. The kidnap was to be carried out by a special unit of the SS, who would seize Hitler in Germany and spirit him away to the Mediterranean coast near Valencia, where the waiting American Military would whip him away to the States. All went smoothly until Winzer's chief courier, Monsieur Letellier, stole papers from his safe and sold them to the British Secret Service. The plan was immediately dropped.

Whatever the truth of this tale, Himmler cast his shadow over multiple peace negotiations throughout the war. He offered a buffer zone between the Allies and Soviet Russia that he would police for the good of Europe. The visits of the anglophile German aristocrat, Adam von Trott, to meet British contacts in Sweden as a representative of the von Moltke peace group, who termed the removal of Hitler as the 'Himmler solution', were so frequent that the British strongly suspected he was Himmler's agent. This did not stop them from continuing to meet him for quite some time, until a final meeting with British Secret Serviceman David McEwan in Stockholm on 21 June 1944 removed any shred of doubt. Even after von Trott's arrest and execution following his role in the failed 20 July plot to assassinate Hitler, the British remained convinced that he had been Himmler's pawn.[33]

It is now clear that both the British and American Secret Services were not only aware of the 20 July plot, but were deeply implicated in assisting it, despite their suspicion of Himmler's involvement. Colonel Claude Arnoud, chief British Intelligence agent in France, has since revealed that only weeks before the assassination attempt his agent Keun visited Abwehr chief Admiral Canaris, flew to London to see Menzies, and then returned to see Canaris at the convent outside Longchamps near Paris on 3 June. This meeting was so secret that not even Keun's chief liaison officer to the French, Wilfred Dunderdale, knew of it.[34] Former agent Peter Tennant has admitted that the British provided direct assistance; SIS officer David McEwan gave Adam von Trott British fuses for the bomb, some of which malfunctioned, and the SIS supplied Abwehr officer Freytag-Loringhoven with the explosive.[35] According to American diplomat Cyrus Sulzberger, American Intelligence had advance knowledge of the bomb.[36] It seems likely that the King of Sweden was also involved. The SD officer who debriefed Raoul Nordling after his meeting with King Gustav saw Nordling again on 19 July, possibly to discuss events planned in Sweden to follow the assassination.[37]

A small anomaly hints Himmler may have played a more direct role in the 20 July plot than previously suspected. It has been assumed that conspirator General Fromm promoted Stauffenberg, who planted the bomb, to the key position on his staff that gave the bomber access to Hitler's quarters; customarily Waffen SS generals were in charge of internal promotions. No one checked. However, opposite the recommendation for Stauffenberg's promotion there is the neat signature of Heinrich Himmler, who had met the young officer only two weeks earlier. Although Reichsführer, Himmler had no official right to interfere with such promotions.

After the plot had failed Gördeler was arrested and no longer available to conduct any negotiations in Sweden. A new envoy came in the shape of Binger Dahlerus, the Swedish tycoon who had had first-hand experience of peace-making between Britain and Germany since 1939. The British government had reacted savagely to these early peace ventures, blacklisting all his companies, so at face value Dahlerus was hardly the ideal emissary. On the other hand, he had been embroiled in secret Anglo-Nazi financial negotiations in Stockholm for over two years. In December 1944 Dahlerus met with Sir Victor Mallet, head of the British Legation in Stockholm. He offered the same proposals as had been connected with Himmler in the past: Germany would provide a Nazi buffer state, with five million men (an inflated figure) at the disposal of the West to counter the Soviet threat. This time, it was promised, any obstacle, including Hitler, would be removed.

As soon as he heard of Mallet's report, in great alarm, Churchill ordered Eden to have nothing to do with the proposals. 'I am seriously concerned about this telegram,' he wrote. Behind their Prime Minister's back, others, including Cadogan, voiced their support for the Dahlerus connection. Sir Frank Roberts, who had received Mallet's telegram at the Foreign Office, defended the negotiations, writing 'there is nothing of which we should feel ashamed'.[38] A strange minute from Sir Frank discusses the possibility of putting Dahlerus' companies on the blacklist (where, of course, they were already), yet they were promptly taken off it; an odd reward for a spurned peace offer.

On 23 December 1944 Eden cabled Mallet in Stockholm: 'I must ask you to ensure that in future no member of your staff enters into discussion of this nature with Dahlerus or anyone else.'[39] This was classic tongue-in-cheek diplomacy. Mallet, not, after all, 'a member of your staff', was later to ensure that the telegram was obeyed to the letter by meeting with Walter Schellenberg and others personally to discuss matters of quite a different nature. Mallet would be involved in an agreement whose terms were so generous to Himmler that it is difficult to conceive what the Reichsführer SS could possibly offer in return.

6

The Stockholm Connection

While Himmler's agents carried out a plethora of peace negotiations, there was an alternative series of talks that show him looking ahead to the need to secure his post-war survival. There is an early strain of realism in this search for insurance against the worst possible outcome. Although Himmler would not abandon the dream of ruling the Reich until the last moment, his comprehensive desire to address every eventuality is expressed by these attempts to ameliorate his position. As ever, fantasy was an equal match for reality in the Reichsführer's multiple plots and plans for the future. Until this point Himmler had shown his talent for picking the right people in his attempt to seize power from Hitler, and a good nose for those people in Allied intelligence who would be most susceptible to concerns about the Bolshevik threat.

In February 1945 Himmler's trusted SD Ausland (overseas) intelligence chief Walter Schellenberg was arrested by the Gestapo. They accused him of being a British agent, and he was charged with giving away or bartering with top secret SD documents known as the Egmont reports: a clearcut act of treason.[1] At about the same time, the Gestapo charged Karl-Heinz Krämer, Himmler's special representative in Sweden, with treason.

Gestapo Chief Heinrich Müller had carefully tracked Schellenberg during his visits to Sweden. He could only prove Schellenberg and Krämer's close association with the British, in itself insufficient evidence of wrongdoing. But when Schellenberg fell ill with pneumonia Müller was quick to act, seizing papers during his absence that should have already been evacuated from Berlin to the mines in Thuringia where the SS stored secret documents. These papers enabled the elated police chief to ascertain the absence of some of the Egmont reports, as Schellenberg had not had time to re-index his papers to conceal their removal. Müller believed he was able to prove that Schellenberg had been carting away documents to Stockholm.

Poor Schellenberg, unable to come up with a decent explanation, arranged for the Hamburg book publisher, Goverts, to alert Allen Dulles that Schellenberg might be interested in fleeing to the Americans immediately. Before they could take this further, Himmler stepped in to save him. Himmler's aides, Dr Karl Brandt and Dr Gottlob Berger, wrote independent reports on Schellenberg's use of the Egmont files, effectively quashing the charges. Free from danger, Schellenberg then cleared Karl-Heinz Krämer from his similar predicament.

The Egmont reports were in fact rather inconsequential, although of considerable post-war interest to the Allies. By the end of 1944, Schellenberg had established a *Zentralauswertungsbüro* in Amt VI, his main intelligence bureau. This department analysed the sub-sectional SD reports that were coming in from every outpost, each one adding another weary brushstroke to the bleak picture of the war's progress for Germany. The reports were collated, edited and reissued under the cover name 'Egmont' to a limited intellectual audience within the SS in order, Schellenberg claimed, to get them around to his way of thinking (sanctioned, naturally, by Himmler). It was a private campaign to convince key personnel that defeat was inevitable.

Thanks to the actions of two Stockholm-based British Intelligence officers, we now know what papers Walter Schellenberg was trading in Stockholm. They had nothing to do with the defeatist Egmont reports that so enraged Gestapo Chief Müller, and everything to do with Himmler and Schellenberg's desire for self-preservation. As the Egmont reports and the SD's gossipy magazine *Reports from the Reich* all agreed, German defeat in the East was likely. Himmler and Schellenberg were busily arranging their own, very special options.

'The atmosphere [in the British Legation in Stockholm] was petty, childish and demeaning,' confessed undercover SOE officer Sir Peter Tennant, the Legation's press attaché, and he was partly to blame.[2] The problems had started when he noticed that Sir Victor

Mallet, Chief of the British Legation, had been holding secret meet-ings with his friend Marcus Wallenberg, the Swedish financier, and Himmler's envoy Dr Karl Gördeler. (Mallet also came from a family of bankers that had ties with the German Kleinwort family who owned the merchant bank of that name.) Gördeler was a constant visitor to Sweden, making some ten trips during 1940 alone, when he was known to have met with Thoma and Calissendorf, wealthy ex-diplomats and prominent members of the Swedish establishment who were involved in peace manoeuvres. According to Tennant, Schellenberg first met with Mallet in March or early April 1943. Before then, on several occasions in January Mallet had met with Himmler's envoy, the lawyer Dr Schmidt, always in the company of Marcus Wallenberg, and Georg Conrad van der Golz, who left Sweden to work at the Deutsche Bank later that year. Tennant immediately sent a strongly worded report to London, which was ignored. Nevertheless, he received great support for his concerns, first from the naval attaché in Stockholm, Henry Denham, and SIS officer Peter Falk. All three were united in disbelief as they watched events unfurl. After sending his first, unacknowledged report, six weeks went by before Tennant first suspected from Mallet's manner that he knew what Tennant had done. It was not until much later that autumn that Tennant was approached by Robert Turnbull, head of the SOE in Stockholm, with a confidential message from Sir Charles Hambro to 'festina lente'. They wanted him to take it easy because Mallet was representing banking interests. By that time relations between the two men were decidedly frosty. Tennant, with some relish, made Mallet a prime intelligence target, while Mallet struggled to maintain his dignity and make life as unpleasant as possible for Tennant.

Tennant thought his position had strengthened considerably when on 23 December 1943 the Soviet government demanded Sir Victor Mallet's recall on the grounds that he had been supplying the German High Command with details of the Soviet Army. But the Soviet request was ignored.

Help arrived in the shape of Peter Falk, a former schoolmaster at Rugby who had been recruited by SIS. After impressing his bosses during a stint at Reykjavik after the Churchill/Roosevelt conference, he was recalled to Britain and trained for his new position as assistant passport control officer in Stockholm. During his March 1943 briefing Falk was told that an important Luftwaffe officer and Abwehr agent, Karl-Heinz Krämer, either had arrived or would shortly be arriving in Stockholm. Falk's *raison d'être* was to combat Krämer's activities, a rôle which was to take precedence over everything else. Under no circumstances was his interest to be broadcast, and no questions about Krämer were to be asked of anyone. (Curiously, after the war Falk learned that Krämer had been an occasional guest at the British royal family's Forest Farm near Windsor – where, as Falk put it, 'assorted Royals cavorted'.)

When he arrived in Stockholm in late summer Falk found that he had inherited a Prussian agent known as 'P' who worked in the press department of the German Legation.[3] She produced a 'Who's Who' of the Legation from which Falk established that Krämer had already arrived the year before with his wife and daughter, and was living in some style at the Grand Hotel. Even after he had officially been settled in Stora Essingen, an attractive suburb, Krämer kept on rooms at the hotel for entertaining.

Falk's job was not an easy one, and was made worse by the extraordinary privileges his target enjoyed. Krämer did not associate with fellow Abwehr officers, called himself 'Himmler's special representative', and had unique permission to use GLYST, the German Air Attaché's message scrambler.[4] Moreover, Abwehr station chief Major Golcher allowed him to see all intelligence information. His personal secretary was the daughter of Prince du Wied, the former German Minister in Stockholm, and he raced about town at breakneck speed in his specially modified white DKW, the Gestapo in hot pursuit. Hated by the Abwehr for his privileges, Krämer's imperious manner and his overbearing wife were the weak points that Falk would brilliantly exploit.

Frau Krämer inherited a German maid with whom she established a disastrous relationship. The maid heartily resented both Krämers, confessing to an Austrian woman friend she actually felt like murdering the wife. The Austrian was happily married to a Swedish assistant at the British Legation. Falk's secretary, Bridget, approached the Austrian and hired her as agent 'Frau E'. Together they recruited Krämer's maid, 'Frau H12' (agent 36704), to help cut her new master down to size. 'Frau E' also became Bridget's home help, even borrowing the Falk silver cutlery service for functions held at Krämer's apartment. It is hard to conceive of a cosier arrangement. 'Frau H12' was very intelligent and resourceful. She soon discovered that Krämer kept a drawer in his desk into which some five messages a week disappeared. It was kept permanently locked, the keys unhitched from his neatly folded trousers and left on the dressing table only when he had his daily bath at 6.45 p.m., in which he would luxuriate for half a hour.[5]

Falk knew they were on to something. Using slightly warmed butter that was immediately replaced in the refrigerator, 'Frau H12' took an impression of Krämer's keys, from which an architect in the British Legation was able to draw a design for duplicates. The copied keys worked, and 'Frau H12' provided Falk with a constant stream of material that was rapidly photographed at the Legation and returned within hours.

The first batch of material that stunned Peter Falk has never before been fully described outside intelligence circles.[6] It included two passports, one Krämer was then using and its predecessor, as well as rough drafts and secret memoranda from the private discussions of Roosevelt and Churchill at the Quebec Conference in late August 1943. These were not copies, but originals that must have been appropriated at the time. The strong language that had amazed Falk at his previous posting, when he found documents from discussions of 19 August 1941 between the two leaders at Reykjavik, was recorded in detail, including Roosevelt's obscene remarks about correspondence received from Stalin. The Krämer material included other unrelated documents from a later date, and a memo from March 1943 regarding American proposals for the post-war trusteeship for 'dependent peoples'. Peter Falk remembered a draft stamped by the American State Department on this subject, signed by an indecipherable Polish name. Its receipt had clearly angered a member of the British contingent or somebody at the

Foreign Office. Presumably believing that such proposals were an attempt at legally dismantling the Empire, that person had scrawled across the report in a bold hand 'Vindictive old woman', indicating the Foreign Office opinion of Cordell Hull, American Secretary of State.

In Falk's opinion, someone present at the Allied leaders' confidential chats, or someone with access to these original drafts, was directly passing them to Krämer, safe in the knowledge that in England they would be presumed destroyed. Falk was witnessing the ongoing work of an agent working at the highest possible level. As if this was not shocking enough, copies of Cabinet documents and War Office minutes nestled in Krämer's drawer alongside Foreign Office letters from the office of Permanent Undersecretary of State, William Strang, and a wealth of other material. Strictly confidential statements of an Air Vice Marshal, high-ranking Air Ministry officials, other civil servants, and an officer serving as an aide to the King at Buckingham Palace were included with up-to-date monthly aircraft production figures for almost all British factories.

The awe-inspiring haul was clearly denoted as having come from Krämer's agent 'Josefine' by three separate telegrams sent back to Berlin. Peter Falk knew he was dealing with material that affected the entire Allied war effort. He hastily made arrangements for the transfer of the first batch of documents by courier to London. Although he had received the material within days of the Quebec Conference's close, arrangements were made, with no apparent urgency, for him to meet with his MI5 liaison officer Anthony Blunt in London, bringing with him all additional relevant material. This was not the response Falk had anticipated. Two months passed before the meeting.

On 23 December 1943 Peter Falk returned to Britain with the material gathered in September, including a second set of Churchill/Roosevelt minutes, as well as the second of the telegrams sent by Krämer to Berlin identifying material as derived from 'Josefine'. At Blunt's suggestion they met at the Reform Club where they spent the whole evening going over the material and discussing its relevance. Blunt's initial reaction had been to doubt the authenticity of some of the material. 'He tried to make out', said Falk, 'that some of the phrasing and the very nature of the obscenities used seemed Germanic, and thus possible forgeries. I pointed out to him that I was responsible for retrieving previous minutes from Iceland, which had proved exactly similar, when I had quickly come to appreciate that such social graces were typical of many Americans. He seemed suitably astonished and at least dropped that tack.'[7]

Towards the end of the evening Falk raised a concern he shared with all the Stockholm SIS section, for whom the fear of a future Soviet threat was more immediate than to their London colleagues. All were anxious that London should not leak the Roosevelt/ Churchill confidences to the Russians. He was completely taken aback when Blunt, a notorious waffler, lost his temper and said in an uncharacteristically firm manner: 'I can categorically assure you there is no cross knowledge. The Soviets know nothing about this, they are only interested in the timing of the second front.'[8] Today we know only too well from released Soviet archives that there were highly placed Soviet moles at the heart of the British establishment, the most important of all being 'Fifth Man' John Cairncross, private secretary to Lord Hankey until March 1942, when Hankey was sacked by Churchill. During this time Cairncross would have had access to all Cabinet papers and telegrams between the two leaders, although certainly not to the other documents forwarded to Krämer. A few months elapsed after Cairncross lost this key position, before he was admitted to the signals intelligence unit at Bletchley Park. Soon he was churning out useful information, literally by the car-load. However, it is clear that the material relating to the Churchill/ Roosevelt talks that Falk presented to Blunt could not possibly have come from John Cairncross, whose access to such material had long since ceased.

Falk's lucky discovery was Anthony Blunt's first glimpse of what might possibly be on offer from Walter Schellenberg and Heinrich Himmler. Secret negotiations were still going on between Schellenberg and Mallet; now Blunt had a cogent reason to take these negotiations more seriously. Blunt's oddly vehement reaction, and unwillingness to credit the material, had disturbed Falk. In a way he was rather relieved to hear no more from him on this matter. This does not mean no further action was taken, but it was not quite as straightforward as one might have expected. The choice of envoy for critical new negotiations with Schellenberg, quite separate from the ongoing financial arrangements with Mallet, was surprising to say the least. Major Ewan Butler's appointment as assistant military attaché to the British Legation in Stockholm was to cause considerable post-war embarrassment.[9]

Ewan Butler was a flamboyantly attractive man who spoke fluent German. He lived for several years in Germany, where he struck up a bizarre relationship with Himmler's dreaded favourite, Obergruppenführer Reinhard Heydrich. The two became 'blood brothers' in a childish ceremony at Butler's birthday party. Very few Englishmen had the dubious privilege of being able to address Heydrich with the intimate 'Du'. Unfortunately, apart from some prestigious royal connections, there was a darker side to this extrovert. He suffered from a distressing facial tic, but this invited far less comment than his alcoholic 'blinders', which occurred every few weeks and proved memorable for everyone apart from the unfortunate Butler. Pre-war work as a journalist had allowed this tendency full rein. Unsurprisingly, marital relations were strained. Although his wife accompanied him to Stockholm in the autumn of 1943, embarrassing quarrels limited their social appearances. They broke up when they returned to Britain after the war.

Butler's marital and drinking problems were the least of it. He suffered manic depression, for which he received treatment at the mental hospital at Virginia Water, outside London. Yet he was to be employed by the SOE, his outlandish idiosyncrasies fitting in imperceptibly with their rag-bag intake of aristocratic mavericks. Dorothy Furse, who was in charge of SOE personnel and related to Kim Philby by marriage, recalls that Ewan had to be 'helped out' just before going to Stockholm.[10] He was in 'an awful state, just having been discharged from Virginia Water where he had spent three weeks'. Furse helped make Butler's personal arrangements, which he was incapable of managing himself. It was an inauspicious beginning to an exacting mission.

It seems extraordinary that this man ever came to be chosen to go to Stockholm, the crucible of wartime intelligence activities. According to Butler, the MP Harold Nicolson, an extremely close family friend and a pal of the Duke of Windsor, was instrumental in his appointment. It is worth noting that Nicolson himself flew out to Stockholm in October 1943 to become embroiled in peace negotiations that involved the Swedish royal family. His diary records that whatever was discussed after dinner with Prince Wilhelm at Urikstal Castle 'was not for repetition'.[11]

Butler's role was all the more remarkable because during his time in Sweden he never used, let alone recruited, a single agent or contact. His remit was unique. Rather like Karl-Heinz Krämer, he enjoyed luxuries above and beyond his official status. He was awarded a large first-floor office in the overcrowded British Legation, at a time when several newcomers occupied temporary huts in the courtyard, and his living accommodation, which boasted a marble floor and magnificent chandeliers, was the subject of much jealous comment.

Mallet initially welcomed this well-connected new recruit, his friend Nicolson's protégé, with open arms and overlooked his unfortunate behaviour. It took a year before he became antagonistic toward Butler. Then Mallet's secretary, 'Aunt Annie', opened 'the Butler file' that was, as Tennant commented, 'full before it was opened'. According to Falk, Mallet was jealous of the way Swedish society readily accepted Butler and horrified by his canoodling with the Swedish princess 'Sibi'. Mallet and Tennant were for once united in this opinion; Butler had some serious explaining to do.

They did not have to wait long. In February 1945 Butler requested leave after a period during which his behaviour had been causing real concern. Janet Dow, Butler's loyal secretary, confided to Falk's secretary and future wife Bridget Pope that she had tried in vain to contact Sir Richard Boord, Butler's SOE boss in London, because Butler needed drying out, only to learn that Boord was unavailable because he was being treated at Virginia Water. To everyone's dismay, one day at the end of that month Butler learnt he had been refused any time off. Already inebriated, Butler sought solace in a bottle of Black & White whisky. He ended up sitting outside Falk's apartment in the early hours of the morning in search of advice, still clutching his bottle. Falk had no alternative but to listen to Butler's blabbings. Falk advised him to make a direct approach to Mallet, persuading Butler that he and Tennant would do their best to see that he got a fair hearing about his leave.

Butler was labouring under a misapprehension. He thought Falk had been fully involved with Mallet's negotiations with Schellenberg because Falk had produced a report on the German for the Legation Chief. (In fact, this was a smokescreen, as Mallet had already met with Schellenberg several times before he requested this report, and negotiations were ongoing rather than about to begin, as Falk was led to believe.) Butler was also under the impression that Falk knew about continuing secret financial negotiations between Mallet, Schellenberg, Marcus Wallenberg and Himmler's legal representative Dr Schmidt that were to secure British, Swedish, German and, by extension, SS monetary interests. As a result, in his anxious, drunken state, Butler blurted out the outline of his own, separate negotiations with Schellenberg, intimating that he shortly faced the nightmare of ensuring the smooth exodus of Nazi war criminals to Sweden and the guarantee of immunity from prosecution to not only Schellenberg, but Himmler himself.

Poor Ewan Butler complained that his expressions of distaste for his mission had been ignored. He had attempted to enlist the help of his old boss, Field-Marshal Gerald Templer, to get him off the hook, but Templer did not return his call. Then, he claimed, he tried unsuccessfully to involve an old friend, Mason MacFarlane, the current Governor of Gibraltar. Would Falk help?

Sceptical and horrified in equal measure, Falk and his astute wife-to-be, Bridget Pope, failed to persuade Butler to go home and sleep it off. Falk reluctantly left Butler behind with his fiancée, and went to meet Peter Tennant at the Legation. Tennant was adamant that neither of them should become entangled in the mess. Considering Tennant's own trench warfare with Mallet and his pending appointment to Assistant Counsellor in Paris, his reaction was understandable. Moreover, inaction meant that neither of them would be known to be aware of the astonishing negotiations, which could have caused them considerable difficulties.

Tennant and Falk chewed over Butler's revelations. The first surprise was that Butler wasn't reporting back to any of his SOE superiors. This explained a lot. They had always been puzzled that SOE chief Turnbull tolerated Butler's often extreme behaviour and had never disciplined him, especially when his frequent clashes with Mallet had led to so much comment. Falk was troubled to learn that Ewan Butler was reporting to Anthony Blunt in person, because he had long suspected that his own battle with Krämer was being undermined by a hidden agenda.

It turned out that Butler was sending material back to London via the Swedes rather than through customary intelligence channels. Butler bragged that this had been arranged 'only for him', at the time of Harold Nicolson's trip in October 1943, a visit that he claimed had laid the groundwork for his 'especial social contacts' in Stockholm. Tennant and Falk suspected this meant that the royal courier was being used, which suggests that the British royal family were involved. Falk also learnt that some of the material passed back to Blunt came from Schellenberg. Schellenberg's material came from General Makoto Onodera, a Japanese spymaster trading secrets in Stockholm, but was Soviet in origin, and would prove very important.

Still drunk, Ewan Butler did not attend the Legation until that afternoon, in what was described as a high state of merriment. Unfortunately, he clearly remembered Falk's mistaken advice to put himself under Mallet's wing. Butler produced a sheaf of Russian documents and quarto-sized SD reports, replete with purple stamps, for the perusal of a startled Victor Mallet (now nicknamed the 'Angry Rabbit' by the Legation for his habit of stamping his feet when enraged). He was promptly ejected from Mallet's office, and the legation was subjected to the sight of a sobbing Butler retreating up the wide crescent of the stairs to the first floor, shedding papers as he sought sanctuary in his corner office.

It took only three days before Cyril Cheshire, SIS head at the Legation, buttonholed an indignant Peter Tennant to tell him any further attempts at questioning Butler were strictly forbidden. Peter Falk was similarly reprimanded the following week by his London SIS boss Keith Liversidge, with whom he had enjoyed a good relationship until that point. It was later ascertained that the warning had come directly from Anthony Blunt. Annoyed at these rather unjustified attacks, Tennant and Falk realised that they had stumbled into a secret game being played out at the highest level. This discovery of a hidden agenda transformed their understanding of the strange tensions at the Legation, and they realised that the stakes were far greater than they had ever suspected.

Peter Falk already knew from an Estonian military attaché, Saarson, who was always in need of extra cash, that Onodera was running a bourse in Stockholm selling top-class material to the Germans, Russians, Americans and British. Falk was only too aware of Onodera's tremendous influence as he had followed Krämer to his house, where he frequently dined. He also knew that both Onodera and Krämer had contact with Mallet. Onodera was extremely friendly with the Free Polish Intelligence Service in Stockholm, running several members as agents under the cover of Manchurian passports, the Finnish General Hallama, whom he had helped set up an intelligence base in Sweden, and Walter Schellenberg. Both the Poles and Hallama brought in Soviet documents, but it became evident that only Hallama was able to obtain Soviet archive material of the highest quality.

According to Saarson and his aide Reinhard Massing, Onodera had offered them some Soviet material to see if they could sell it to the British, as it contained British War Cabinet minutes and Onodera knew they had a good British contact.[12] However, this contact was Harry Carr, a Russian-born SIS agent at the British Legation in Stockholm. He was a fit hypochondriac who relished his putative ill health, and was so secretive he was said to handcuff his own shadow. Once he had made up his mind he would not be moved. Carr decided that he did not even want to see 'Cabinet Papers'; the whole idea was too incredible to be contemplated.

We now have a fair idea what Schellenberg had to offer Blunt. There were British documents relating to Roosevelt/Churchill talks and secret Cabinet papers that Krämer had obtained from an as yet unidentified mole at the highest level. Then there was material from Onodera that had been leaked from NKVD (KGB) central archives, some of which was probably obtained thanks to the 'Fifth Man', John Cairncross, and other moles in the British establishment. This Soviet material came with SD analysis of its contents.

Blunt had positioned himself to field Falk's material from Krämer. Now, through Butler, he was in a position to make a deal to ensure his own security within the British establishment and, of course, Heinrich Himmler and Walter Schellenberg's immunity from prosecution.

Colonel Christie had provided British agents to help the German army take Hitler prisoner in the unsuccessful Venlo incident, in Holland in 1939. Two agents were captured by the SD and under interrogation revealed the whole structure of the British Secret Service. After that, one of Himmler's favourite party tricks was to quote the names and even the offices occupied by various Secret Service personnel. While the entertainment value of this trick is questionable, it clearly demonstrates that an intimate knowledge of British intelligence agents was considered by him to be a priority. Added to that, SD analysis of material in the Onodera papers showed that Soviet agents operated in British intelligence. Certainly, Himmler used stolen documents to discover those most likely to share his concerns about finance and the implications of Soviet power for the progress of global capitalism, as will be seen in the next chapter. It is unimaginable that Himmler would not have used such information to exploit Soviet sympathisers as well. So it was that Anthony Blunt took a particular interest in peace offers that were supposed to have come from Himmler.

Ever since his appointment as Reichsführer SS, Himmler had shown deviousness, ruthless persistence and, for the most part, caution in his campaign for power. Peace moves were just another strategy to exalt his position. From 1943 Himmler alone of the leaders of the Third Reich started acting upon the recognition of Germany's likely defeat and set out to provide himself with a life insurance policy. Thanks to Falk, Tennant, and the indiscretions of Ewan Butler, we at last know at least one of the reasons for the extraordinary British offer to Himmler and Schellenberg of immunity from prosecution at the end of the war. When Himmler made his approaches he was far from empty-handed.

7

The Maison Rouge Meeting

Himmler's plans for a post-war future encompassed more than deals
to ensure his personal survival. As Germany edged towards defeat
the SS was busily engaged in securing assets on a vast scale, shoring
up Himmler's power to a degree that would have made the prospect
of negotiating with him enormously attractive to some. A meeting
in Strasbourg in August 1944 reveals how much the Reichsführer
SS had to offer.

Was it Hôtel de la Maison Rouge, Strasbourg or Grand Hotel
Rotes Haus, Strassburg? To the people of Strasbourg the dual identity
of their grandest hotel encapsulated a century's schizophrenia for a
borderland population divided in its loyalties to France and Germany.
The hotel stood at the heart of Strasbourg just off the grand Place
Kléber. All the old antagonisms seemed to condense there, with street
signs and shop fronts bearing witness to whoever owned Strasbourg at
the time. Widespread deportations of French-speaking citizens from
Alsace and Lorraine had weakened the French hold on the city's
culture and its soul, while despite vehement protests from the Vichy
government, the transplantation of German families from the Saar
had carried on apace.

Those French remaining, under petty pressure to Germanify their
names, sought solace in their glorious past, embodied in the Place
Kléber's oversized statue of their hero, General Jean-Baptiste Kléber,
whose proud features seemed frozen in disgust at the current occupants of his square. He was soon to be put out of his misery; a
solitary cluster of British bombs knocked him off his pedestal on 10
August 1944.

Until that August Strasbourg had led a charmed existence. No bombs rained down on what the Allies regarded as a French city. Thanks to Allied indulgence, the centre of Strasbourg was one of the safest places in Europe and its strategic importance made it a unique bubble of calm. And there was no safer place for peaceful revelry than the Hôtel de la Maison Rouge.

The Maison Rouge had come to prominence in 1837 following its description by Victor Hugo as 'the centre of Strasbourg society'.[1] Its terrace, furnished with a grand piano and orchestra, dominated the lively plaza. All the grandest visitors flocked to join the merriment, as well as less salubrious guests. Before the First World War it was already being described by advertising posters as 'the Hotel of the German Officer Class', a fact quickly endorsed when war came.[2]

During the Second World War the hotel continued to hold its attraction for the German High Command. But by that time its heyday was past. Just prior to the war it had become the favoured resort of Europe's rich industrialists and bankers. It was also a magnet for celebrities such as the famous tenor Richard Tauber.[3] 'Julia', the legendary 'Queen of the Bar', was visited there regularly by King Leopold of Belgium, complete with discreet entourage.[4] Not to be outdone, the French President Alexandre Millerand had a special exit prepared from his first-floor room for those of his lady visitors who wished to avoid unnecessary contact with the police. He joined more notorious flamboyants such as Mistinguette and Cécile Sorel in giving the Maison Rouge a reputation to match its Paris rivals.[5] Rudyard Kipling and Winston Churchill were to add a note of pre-war sobriety. The famous French comic actor, Fernandel, who obviously did not find the prices funny, ate in the somewhat cheaper Hannong restaurant elsewhere in the city. Nevertheless, he would humour the hotel with an amusing habit of leaving without paying the bill.[6]

On 10 August 1944, the night of the Allied bombing raid, the Maison Rouge was to add to its illustrious heritage with far more serious implications. That night it was the site of one of the most remarkable and dramatic meetings of the war. Even now the rumours surrounding the meeting and its consequences remain to be clarified. Immediately after the bombing, dazed people walked around the rubble of Rue du Fossé-des-Tanneurs, looking in disbelief at the gaping hole that was number 6, a house now completely destroyed. More destruction greeted them in the Rue du Vieux-Marché-aux-Vins. A picture shows the crowd's stunned reaction as they gaze on the ripped canopy of the Elka department store.[7] They were confused. Strasbourg was a historic city, until then spared any serious Allied attack. What had changed?

As dawn broke on 11 August, injured deputy manager Eugène Haller was receiving treatment from the hotel's resident physician. He had been injured while carrying out special security duties at his desk in the hotel foyer, which had imploded around him when the hotel itself was struck. While the doctor got to work, Haller watched SS officers tramp over the rubble, systematically searching every room. They worked so diligently that an onlooker would have thought they suspected sabotage rather than the somewhat obvious cause from the skies above. SS guards ringed the hotel's three entrances, letting none pass in or out without question. No other building in the square seemed to merit such dramatic attention.

The implications of the heavy SS presence in and around their grandest hotel were not lost on the Strasbourgeois. When the bombing was repeated the following night, suspicion hardened to certainty. All the people of Strasbourg wanted was for the guests, whoever they were, to leave Strasbourg so they could live in peace. They soon realised that the Maison Rouge had been the focus of the bombing of Strasbourg's centre, well away from strategic targets. Remarkable accuracy and, it was said, no coincidence.[8] It was rumoured that a secret meeting[9] of high-ranking Nazis had taken place at the hotel that evening and the following day. It was believed that Churchill had been tipped off about the meeting, and had ordered the air raids as an emphatic reminder that it would be their last get-together. Locals were in no doubt: the bombing was retribution. Rumours seeded local legends that Jodl, von Ribbentrop, and at least three-quarters of those later condemned at Nuremberg had either stayed or dined at the hotel.[10]

At the hotel itself, the management were confronted with an interesting situation. It seemed that during the night someone had drilled fine holes in many of the doors to the more expensive rooms, even though armed SS men had been guarding each of the three staircases on every floor. These strange perforations were later put down to the insatiable activity of a determined voyeur, 'because he left hastily in the early hours of the morning'.[11] It would have been a brave man who could run such risks. The professionalism reveals the handiwork of a secret agent. Later it was thought that the agent could have had Communist sympathies. During the Nuremberg trial, it was discovered that Soviet Intelligence not only knew soon after about proceedings at that fateful Maison Rouge meeting, but deemed the information important enough to use in their interrogation of Harald von Bohlen, one of the Krupp armaments family whom they had captured shortly afterwards in Romania.[12]

Some aspects of the rumours may not have been all that far-fetched. It is conceivable that Churchill could have personally initiated the bombing, as Allied intelligence knew in advance about the meeting at the hotel. Moreover, in addition to the hole-drilling voyeur, 'Mr Waddington' (not his real name), a well-respected agent of the French Deuxième Bureau, attended the meeting from beginning to end, and his detailed account was soon circulating among top members of the British and American Secret Service. Colonel John W. Austin, who worked for US Military Intelligence, considered him 'reliable, he has worked for the French on German problems since 1916, and was in close touch with the industrialists'.[13]

Those who thought the war would end with Hitler's fall were in for a surprise as they read the British 'Report on a meeting of German industrialists to make post-war plans – Strasbourg August 10th 1944'.[14] The title of a later, less detailed, American version of this report spells out the threat in bolder terms: 'Plans of German industrialists to engage in underground activity after Germany's defeat; flow of capital to neutral countries.' The last-ditch reunion of the damned was indeed a myth, but the truth of what went on that night was even stranger than the Strasbourgeois' wildest imaginings.

The plucky voyeur would have seen the SS guarding and hosting a meeting of Nazi Germany's top industrialists in a display of pragmatic defeatism, at a time when to acknowledge defeat was considered an act of treason. (Three army officers were shot for defeatism that month; in one case the victim had only pointed out the overwhelming material superiority of the Allies. This information was spread in a circular, 'For General Staff Officers only', to warn off those who might be tempted to espouse and act on such views.) Himmler's representative, SS Obergruppenführer Scheid, who chaired the meeting, was also a director of the HECE, Hermandorf and Schönburg Company. The high-ranking industrialists in attendance included representatives from megalithic German armaments and engineering firms: Dr Kaspar represented Krupp; Dr Tolle came for Röchling; Dr Sincoren was there for Messerschmitt; Drs Ellenmoyer and Kardos attended for Volkswagenwerk, and Drs Kopp, Vier and Beerwanger represented Rheinmetall. They were accompanied by engineers Drose, Yenchow and Koppsheim, who represented the firms Drose, Yenchow & Co, Brown Bovari, Herkülswerke, and Stadtwerke. The presence of Dr Mayer of the German Naval Ministry in Paris, along with his Paris compatriot Dr Strössner of the Armaments Ministry, signified that the SS proposals had already gained very influential support among some key military leaders.

'Mr Waddington's' secret report on this meeting became part of American and British files on the 'Red House report'. Their files were later expanded to include Allied Intelligence information about a follow-up meeting some months later between representatives of HECE, Krupp and Röchling that confirmed agreements made at the Maison Rouge.[15] Dr Bose took the chair this time, as a representative of the German Armaments Ministry, an industry that was mostly under Himmler's control – again we see treason receive awesome official support. Once again, trusty 'Mr Waddington' leaked all the details. There is no question that all present at both meetings were fully aware of the nature and gravity of the matters under discussion; everything had been carefully pre-arranged with a set agenda that Dr Scheid would certainly have discussed with Himmler. The tone was uncompromising: Scheid's first words were a categoric statement that not only the battle for France had been lost, but the whole war.

Our information about the second meeting is more detailed. Dr Bose reiterated and expanded on the SS view. The war was lost, and he reminded them that the SS had gone to some lengths to inform industrialists that this was their official – that is, Himmler's – opinion. He announced the new policy: 'From now on government will allocate large sums to industrialists so that each can establish a secure post-war foundation in other countries.'[16] The prohibition against the export of capital, which had been rigorously enforced until that time, 'has been completely withdrawn and replaced by a New National Socialist policy whereby industrialists, with government assistance, will export as much of their capital as possible'.[17] This policy would have come as a surprise to Hitler; the SS claimed an authority to speak for the government in a sleight of hand that, given their inordinate power, was not far from the truth. By this stage, Himmler's will was Nazi policy.

At the Maison Rouge, Scheid handed out a list of mainly American addresses for companies such as the Hamburg-America Line, the Chemical Foundation Inc., and the US Steel Corporation. The good doctors should contact these firms 'individually and without attracting attention' for further assistance in cloaking their companies' assets.[18] If transferring their capital abroad proved impossible, they were told to buy agricultural land in Germany. Large factories and industrial concerns were advised to set up small technical offices and research bureaux in cities where they could be hidden and have 'no known connection with the factory. These bureaux will receive plans and drawings of new weapons as well as documents which they will need to continue their research and which must not be allowed to fall into the hands of the enemy.'[19] The nit-picking instructions are so characteristic of Himmler that he might have written them himself. Consider the fantastical, irrelevant detail of the following:

> These research bureaux are to be located in little villages near sources of hydroelectric power, where they can pretend to be studying the development of water resources. The existence of these is to be known only by very few people in each industry, and by chiefs of the Nazi Party. There will be liaison with the party and as soon as the party becomes strong enough to

re-establish its control over Germany the industrialists will be paid for their effort and co-operation by concessions and orders.[20]

Fantasy may have been a strong element of their future plans, but the stark truth was that the SS was methodically stripping the wealth of the Reich. Germany's resources were to be transplanted out of Germany into foreign lands, where they could be used to form the industrial and financial basis for the resurrection of a Fourth Reich. It was blatant high treason. Himmler wanted nothing less than total control of Germany's financial future, to be dictated by the SS under his unbending rule. Bose explained, 'Existing financial reserves in foreign countries must be placed at the disposal of the Party so that a strong German empire can be created after the defeat.'[21] Extra Nazi funds were placed at the firms' disposal to facilitate such transfers. However, wherever the firms were destined to re-group (in property acquired for them by each host company at a nominal charge of 5 per cent), their wealth was to be handed over to the SS under the charge of trusted individuals. It may seem extraordinary that businessmen could be relied upon to comply with such demands. Yet they were a typically German, loyal bunch, many of them affili-ated with the Party over long periods, with SS-trained personnel in place to guarantee the use of assets in accordance with Himmler's plans. Here was proof of the extent to which the industrial might of Germany was in Himmler's hands. He effectively controlled the profitable sections of the German Armaments Ministry in the whole of the Reich. There was no place in this financial masterplan for the old-guard Nazis who were not under SS rule, let alone Hitler. Once Himmler had dispersed the industrial assets, the Third Reich was almost bankrupt.

By the time of the first Maison Rouge meeting on 10 August, arrangements had already been completed for most other major industrial firms in the Reich to covertly transfer their assets abroad. Himmler had allowed the circulation of Ohlendorf's defeatist SD magazine, *Reports from the Reich*, which had started as early as August 1942 to spell out the unpalatable facts of Germany's untenable military and political ambitions. Ex-Ambassador Ulrich Von Hassell was writing in his diary by early 1943 that the war certainly could not be won and that the chances of acceptable peace terms were slim.

Even before these views had gelled into a tacit understanding that defeat was inevitable, Himmler had started putting in place the infrastructure to ensure post-war financial survival. He was the first intelligence chief in world history to set up two research institutes within his own SS organisation. The first, Gruppe VI wi, studied world economics under Amt VI in a large, scientifically-run institute in Hamburg, and the second, based in Kiel, focused on world markets and trade. Gruppe VI wi was created to train hand-picked SS men in finance according to strictly agreed requirements of individual businesses and industrial firms. In other words, Himmler set up an impressive production line of knowledgeable SS men planted in selected businesses. In addition to these institutes, a Central SS Economic Evaluation Department was established to work closely with the Ministries of Economics, Armaments, and Economic Warfare.[22] Key industrialists met with trainees in a business club that was described as a 'social pooling of interests'.

Through these enterprises Himmler learned the best means to cloak German assets abroad. Using this machinery he had, by 1943, examined all major German companies; their personnel had been evaluated and their weaknesses exposed. The SS moved in to most firms to establish control, manipulating men into top positions of influence. Dr Werner Naumann represented Himmler's interests at the massive chemicals firm of Kali; Georg von Schnitzer was placed in IG Farben; Lyschen at Siemens, Kirschfeld at Ferrostahl and Otto Wolf steel company, Fischer at Conti Oil, Backe at Zucker, Karl Blessing at Unilever, and so on. The list was seemingly endless – with the exception of the firm of Krupp, which managed to avoid having SS personnel thrust upon them.

The firms that gathered together on 10 August at the Maison Rouge seem to have been the last main businesses to succumb to Himmler's plan for the transfer of wealth abroad; they were understandably reluctant to comply with his directives. Hitler's official policy – to fight on until victory – had been a convenient shield for these few remaining firms, particularly Krupp, to shelter behind, hoping to avoid the suffocating embrace of the SS. The timing of the meeting coincided with Himmler's apparent victory in an internal battle at Krupp. A gifted young Luxemburger, Eduard Houdremont, had been professor of metallurgy at Aachen University before moving to Krupp, where he swiftly rose to become managing director. A favourite of Hitler's, he had been decorated by the Führer for services to the Reich. When Albert Speer took over the Ministry of Armaments and Munitions Houdremont was appointed co-ordinator of all private, semi-private and public agencies and cartels that were engaged in finding substitutes for scarce metals. This position made him responsible for all military aspects of metallurgy within the Reich.

After many blandishments, Houdremont had been won over to Himmler's faction by August 1944. Now the Krupp firm seemed prepared to fall into line and start transferring its assets abroad. But the new owner, Alfred von Krupp und Bohlen, proved to be an exception. He was used to managing his own affairs and was not about to let Himmler dictate how he should run the company. A grateful SS was flooded with worthless bonds in a mountain of paperwork, while Krupp retained the bulk of his family fortune. However, fear and an inculcated sense of duty seemed to compel all the other firms to co-operate fully.

Just as the end of the Second World War looked inevitable and the longed-for peace at last attainable, the Maison Rouge meeting of August 1944 opened a horrifying new vista to the watchful Allies. Albert Speer expressed their problem best: 'I pity anyone attempting to unravel any enterprise set up by Himmler – the layers of deceit and the breathtaking imagination that this unlikely man was capable of were unreal.'[23] The disbelieving Allied Intelligence services were soon to discover how right Speer was.

Hints of Himmler's plans for a post-war Fourth Reich started filtering into the Allied consciousness long before the bombing of the Place Kléber. In mid-1943 British Intelligence intercepted a cache of mail in Gibraltar directed from IG Farben to its subsidiary Bayer in Argentina. This revealing correspondence discussed the transfer and cloaking of IG Farben's German assets, alerting the Allies to the role of the SS in these plans, and giving them an insight into Himmler's ambition. At this stage they had no idea of the imaginative scale of his enterprise, the vast scope of his goals, nor of his intuitive understanding of the power achieved by fusing together the worlds of finance and intelligence.

Then in October 1944, just before they received the Red House report, British SIS received a disturbing communication from the French Intelligence Service. Himmler had appointed SS Obergruppenführer Erich von dem Bach-Zewelski, infamous for his brutal efficiency in putting down the Warsaw ghetto uprising, as Commander-in-Chief of post-war Nazi resistance. Approximately half a million members of this 'movement' were given false identity cards that had belonged to people who had gone missing after air raids. SIS passed this information on to the SOE.

Some idea of the importance the British government now accorded Himmler is indicated by the fact that of all the leaders of the Third Reich other than Hitler, Himmler was the only one subjected to the SOE German Directorate's 'analysis' – meaning he was considered for assassination.[24] Meanwhile, war with Japan added urgency to the American Secret Service's concerns about Himmler: the Japanese obviously considered him rather than Hitler to be the man in power. In May 1944, a delegation comprised of Admiral Abe, General Komatsu and General Kojima had visited Himmler in Salzburg, pointedly ignoring all other Nazi leaders. The Americans made a similar report to the Directorate's:

> Himmler, profiting from Hitler's illness, has been working to divide the Generals. Himmler is reported to have made a pact along these lines. Withdrawals can be effected independently of prestige considerations or any wild orders of the Führer. The military will participate with the SS in perfecting Nazi underground organisations.[25]

While they were considering the Red House report the Americans received another British report on 8 December from the SIS in Madrid: 'Diplomats in Madrid have recently received orders from

Himmler not Hitler – causing them to believe that he has gained supreme command.'[26] It went on to say that German diplomats in Madrid, who were pro-Abwehr and Canaris, had reacted with horror because they feared that under Himmler's regime Nazi resistance would be more organised and fanatical. Similar reports came in from Paris. On 11 December the SIS concluded that those who knew Himmler regarded him as 'a thousand times worse than Ivan the Terrible – the most frightful monster that ever lived on earth'.[27]

The Allies could not ignore a man who evoked such fear and loathing, but they were hopelessly wrong-footed by Himmler's determined acquisitiveness. They were about to find out how instinctive a feel he really had for the power of finance. As they were later to learn from von Papen's testimony at Nuremberg, Himmler had introduced financier Wilhelm Keppler to Hitler in 1929. Keppler became a constant member of Hitler's entourage. Through this contact Himmler arranged the meeting in Cologne on 4 June 1933 between Hitler, von Papen and the banking colossus Kurt von Schröder, where they plotted Hitler's succession to Chancellor, which came to pass at the end of that month. In gratitude for this direct line to the Führer, Keppler set up the 'Circle of Friends of the Reichsführer' that made generous donations to the SS. Thereby Himmler and his organisation received the backing of powerful financiers and industrialists; members included Steinbrech of Flick Steel, Bingen of Siemens, Bütefisch of IG Farben, Olschner of Kreditbank, Meyer of Dresdner Bank and von Halt of Deutsche Bank. In addition to contributions to the SS, Himmler had a personal 'S' fund. On 1 September 1943 he coolly transferred a million marks to this account.

By 1944 Himmler's talent for putting his hand in the till had filled several private bank accounts with diverted funds. He also set up a special loot-plundering unit, the *Devisenschutzkommando*, to acquire gold for the nation – that is, for the SS. The unique 'Melmer' system was devised to cream off the best of this national treasure and divert it into SS coffers. Capital was paid into the humorously named Max Heiliger ('Max Saint') account, that was thought by Allied Intelligence to belong to Himmler. When the American Army overran the Plauen branch of the Reichsbank at the end of the war, they found one of Himmler's many kleptomaniac accounts. It contained thirty-five bags of gold and millions in foreign currency, including 250,000 US gold dollars. The Dresdner Bank, known in financial circles as the 'SS bank', readily and repeatedly contributed to a personal account set up in Himmler's name by Schellenberg's friend, Colonel Karl Rasche. Rasche also set up a slush fund for Himmler in Sweden as part of his duties in trying to arrange last-minute peace talks in Stockholm. There were doubtless other accounts elsewhere. By 1944, Himmler's obsession with the power that money conferred was tinged with an obsessive cupidity.

In response to the Red House report, British and American investigators started working in concert from the end of 1944. As they delved deeper into Himmler's financial maze, they discovered a multiplicity of complex yet expertly concealed transfers of much of Germany's wealth. The sheer magnitude of Himmler's enterprise and its breathtaking purpose astonished them. As they mined for information, they were also perplexed by the extent of personal wealth that he had stashed away, minor in comparison with the business ventures, yet disturbing evidence of compulsive personal greed. But Himmler's ambition for the transfer of Germany's wealth was the main focus of the British and American governments' anxiety. They responded in very different ways. In America, the FBI and OSS were the main investigators, backed up by the US Treasury Department and US State Department. They threw massive resources into a top-priority operation in the United States and Latin America, reporting their progress to the Sub-committee on War Mobilisation for the Committee on Military Affairs. In November 1944 their first report, by Senator Harley M. Kilgore, emphasised the gravity of the situation:

> At the end of the First World War Germany was outwardly a defeated nation. But this was not the case. The war had greatly expanded industries to [sic] which Germany had depended to supply the armaments and raw materials for the war machine. Defeat did not permanently reduce the productive capacity of

their industries, nor did it alter their degree of concentration, or impair their position of dominance in the German economy.

The German aggressors have begun to pursue the strategy which they found successful a quarter of a century ago. They are already deploying their economic wares throughout the world in preparation for a third attempt at world domination.[28]

By January 1945 they had made considerable progress in countering the explosive expansion of firms such as Tubos Mannesman, IG Farben, Ferrostahl, AEG and Siemens Schückert in Latin America. Their task was simplified by the impending defeat of Nazi Germany. Huge pressure from the American State Department compelled the government of Uruguay to seize the offices of the Deutsche Bank, the Banco Aleman, where they recovered papers that were immediately passed on to the FBI. These caused 'real concern' because they revealed the extent of the operation set up by the SS in Uruguay alone.[29] William L. Clayton, Assistant Secretary of State on the Sub-Committee on War Mobilisation, reported to the Committee on Military Affairs on 25 January, 'Axis penetration in the American Republics is very serious.'[30]

The problem remained serious. Further American successes had a limited impact. Covert wealth transfers did not become too overt because of the risks attached to offending the United States, but the economies of Brazil, Argentina, Chile and Paraguay were suddenly substantially upgraded, despite American scrutiny. The SS's transfer of wealth to Latin America was broadly successful, as was suggested by the lack of any final progress reports from US investigators to assess the success of follow-up work to the Red House report. Apparently, they simply forgot about it.

Latin America was not the only focus for SS wealth transfer. It was a worldwide problem. In Europe, where co-operation between the British and American secret services had already proved useful, an atmosphere of defensiveness, irascibility and even defeatism began to infect the investigations. This pessimism was discernible as early as two months before war in Europe ended.[31] OSS and, later, CIA operatives in Europe displayed unease and a lack of openness in their investigations of buried SS wealth because they were embroiled in a high-level battle of both national and very much self-interest with the FBI, the US Treasury and the State Departments. This internecine warfare was heavily influenced by some of the world's biggest industrial concerns. Against this backdrop, individual agents, who were often personally involved in finance, behaved warily and wearily.[32] The FBI started investigating a multitude of American companies that were cloaking Nazi assets. They found themselves largely thwarted in their efforts against an extensive network of linked companies they dubbed the 'Schröder/Dulles network'.[33]

The all-powerful Schröder Finance House, working mainly from New York, London and Hamburg, enjoyed extensive influence in Latin America. Kurt Schröder, a generous member of the 'Circle of Friends of the Reichsführer', had set up yet another special account for Himmler in the Stern bank, and was promoted to SS Brigade-führer by a grateful Himmler. Schröder was the German half of an unholy alliance with American intelligence chief Allen Dulles, who sat on Schröder's board. Through the German brokerage company Albert and Westrick, and Dulles' legal firm, Sullivan and Cromwell, they created an impenetrable web of companies that siphoned off the concealed SS assets. In Germany, broker Dr Heinrich Albert represented vast American corporations such as Ford, Gillette, Kodak and ITT. Although just after the war the FBI uncovered key links between Dulles and Schröder in New York and the diversion of IG Farben and Stahlwerke's assets, they were unable to mount effective counter-action in the US itself.[34] Despite furious representations by FBI Chief J. Edgar Hoover, the new President Truman was successfully lobbied by Ford, General Motors, Gillette, Kodak and ITT, whose chairman Sothenes Behn had contributed to the 'Circle of Friends' fund and was vigorously engaged in laundering SS capital.

Matters were not helped by the fact that, in Europe, the OSS and, later, agents from the fledgling CIA were actually employed by Allen Dulles, in his capacity as Chief of Intelligence. Working from his comfortable flat at Herringasse 23 in Bern, he continued to meet openly with his German collaborators, such as fellow Schröder Finance House director, Valerian Mocarski, a close personal acquaintance of former German finance minister Hjalmar Schacht. According to Swiss Intelligence Chief Colonel Roger Masson, Dulles described his flat as 'a financial research unit'. In the interests of his research, he continued to receive representatives from the Dresdner Bank. Dulles was an insurmountable obstacle to any effective challenge to Himmler's plans.

American intelligence agents in Sweden soon discovered that Dulles, along with Swedish bankers the Wallenberg brothers, had brokered deals with the Swedish firm Bofors to conceal similar Nazi assets. In effect, Allen Dulles had rubber-stamped the transfer of a sizeable portion of Nazi Germany's assets by the SS. Thanks to his unique position he was empowered to abort any investigation, by his own employees, of his actions. It was like asking a detective to solve a murder that he had committed. American embarrassment was to become acute when, shortly after hostilities had ceased, Colonel Bernard Bernstein, Chief of the Financial Division of the US Military Government, found a cache of six boxes of Bosch files hidden in 6T Ablagen, a shelter in the mountains near Stuttgart. These exposed the detailed involvement of both Dulles brothers, as well as that of George Murnane.[35]

The correspondence between the US Treasury and the US State Department gives us the first insight into the extent of British involvement in cloaking Nazi assets. Up to that point numerous US Treasury reports had condemned the Enskilda Bank and the Wallenbergs out of hand, implying that the British were heavily and secretly involved. After Colonel Bernstein's discovery, Ivan Olsen of the US Treasury met with John Foster Dulles, and suddenly the previously belligerent US Treasury were expressing the need for caution, especially since 'We would never get Britain's concurrence in the blacklisting of this bank'.[36]

But FBI Chief Hoover could scent the blood of his arch-rival Allen Dulles. His fury increased when he found out that Dulles had asked Sir Charles Hambro, his British brokering partner-in-crime, to write a letter to President Truman falsely claiming that the Wallenbergs were pro-British and had not been involved in profitable activities in Germany during the war. Sir Charles Hambro had shared much with Marcus Wallenberg (including Wallenberg's ex-wife), and willingly obliged. Hambro held IG Farben shares in conjunction with Standard Oil, and had helped Marcus Wallenberg cloak the IG Farben shares held by the Enskilda Bank. Here was a British financier with American and Canadian interests, implicated in international collaboration with the Wallenberg and Dulles brothers, the facilitators of Himmler's scheme. Cheekily, Hambro even used the British SOE to send his personal financial representative, SOE agent John McCaffrey, to work with Allen Dulles in Bern, at a time when the SOE had no official role in Europe.[37]

Unfortunately for the conspirators, Hoover had just finished investigating the affairs of the finance house of J. P. Morgan and the National City Bank, both beneficiaries of Marcus Wallenberg's dealings. Hoover rapidly countered by declaring Wallenberg to be nothing more than a paid agent of the Reichsbank. Under renewed FBI pressure, the US Treasury reversed their stance yet again and officially asked for the Enskilda Bank to be blacklisted. True to form, the British refused. The fury behind the scenes continued unabated. General Lucius Clay, in charge of the American Occupied Zone in post-war Germany, called for Marcus and Jacob Wallenberg to be prosecuted as war criminals. (Clay was hardly in a position to seek the moral high ground, having used his personal plane to fly out stolen art treasures from Germany to Miami.) The US Treasury took action, initiating a case against the Wallenbergs at Nuremberg – only to see this stopped by John Foster Dulles in the US State Department.

Even as open warfare raged between Hoover and the Dulles brothers, and all attention was centred on the wartime activities of the Wallenbergs, particularly Marcus, the King of England stepped in. At what proved to be a most opportune moment, George VI honoured Marcus Wallenberg, making him a Knight of St Michael and St George. This sign of royal interest effectively silenced any further argument. Sir Edward Playfair worked in the British Treasury from 1943 to 1946 and helped organise British opposition to the American proposals to blacklist the Enskilda Bank and punish the Wallenbergs for their role in the cloaking of Bosch's assets. When questioned in his nineties about his reasons for doing so, all Playfair would say was that 'It [blacklisting] was entirely out of the question; ruled out from on high'.[38]

American anger surfaced quite quickly – surprisingly, through a visit to the British Legation in Stockholm by the normally affable George Brewer of the OSS, who worked under Allen Dulles. Sir Peter Tennant's successor as Assistant Military Attaché in Stockholm, Jasper Leadbitter, relates how Brewer's anger was focused on Sir Victor Mallet, and that the Americans 'seemed to know more than we did about the meetings he had held'.[39]

Tennant, then in Paris but still keeping a close eye on affairs in Stockholm, was contacted by his former deputy Leadbitter.[40] His understanding at the time was that everyone thought Ewan Butler, who had been one of Brewer's best friends, had yet again been decidedly indiscreet. According to Tennant, the Americans thought that 'whatever Mallet had been up to in his meetings with Schellenberg and Brandin (Director of the Swedish Match Company) involved the Wallenbergs and involved the Swedish royal family either directly or indirectly'. Both Brandin and Marcus Wallenberg had immense business interests in the Soviet Union; the Americans would hardly welcome Swedish and British involvement with the Bolsheviks. 'They [the Americans] obviously drew their own conclusions, a lot of it was sour grapes,' Tennant concluded.[41] His view that the Americans were only interested in secret financial arrangements that disadvantaged them has the ring of truth; they could hardly have been upset by pure peace negotiations if, after all their efforts, Churchill had at long last lifted his veto on Anglo/Nazi peace deals.

American representations obviously did not stop at personal remonstrances in Stockholm. Worried queries from the British Foreign Office in London prompted Mallet's post-war successor Jerram to report to Foreign Secretary Ernest Bevin in London that Mallet's dealings with the Wallenbergs 'would in many quarters make Mallet appear a fool and perhaps a dupe'.[42] This hardly reflected the true situation. Apart from his frequent, childish displays of unbridled temper, Mallet was not generally considered a fool. When he had first taken over the Stockholm Legation in 1940 from Sir Edmund Monson 'Debonair' Bart, a strutting peacock of a man, the Legation had welcomed Mallet with open arms. A career diplomat who was by nature cautious and proper, Mallet had displayed astonishing courage in combating Churchill's direct orders against any further discussions with Schellenberg. Such bravery was probably bolstered by his royal connections. Victor Mallet was a godson of Queen Victoria, his mother one of her ladies-in-waiting, and a favourite in the royal household. That background, combined with his marriage to Peggy Andreae, daughter of Herman Andreae of Kleinwort, and a personal friend of the Swedish royal family, made Victor Mallet an ideal confidant to manage royal financial interests. According to Sir Peter Tennant, 'Mallet was on intimate terms with the Swedes, some thought too intimate.'[43] As a banker himself, Mallet would have been a saint among sinners had he not nurtured an element of self-interest in his discussions with Schellenberg and the Wallenbergs.

Tennant thought Mallet had arrived at some kind of agreement with Churchill. When he was ordered back to London in March 1944, Mallet was asked to lunch at the Prime Minister's country residence, Chequers, during which he was dismayed to learn that he was to be posted to Brazil immediately: a clear indication of Churchill's displeasure. He duly broke down and, in tears, begged Churchill to be allowed to continue in Stockholm until the end of hostilities. The request was granted.[44] Mallet was eventually moved to Madrid. What ambassador is invited to Chequers to be put in his place? It all reflected Mallet's unusual personal status and, possibly, British royal interests. In retrospect, Tennant felt that Churchill's reaction had been an automatic, instinctive response to preserve the status quo. Rather than overtly counter Mallet's ongoing negotiations which continued until May 1945, he left his trusty friend Monckton to quietly keep an eye on things. It was entirely in keeping with Churchill's previous reactions to Sir Samuel Hoare's treachery, and revelations of the Duke of Windsor's gross profiteering during the war and large-scale currency frauds. Rather than rock the boat, and risk upsetting his own position, records were destroyed or buried and the culprits escaped harsh censure.

So what linked German Bosch shares; Himmler's envoy, corporate lawyer Dr Schmidt; Deutsche Bank representative Conrad van der Golz; Marcus Wallenberg, their constant companion when in Sweden, and Sir Victor Mallet? What grounds did the Americans have for believing that the Swedish royal family was involved, and why did Sir Peter Tennant think that Churchill's hands were tied because of possible royal involvement? Scant details are available of the British royal family's investments in the Bank of International Settlements in Switzerland, a secretive bank set up after the First World War to deal with reparations. It had become something of a vehicle for the transfer of large amounts of shares without much scrutiny – like an offshore fund. Montagu Norman, Himmler's friend Hjalmar Schacht, and numerous Americans sat on the board. Its wartime chairman, Thomas McKittrick, claimed to be 'the most neutral man in the world'.[45] He described the Bank as 'a sort of club for the world's leading central bankers, a little group of like-minded men who understood and trusted one another'.[46]

Concerning the British royal family's involvement, we know only that substantial amounts were deposited in 1937 and reinvested by the bank on their behalf in shares, many of them in German companies. Nor is much known about the 1943 transfer of Bosch shares from this bank to the Wallenbergs' Enskilda Bank. We are left with the frustration of the American Treasury agents as they attempted to uncover the dispersal of Bosch shares as revealed by the Red House report. The trail stopped at the offices of three Stockholm lawyers, Hans Hohm, Herbert Luckfest and Stenbeck.[47]

Once again, American investigators' attempts to discover the beginning of the trail and the transfer of assets from the Bank of International Settlements and to blacklist the bank were blocked by the British Treasury, under pressure from the Foreign Office, thanks to Mallet and his influential friends. As before, Sir Edward Playfair played a key role in obstructing the Americans. According to him he had no choice: 'The amounts of British capital invested were so great that it made it impossible for a nearly bankrupt Britain to even consider sanctions.'[48] Even today it still cannot be determined exactly what amounts of British capital were involved, nor whom it belonged to. It is interesting to note that after the war, Swedish Princess Louise Mountbatten received a gold cigarette case shaped like an envelope from the British royal family to commemorate her role as go-between in difficult negotiations with the Nazis. Margarette Mountbatten was married to Prince Gottfried von Hohenlohe-Langenburg, and Prince Christopher Mountbatten had joined Himmler's staff, enlisting as an agent.

Mallet may well have been party to unusual financial arrangements and the concealment of Bosch assets in 1943 with Himmler via Schellenberg. (This could be reflected by the Allied investigators' discovery, when investigating Bosch files in Stockholm, of numerous Bosch shares held in a deposit box opened for Schellenberg's contact Karl-Heinz Krämer at the Enskilda Bank.) Though shocking, this pales in comparison with the intrigue surrounding Ewan Butler's discussions with Schellenberg, though it presents further compelling reasons for the British to offer immunity from prosecution to Himmler and Schellenberg. As ever, the activities of Himmler's agents displayed his unerring ability to understand where power and influence really lay. Himmler's organisational skills and his political and financial knowledge were greatly in evidence in the last-minute bargaining led by Schellenberg in Stockholm.

Embarrassment on the American side was equalled on the British, whose investigators, in addition to the compromising situation in Stockholm, found two of their own pale imitations of Allen Dulles, not to mention Sir Charles Hambro. Viscount Bearsted of Hill Samuel, Lloyd's, and Sun Alliance, and the late Sir Henry Deterding of Royal Dutch Shell, were linked through Lazards and Lee Higginson Investment Bank with some of Schröder's closest associates.[49]

In contrast to the initial enthusiasm of the American Secret Service, the immediate reaction of the British SIS was one of exhausted despair. They had unsuccessfully attempted to counter similar German ambitions and trickery at the end of the First World War – and that was without someone like Himmler to reckon with. Senior operatives remembered only too well how at that time a young lawyer, Allen Dulles, had perfected brokering techniques for his personal financial gain, techniques that he was using once again with great success. The British Secret Service had nothing like the political or financial back-up enjoyed by their American counterparts. Making the best use of limited resources, individual financial experts were called in to handle the affair at probably the most efficient level; mid-civil servant grade. Archives reveal the likes of Mr Shaekla, Mr James, Miss Kilroy, Mr Welch and Mr Andrew, faceless signatories, whose relatively lowly status did not stop them from coming up with several interesting points that were to guide subsequent actions. They observed how German reports of the arrests of key industrialists, such as Gustav Krupp von Bohlen und Halbach, for 'defeatist attitudes and organising anti-Nazi resistance groups', and similar reports of the arrest of Alfred Krupp von Bohlen und Halbach and the violently Fascist I G Farben director Georg Schnitzer as 'alleged anti-Nazi conspirators', were obviously intended for Allied consumption.[50] These individuals were targeted to ensure they retained their critical positions at the head of their industrial concerns in a post-war Germany dictated to by the Allies.

Although such mock arrests were too obvious to fool most people, the British warned that other such cases might not be so conspicuous. The Nazi fires would be kept burning, albeit underground, 'nourished and supported by the trustees of German economic and financial interests within and outside Germany'. 'They are the true underground. Other evidence indicates that minor officials reported executed for treason are reappearing in neutral countries with fake passports.'[51] It was a remarkably accurate assessment, as we shall see.

British investigators acted as the main catalyst in the launch of combined operations between the OSS and SIS to counter the deployment of Himmler's plans in Europe. Two Swiss banks named in the Red House report were immediately placed under scrutiny. Employees were bribed, telegrams surreptitiously copied, and letters intercepted. They were not the banks normally associated with receiving Nazi gold, but were found to be engaged in forwarding suspect currency to Lisbon, Madrid, and even as far afield as Shanghai. Himmler's plans for his own pension fund and for the dismemberment of a defeated Germany were working. As soon as the Red

House report reached Allied Intelligence in November 1944 the results had a fascinated, impotent audience.

In parallel with their American colleagues, British activity to combat Himmler's master plan reached its peak in the early summer of 1945. After some small successes, the British researchers found their commonsense suggestions often inexplicably blocked by government departments. Everything ground to a halt, stymied by strange inertia at Treasury level and above. Embarrassed silence on the American side was matched by British passivity. The lack of any final summary of action taken in response to the Red House report said it all. It is easy to see why so little was done. Many people with vested interests in Wall Street and the City of London stock exchange were incapable of seeing the flood of hidden German investments and money as anything other than a sea of opportunity. Moral questions were beside the point. But amongst the financiers of the time there was a colossus whose outspoken views on the dangers of a resurgent Nazi state took several committees and a dozen sub-committees to 'rationalise'.

Wartime US Secretary of State Henry Morgenthau Jnr was known as the 'Nostradamus of Finance' because his economic forecasts were always devastatingly accurate. Buttonholed by the FBI very early on, he was appalled by what he read in the Red House report. The FBI secured tell-tale correspondence from Schmitz, a key figure in the Heidelberg branch of IG Farben, that revealed the decisions taken at the final meeting of the IG Farben board. Assets had been buried away from the Allies' reach and suspicion, and a healthy investment had been made in the purchase of the Bayer Company's foreign intelligence network. They agreed on proposals that had been put forward to Mann, the director of IG Farben's overseas sales, by Brigadeführer Walter Schellenberg. The FBI's assumption was confirmed; Schellenberg was the mastermind behind many of these covert overseas ventures under the instruction of Himmler. (It is interesting to note that Schellenberg's term for the size of the IG Farben finances was that they represented a 'state within a state'.)[52]

Annoyed at the way their investigation into IG Farben in America had been blocked, the FBI had turned to a man who would not need to be convinced of the need to investigate Himmler's financial master plan. Like their chief J. Edgar Hoover, Henry Morgenthau Jnr was vehemently opposed to anything the Dulles brothers ever favoured.

Morgenthau saw the Red House report as a prophecy of the Allied governments' failure to address the problem of German nationalism for the second time. The carrion crows of international finance would ensure success for Himmler by their sheer numbers, influence and rapacity, even if the cloaking was removed. Morgenthau forecast that subsequent aid to post-war Germany, such as the Marshall Plan, would prove totally superfluous, thanks to the immense flood of capital that would eventually and inexorably return to the Fatherland. His standing ensured that he had a voice on the various panels established after the war to debate the rebuilding of Germany, but he was always outnumbered in his opposition to financial assistance. Morgenthau wanted to turn Germany into an agrarian economy that would act as a buffer zone against the influence of Soviet Russia. Understandably, this view was considered too extreme. Nevertheless, his economic forecasts were to prove correct.

Sure enough, in the 1950s, the German federal government shifted the responsibility for the prosecution of any war criminals who might surface to individual *Länder*. Before the end of the decade Germany duly saw an influx of capital and a marked increase in prosperity, which within only ten years had made Germany the stable economic centre of Europe. We cannot know how much of this economic miracle was due to sheer hard work or could be ascribed to the Marshall Plan; it has never been quantified. No Western historian has explored the reasons for Germany's rapid success as Europe's post-war economic leader. East German historians were, understandably, more interested in examining the background of their neighbour's triumphs. By the 1970s they had produced a 'Brown book' that purported to list all Nazi war criminals living freely in Western Germany.[53] Each entry sketched their wartime status, describing the crimes they had allegedly committed, their current whereabouts and occupation. Many worked in the judiciary and the civil service, and a large proportion held high positions within the *Länder* police forces

– *Länder* that now proved even more reluctant to prosecute war criminals. Alongside this startling information, the book featured the first estimates of the sums of money returned to West German *Länder* from many countries, including those of Latin America, Turkey, Egypt, the USA, Britain, Sweden and Switzerland.

The 'Brown book' was dismissed as propaganda. Western historians could not countenance the East Germans' claims, incredulous at the vast sums they cited. There has been no full investigation of the flow of capital to Germany from abroad. This seems surprising when you consider that the amounts were similar in scale to those listed in a similar 'Blue book' produced by the American CIA, aimed at specifying Nazi funds salted away in Argentina. (It has never been released. I have been shown it by a CIA contact.) Furthermore, this book credited much of Argentina's post-war wealth to the injection of such Nazi capital.

There are reasons to be cautious about these books. Both seem to fall far short of their aims to uncover all arrangements – their investigations seem woefully inadequate compared to the scope of the ambitions recorded in the Red House report. If you strip away the political bias – anti-British in the case of the Americans – and allow for a certain amount of exaggeration, the fact remains that these reports add great weight to the suspicions of Henry Morgenthau Jnr in 1945. He was so exercised by his concerns at the Red House report that he uncharacteristically wrote a book immediately after the war, called *Germany Is Our Problem*. This advocated a decentralised, deindustrialised post-war Germany, citing the Red House report as evidence of evil intent. Morgenthau even named the two Swiss banks involved in turning Himmler's grandiose plans into hard reality. Crédit Suisse of Zurich and the Baseler Handelsbank were decried for allowing 'these funds to be at the disposal of the Nazis in their underground campaign'.[54]

Although the author enjoyed great repute, the immense size of the financial transactions his book revealed was unacceptable and unwelcome to establishments heartily sick of constant vigilance. Historians refused to entertain the notion that 'timorous' Heinrich Himmler was behind this master plan. As Hugh Trevor-Roper condescendingly put it when criticising Schellenberg's memoirs, 'Imagine poor Schellenberg ever thinking that Himmler would be party to plotting against the Führer.' Those that had known the ruthless Reichsführer personally, who considered him 'capable of setting Dresden alight', were derided.[55] Even more risible was the thought that Himmler, a man who constantly advertised his meagre circumstances and honesty, could ever have been interested in finance, let alone capable of personal deceit. After all, had he not borrowed from Martin Bormann in 1942 to finance his house?

The legacy of embarrassment at the time, and the vested interests that caused that embarrassment, live on. Official historians (those chosen by the British government to look at carefully selected archive material and produce reports and books for public consumption) have been reluctant to acknowledge that the Red House report ever existed, let alone admit the possibility that its contents might be genuine or significant. Indeed, two who were involved in handling the Red House report when it first came into Allied hands continued to deny its very existence until the day its yellowing pages were released, somewhat belatedly, in 1996 from Washington archives under the Freedom of Information Act.

Those historians who first read the report said the experience was quite unreal. With the benefit of hindsight they were able to savour at least some of the flavour of a meeting that saw the economic heart of the Reich transplanted abroad in a bold gesture which ensured, at the very least, Germany's survival, and at most, its future prosperity. They could at last understand what had inspired dread in the imagination of men like Henry Morgenthau Jnr, and caused such wild excitement among financiers such as the Wallenbergs, international brokers like Westrick and the Dulles brothers. Perhaps the greatest irony of the Red House report is that its very existence drew an unrivalled financial opportunity to the attention of a number of financiers who worked for Allied Intelligence services. Their knowledge of Himmler's plan in some ways operated to guarantee its success. And the report disclosed that Heinrich Himmler commanded the finances of the Reich, one of the greatest bargaining tools of the twentieth century. He was in a position not only to negotiate the Reich's future, but also his own survival, ready to engage in final discussions with Allied Intelligence.

As Sir Peter Tennant put it, 'At the very time when we in the Secret Service were railing against the stupidity of the "unconditional surrender" terms on offer, there were several figures in Stockholm who would have married Himmler off to their daughter to get a piece of the action [. . .] there was a frenzy about what was on offer.'[56] It all adds another dimension to the urgency of the British desire to come to an understanding with Himmler and Schellenberg in Stockholm, and their extraordinary offer of immunity.

The meeting of industrialists at the Hôtel de la Maison Rouge started in the early evening of 10 August 1944. Proceedings commenced in the dining room; after dinner they retired to room 23, the private salon on the entresol with chairs around the massive square table, offering a fine view through high-arched windows of the mature palms of the Jardin d'Hiver. With the onset of the Allied bombing the meeting had quickly resorted to the large purpose-built air-raid shelter. As 'Mr Waddington' quietly sat with the conspirators, the mystery eavesdropper, having earlier listened in satisfactorily to conversations in Dr Scheid's suite (rooms 6/7), Kaspar's, rooms 68/9 on the floor above, and Dr Strössner's (rooms 104/5) on the top floor, was having a field day in the deserted corridors, turning fourteen more of the delegates' double rooms upside down before making a getaway past the statue of General Kléber.

The last words of the Red House report look unblinkingly at the future faced by Himmler and his partners in crime:

> After the defeat of Germany the Nazi Party recognises that certain of its known leaders will be condemned as war criminals [. . .] However, it is arranging to place its less conspicuous but most important members in positions with various German factories as technical experts or members of its research and development offices.[57]

Eight months before the inevitable happened, the SS acknowledged it faced total defeat, and was arranging hiding places for its key members well in advance of necessity. Such pragmatic realism leaves a sour taste when one considers the success of so many other aspects of Himmler's plan. The Red House report provides ample testimony for Himmler's determined, systematic financial realism, and offers an insight into his thoughts on post-war survival.

On 5 November 1944, just two days before the Red House report was submitted to Allied Intelligence, another meeting took place at the Hotel Savoy in Baur en ville, Zurich, that shares startling correspondences to the meeting at the Maison Rouge. It was to be the culmination of many prior meetings. Financiers, bankers and the SS were involved in providing assistance to foreign governments that ultimately did them no favours. Once again, it resulted in personal gain for the Reichsführer. It was 'one of the most bizarre meetings of the Second World War'. It provided another fascinating insight into the mind of Heinrich Himmler, bent on using another tack in his battle for survival, tying up loose ends and clearing away obstacles to his post-war future.

8

Loose Ends

The Soviets mastered the paradoxical art of following from in front. They would overtake other traffic so swiftly that the car under surveillance had difficulty keeping up. It was a demanding technique to master and required a lot of preparatory work. Nevertheless, it was the NKVD's proud boast that in wartime Switzerland, with the Americans at least, they were consistently successful in tracking agents. On 5 November 1944 they would have arrived at the Hotel Savoy in Zurich in good time to watch an extraordinarily indiscreet delegation.

The large and obtrusive presence of the Americans at Allen Dulles' 'secret' Bern HQ was a subject of national amusement to the Swiss. This was not helped by their habit of having excessively 'protected' delegations in conspicuous attendance at every major meeting. When President Roosevelt's personal envoy, the eminent Quaker leader and financier Roswell D. McClellan, arrived at the Hotel Savoy surrounded by a clutch of OSS heavies, it must have narrowly avoided ending up on the cover of *Time* magazine.

McClellan had been chosen for a difficult mission. As if to emphasise the point, he was escorted by Swiss Military Intelligence Chief Roger Masson's smart, green-buttoned security men, while his swaggering American guards jammed open foyer and elevator doors to keep tabs on potential spies. The next arrival was dead on time, as one would expect from an SS Obersturmbannführer. His dirty Opel was decidedly downmarket for the five-star venue, but at least he arrived without the advertisement of an entourage. The officer only had his handsome appearance to recommend him, but this more than compensated for any four-wheel deficiencies. Kurt Becher, a

well-connected businessman's son from Hamburg, had risen through
the ranks of the SS cavalry to become one of Himmler's special
envoys. Signing his letters 'the Reichsführer's most obedient Becher',
he enjoyed the rare honour of being one of Himmler's few trusted
personal agents.

The taciturn American and his German counterpart were escorted
to a luxurious suite where they were greeted by Saly Mayer. Mayer
was a banker who headed the Jewish community in neutral Switzerland. This status-obsessed individual has been much criticised by
Jewish historians for his unpleasant combination of inaction and
greedy self-interest. He came to the meeting armed with a promissory
note of $5 million that purported to come from US Secretary of
State Cordell Hull. They made an odd trio. Here was an American
financier, supposedly personally representing the American President,
ready to draw up a bargain between the SS and a Jewish leader,
while war raged on outside Swiss borders. As writer Andreas Biss
put it, 'That the meeting took place at all – when the Allies had
agreed that all negotiations should be tripartite and based on unconditional surrender – must have seemed to Himmler an important, if
not the most important result of his constant intrigues. Technically,
however, this meeting was a breach of the agreement between Stalin
and the Western Allies to maintain a complete boycott of the Third
Reich.'[1] Biss amusingly catalogued the bizarre sequence of events
that led to a US President apparently agreeing, through a Quaker,
to broker the purchase of Jews from the Nazis.

The peculiarity of this meeting was heightened the following
year, when the atrocities of Auschwitz concentration camps were
discovered by horrified Allied troops. McClellan responded to a
public outcry in the US by issuing a remarkable defensive statement
from Bern on 6 February 1945. He claimed that all meetings between
Mayer and the Germans to trade Jews for cash or, worse still, military
hardware, had been made with the American State Department's
approval. Moreover, the British and Russian governments had been
kept fully informed (while the former is quite possible, the latter
claim is quite untrue). Not to be outdone, the White House immediately denied that the American government would ever have been

engaged in such tawdry dealings, claiming they had never made any money available.[2] It was understandable that Roosevelt and McClellan should jump to the defensive. They were caught up in an affair that ultimately achieved little other than to promote hypocrisy, self-interest and greed, the main beneficiaries of this sleaze being Mayer and Becher.

Himmler had long been well aware of the gain to be made from the sale of that elusive commodity, freedom, to a people he despised for their financial acumen. Indeed, that November he had only just finished using Becher on a mission based on just that premise. While in Hungary, representing the SS Führungshauptamt's Armaments Commission on a mission to acquire 20,000 horses for the Waffen SS, Becher completed an extremely advantageous takeover of the huge Manfred Weiss industrial concern. The Jewish Weiss family's safety was exchanged for a governing 55 per cent share of the works. Much effort was expended in ensuring that the deal had the correct veneer of legality in classic Himmler style. The agreement was stuffed with clauses, definitions and caveats designed to give the post-war impression that the deal had been argued over, considered in detail then freely signed. The Weiss empire was another perfect vehicle for shifting Himmler's wealth into neutral countries.

The meeting at the Hotel Savoy promised much more than mere wealth. Becher and Mayer exaggerated the importance of McClellan's presence, so it seemed to Himmler that he was being offered a direct line of communication to the White House. It also highlighted the whole Jewish question, revealing an unexpected level of Allied concern and its possible usefulness as a bargaining ploy. Constant reference to Roosevelt as Mayer's benefactor was successfully designed to keep Himmler's interest alive.[3] In 1944, the Jewish question had shed any ideological baggage as far as Himmler was concerned. His main interest was to work out how the Holocaust might affect his acceptability to the Allies. As war approached its inevitable conclusion, the murder of millions presented a loose end that, he must have been painfully aware, threatened to unravel any hopes he had for a future public rôle. There is plenty of evidence to suggest that by this stage he was approaching this issue with the same pragmatism with which he had insured his post-war financial survival. Himmler made out that the substantial amounts of money received for Jews were destined for the Reich armaments industry (in fact, most of it was paid direct into his account). This provided him with a useful shield against criticism from his many enemies within the Reich for negotiating with the Americans. He had already established a precedent for this argument with a 1941 order stopping the emigration of Jews except in isolated instances financially beneficial to the Reich.[4] Looking ahead to defeat and the ignominy of indictment for war crimes, he would have recast these actions from an alternative perspective. Surely, he must have striven to convince himself, such 'humanitarian' gestures would weigh against any charges of genocide. This logic was ultimately successful for Kurt Becher who, after his post-war arrest, was freed thanks to the testimony of Jewish Dr Kasztner, with whom Becher had collaborated to send rich Jews to Switzerland.[5] Himmler may well have harboured the illusion that he might receive the same benefits, or at least thought such bargains would make him appear more acceptable in any final peace negotiations.

Himmler had already entered into less official deals with Hungarian Jews, and on 26 July 1944 ordered 'No more deportations from Hungary [to Auschwitz]'.[6] Indeed, earlier intimations that he might find a direct route to Roosevelt's ear through such generosity to the Jews had resulted in an extremely limited, orchestrated Red Cross visit to Auschwitz. In September 1944 he had issued this magnanimous command to Pohl and Kaltenbrunner: 'By this order, which becomes immediately operative, I forbid any liquidation of Jews, and order that on the contrary, care should be given to weak and sick persons. I hold you personally responsible, even if this order should not be strictly adhered to by subordinate officers.'[7]

The tone of Becher's orders and communications dramatically alters in 1944. Where he had previously shown a pedantic preoccupation with the details of the quotidian horrors of the SS regime, suddenly the language becomes punchy and concerned, as if designed for the eye of the inevitable war crimes tribunal. The sudden absence of intricate orders appears to establish a distance from the atrocities, in stark contrast to the previous microscopic attention that under-mined any argument that the Reichsführer might not have been aware of what was going on in his empire. Becher became a personal notebook for his master, graphically recording Himmler's considerate nature and the unfortunate problems he faced with Kaltenbrunner and Pohl. On 26 November Becher wrote, 'The crematoria in Auschwitz are to be dismantled. The Jews working in the Reich are to get normal Eastern rations. In the absence of Jewish hospitals, they may be treated with Aryan patients.'[8] This pathetic missive, drafted two months before the Russians were at Auschwitz's gates, was designed to show that the Reichsführer, sadly misinformed, had no idea that there were not any Jewish hospitals in the death camp. This sheds light on to Himmler's thinking, still clutching at straws with a naivety that seems extraordinary.

Further evidence of such childish delusion lies in his treatment of the concentration camp at Theresienstadt. This was Himmler's pet camp; he personally signed all orders, representing it as the 'Altersghetto', where elderly Jews could live out their lives in peace and quiet. He was furious when news leaked out of mass deportations to Auschwitz, deportations he had insisted should be carried out under the strictest secrecy. Through this 'model camp' (there were, naturally, many atrocities here too) that he personally commanded, Himmler attempted to shift all responsibility for the excesses in other camps on to the broad shoulders of Pohl and Kaltenbrunner. Not everyone was impressed though. Rudolf Hess's wife, Ilse, was appalled by her visit: 'There were Jews hanging around, idling about, and I said to Himmler, "You should get these people to see to the paths and the flower beds, you are far too soft."'[9]

Roosevelt's concern, exaggerated by the cash-hungry Mayer and Becher, was a far bigger priority by late 1944. According to evidence produced by Baldur von Schirach at Nuremberg, Himmler announced, 'I want the Jews now employed in industry to be taken by boat or bus, under the most favourable conditions, and with the best possible medical care, to Linz or Malthausen. Please take care of these Jews, they are my soundest capital investment.'[10] Von Schirach corrected the monetary slant to this statement by observing that he had the impression that Himmler wanted to redeem himself with this good treatment of the Jews. On the other hand, Himmler knew full well that the living evidence for how the Jews had really been treated lay there in the camps. Although the crematoria at Auschwitz had been blown up, leaving only 3,000 sick for the Russians to find, over one hundred camps in Germany still held 500,000 Aryans and 200,000 Jews in horrendous conditions that were deteriorating by the day. The typhus at the research station at Belsen had spread and taken over the entire camp.

Eventually a vacillating, panicky Himmler issued the order in spring 1945 that 'No camp inmate in the southern part of Germany must fall into enemy hands alive'.[11] Simultaneously he told Adolf Eichmann, who was in charge of Jewish Affairs, to preserve 300 prominent Jews 'for hostage purposes'.[12] It was too little, too late, and the Allied advance just too rapid. Himmler quickly decided to prevent further atrocities in the camps at Belsen and Buchenwald – as all discipline had broken down in anticipation of the arrival of the Allies.

Further attempts to use the Jews to secure post-war favours were led by Himmler's trusted intelligence chief Walter Schellenberg. On 16 February 1945 Schellenberg met with Count Folke Bernadotte, the well-connected cousin of Swedish King Gustav who was President of the Swedish Red Cross, to discuss the fate of Scandinavian Jews and Swedish prisoners of war. (Peter Falk believes that they had known each other for some time, at least since Schellenberg paid a visit to Stockholm in 1943, although this cannot be proven.)[13] Two days later Schellenberg drove Bernadotte out to Himmler's headquarters at Hohenlychen for the first of a series of negotiations. The last recorded meeting between Bernadotte and Himmler was on 23 April at Lübeck. It had taken them two months to arrange the release of most of the Scandinavian Jews, although the precise terms of the agreement remain unclear. However, after the war Israeli Intelligence became aware of a deal made with Sweden that sounds uncannily similar to that which caused Ewan Butler distress: 'At the time Bernadotte had conducted the discussions with elaborate (and in the eyes of the Jews unforgivable) caution and circumspection, refusing until

the last moment to promise Himmler immunity from Allied retribution.'[14] This makes it clear that Himmler was aiming for immunity
from prosecution at least months in advance of defeat. Over the
course of the negotiations, Schellenberg built up a strong relationship
with Bernadotte and, as war ended, he would find he could rely on
Bernadotte to do everything in his power to make the deal hold. It
seems likely that the British would have known of, and possibly
approved such an agreement; that this deal was made at all shows
that the British offer of immunity to Himmler and Schellenberg was
not as aberrant as it first appears, however distasteful.

The Swedes were extremely grateful to Himmler. He had also
granted freedom to seven Swedes, five of whom had been condemned to death in 1942 after their arrest in Warsaw for passing on
information from the Stockholm-based Polish resistance movement.
This clemency bought Himmler expressions of gratitude from King
Gustav and Brandin, the Swedish Match Company director who
was active in various secret negotiations.[15] Himmler followed this
up with a proposal to repatriate twenty British officers, already hand-
chosen by Becher, but this scheme never came to fruition. More
humanitarian gestures targeted at Switzerland and Sweden followed,
the most important release being Polish General Tadeusz Bor-
Komorovski, who was conducted into sanctuary in Switzerland from
Ravensbrück concentration camp.[16]

As the Reich quickly dwindled to a rump in the north of Germany,
Himmler met with the director of the Swedish section of the World
Jewish Congress at Hartzwalde for an hour at 2 a.m. on 21 April
1945. He began by claiming that had the Allies agreed to accept the
expulsion of Jews from Germany before the war started, the Jewish
problem would have been avoided and it would have actually been to
the Jews' advantage. The concentration camps were, in his opinion,
merely 'work training centres where work was always found for idle
hands and the treatment had been fair; any SS atrocities had been
punished'. Himmler then bitterly complained of the false propaganda
of so-called atrocities that the Allies were making out of Belsen and
Buchenwald, which he had 'handed over as agreed':

When I let 2,700 Jews go into Switzerland they were made the subject of a personal campaign against me in the press – asserting that I had only released these men in order to construct an alibi for myself. But I have no need of an alibi. I have always done only what I considered just – what was essential for my people. I will answer for that. Nobody has had so much mud slung at them in the last ten years as I have. I have never bothered myself about that. Even in Germany today – anyone can say about me what he likes. Newspapers abroad have started a campaign against me which is no encouragement to me to continue handing over the camps![17]

The language is that of an aggrieved letter to a newspaper. This was not just evidence of Himmler's psychopathic lack of feeling and a revolting exercise in denial; more significantly, it displays his full realisation that the international furore over the fate of the Jews severely limited his horizons and his options for post-war public survival. Two days later he confirmed this shift in his thinking, telling Count Folke Bernadotte that he knew the West regarded him as a war criminal.

Himmler used his relationship with Bernadotte to try to open negotiations with General Eisenhower. He sent a letter on 23 April that offered to capitulate in the West so that the Allies could occupy the remainder of Germany before the Soviets. This appeared to presuppose his acceptability as negotiator and potential for some legitimate post-war rôle. Against the backdrop of Himmler's recognition of the extent of the world's hostility towards him, this offer must at best be seen as suspect, especially when there remained other potentially viable alternatives. He was testing the water, but perhaps he was also attempting to give the impression that he had not realised the game was up. The Jewish question had destroyed the possibility of any future participation in world affairs and Himmler knew full well that there were other, alternative, far more pragmatic courses of action still open to him.

Despite all the effort Himmler had made to resolve his problem over the Jews, it remained a loose end that increasingly resembled a noose. Nevertheless, right until the last moment Himmler would strive to tie all other loose ends that could possibly endanger his future, doing so with his usual calm, reasoned malice. The resistance in Germany presented the Reichsführer SS with a multitude of problems. After the failure of the 20 July plot to assassinate Hitler, attention was focused on the resistance groups, among some of whom Himmler's patronage could be discerned. Investigation by any one of Himmler's rivals could lead to exposure as a traitor, losing Hitler's trust and depriving him of the right to succession. Himmler was determined to get there before his enemies.

Himmler's financial emissary, Dr Carl Langbehn, was his neighbour and his confidant during critical peace negotiations in Sweden and Switzerland. This friendly, genial man and excellent linguist was also a close associate of Wilhelm Canaris, head of the Abwehr, and in close contact with the resistance movements through both Johannes Popitz and Von Hassell. In short, he was a total liability. He had once persuaded the sympathetic Reichsführer to allow, on the usual financial terms, the release of his old Jewish university professor Fritz Pringsheim from a concentration camp and his safe passage to sanctuary in Switzerland. However, Langbehn's indiscretions about Himmler's covert backing of German resistance groups' peace manoeuvres endangered their relationship.

In response to information from his spies, as early as April 1942 Italian Foreign Minister Galeazzo Ciano recorded in his diary that 'Himmler, who was an extremist in the past, but who now feels the pulse of the country, wants a compromise peace'.[18] That May, Ciano commented on rumours that were being spread by Prince Otto von Bismarck in Rome 'That Himmler is playing his own game by inciting people to grumble'.[19] Whatever game Himmler was then playing, doubtless one of power-hungry self-interest, it was sufficiently well known to encourage Von Hassell to write, 'All sorts of things are being planned around Himmler.'[20]

Langbehn also witnessed the critical meeting on 26 August 1943 between resistance leader Johannes Popitz and Himmler, when Himmler was told of Popitz's intention to conduct negotiations with the Allies behind Hitler's back. According to Popitz, 'Himmler did not oppose' this proposal.[21] Langbehn told Marie-Luise 'Puppi' Sarré, who worked with Von Hassell's resistance group, that 'Popitz had touched upon the elimination of Hitler [. . .] Himmler had been quite serious and had asked factual questions but had not tried to find out names.'[22] After Langbehn left for Switzerland to complete Popitz's peace negotiations, a radio message picked up by Müller's Gestapo incriminated him. All attempts by Müller or Kaltenbrunner to bring Langbehn to trial were overridden by Himmler until the 20 July plot left Himmler vulnerable to exposure. Langbehn was just too dangerous a witness. He was executed on 12 October 1944, sacrificed by an old friend who scornfully distanced himself from Langbehn and his indiscretions. Himmler reproached himself with mock-regret, 'We let this middleman chatter, we let him talk.' He went on to coldly describe his amusement at the group's discomfiture:

At last I pulled in the middleman. Since that time nine months ago Herr Popitz looks like a cheese. When you watch him he is as white as a wall; I would call him the image of a guilty conscience. He sends me telegrams – he telephones me – he asks me what is the matter with Dr Langbehn, what has happened to him? I give him sphinx-like replies so that he does not know whether I had anything to do with what happened or not.[23]

This was Himmler's public image, a front put up for his SS audience; behind the scenes he had been careful to ensure that the trials of Popitz and Langbehn were kept as secret as possible. When the hearing occurred in the autumn an ominous letter was sent to the Minister of Justice:

I understand that the trial of former minister Popitz and the lawyer Langbehn is to take place shortly before the People's Court [*Volksgerichtshof*]. In view of the facts known to you, namely the conference of the Reichsführer SS with Popitz, I ask you to see to it that the public be excluded from the trial. I assume your agreement and I shall dispatch about ten of my collaborators to make up an audience.[24]

It was an ultimatum that would not brook refusal. As Popitz's knowledge of foreign dignitaries was extensive and potentially useful, he was kept in prison until his death by hanging on 2 February 1945.

When questioned by Allied Intelligence after the war, Walter Schellenberg admitted that Himmler had known all about the 20 July plot and become anxious after Kaltenbrunner and Müller discovered his involvement in the course of questioning suspects. Fortunately, the proof was insufficient to risk any action against him.[25] General Fritz Thiele was one reason for Himmler's disquiet. At 1800 hours on that fateful day he had rung Schellenberg on an open telephone line to declare 'everything has gone wrong'. Terrified he was being bugged by the Gestapo, Schellenberg immediately called Müller to say he had just had a telephone call from Thiele, receiving the threatening reply, 'Fancy that – from your friend Thiele!'[26] Thiele called him again with the indiscreet suggestion that Himmler would look after them both. It was more of a relief than a surprise to Himmler and Schellenberg when Müller arrested Thiele on 24 July.[27]

At this time of crisis the umbrella of Himmler's power extended to shield Schellenberg and Baldur von Bismarck, grandson of the founder of the German state. Bismarck had been involved in peace negotiations and financial arrangements in Sweden between Himmler, Schellenberg and the Wallenberg brothers. Meetings were held on his estates, and in his house in Potsdam. Deeply entangled in the 20 July plot with Abwehr member Hansen and Schellenberg, he was another dangerous loose end. Himmler's intercession succeeded in obtaining an acquittal by the *Volksgerichtshof* despite Müller and Kaltenbrunner's efforts. Under the impression that Bismarck was potentially an acceptable post-war figure to the Allies and that he would back him when he assumed total power, Himmler allowed him to return safely to his estates. In so doing, Himmler increased the debt of gratitude owed him by Bismarck's close friend, Møller, Brandin's co-director at the Swedish Match Factory.[28] As ever, mercy was the handmaiden of self-interest.

Criminal police chief SS Gruppenführer Artur Nebe was not so useful to the Reichsführer. He had independently sought peace through his personal contacts in Sweden. Unfortunately, these contacts also knew of the extent of Himmler's own dealings in Stockholm. Nebe paid the price for this information, even though he had been one of Himmler's own appointees. He died on 3 March 1945.

Carl Gördeler was the gadfly of the 20 July plot. Ever since his resignation as Mayor of Leipzig in 1937 over the destruction of Mendelssohn's statue, he had been rather too openly at the centre of resistance to Hitler. Gördeler was a figure of immense political standing. He had known Churchill and Vansittart, and striven to prevent the onset of war. His contacts with Wilhelm Canaris, General Beck and financier Schacht, and his meetings with Moltke at his estate at Kreisau, made him party to everyone else's plots. His vainglorious lack of caution ensured he broadcast his involvement in opposition. Himmler had cause to fear his indiscretion for more particular reasons, as he had shamelessly exploited Gördeler's international standing to influence peace moves and financial accords centred on discussions in Stockholm. Yet Gördeler was someone whose connections might still prove useful to Himmler after Hitler had been removed.

Gördeler languished in prison after being betrayed in August 1944. His prison warder Wilhelm Brandenburg became his confidant and smuggled out uncensored sections of his manuscripts and letters. Gördeler had visions of his essays being published worldwide as a social commentary on the Nazi regime. Himmler had encouraged him to write deprecatingly of Hitler, intending to use the essays for home consumption as moral justification for any act against the Führer. It was not to be.

Admiral Wilhelm Canaris, the likable, cultured Abwehr chief, was an even more dangerous loose end. Canaris held Hitler in utter contempt, expostulating 'What HIM!' when told that Chamberlain had visited Hitler in Berchtesgaden. Canaris was always more interested in acting as an unofficial Foreign Office official than a security chief. He had his confidants – Hans Oster, Hans Rickenbrock, Georg Hansen, Colonel Wessel von Freytag-Löringhoven and Egbert Bentivegni – who kept their own counsel, but despite his security training, Canaris was naive enough to conspire with a resistance group that seemed straight out of a Shakespearian tragedy. The conspirators talked more openly than Hamlet and, like Brutus and his cohorts in *Julius Caesar*, they seemed totally unprepared for the inevitable outcome. Moreover, Canaris had collected damning information on Himmler's concentration camps, comprising an appalling dossier stored in canisters of microfilm buried in his son-in-law's garden. His carelessness in mixing with the resistance groups led to his investigation by Schellenberg, who repeatedly gave Himmler enough evidence to warrant Canaris' arrest, yet no arrest was forthcoming. In Schellenberg's opinion, 'I am quite certain that at some time or other Canaris must have got to know something incriminating about Himmler, for otherwise there is no possible explanation for his reaction to the material I placed before him.'[29]

Himmler might have been nervous about how Canaris might react to arrest, but nevertheless he drip-fed other of the Abwehr chief's enemies with titbits of information that strengthened opposition against him. Himmler wanted rid of Canaris, but without Canaris' realisation of his rôle in his downfall. The subterfuge worked. When he was eventually arrested by Schellenberg, Canaris begged him to arrange an interview with Himmler rather than the 'butchers' Kaltenbrunner and Müller. Himmler never came. Not afforded counsel at his precipitate trial at 8 p.m. on 8 April, he was kept overnight to savour the death penalty, before walking naked to the gallows. A fellow prisoner recorded, 'Fragments of unburnt skin in the air were my last physical contact with my friend.'[30]

The concentration camps presented Himmler with a raft of damning evidence of his brutal regime. Nuremberg exposed camp commandants of a terrifyingly bestial mindset, with one remarkable exception. Whereas through their coarse testimony others unwittingly assumed responsibility for the camps, becoming the patsies Himmler had intended, Auschwitz Commandant Rudolf Höss's carefully considered statements and straightforward testimony granted the Reichsführer no favours. Höss had relished the challenge to set up 'By the will of the Reichsführer the greatest extermination centre on earth'. He proudly declared, 'I lived only for my work.'[31] There were others of the same ilk. Three hundred and fifty doctors who had experimented on concentration camp inmates seemed bewildered at finding themselves at Nuremberg, being charged with doing their duty. Amongst them was Himmler's own surgeon, Professor Karl Gebhardt, who was taken aback at even being questioned. Gebhardt was one of Himmler's intimates, and his ready professional accept-ance and participation in the experimentation must have made Himmler think that the morality of these activities was unimpeach-able. However, he was all too aware of one doctor whose activities had caused outrage within the Luftwaffe and the SS.

Dr Sigmund Rascher was an acute embarrassment. Quite apart from the loathing he inspired with his revolting experiments at Auschwitz, Himmler was disturbed that he had been duped into lending the charlatan personal support. His diary ecstatically records in green ink the receipt of large, still-warm tissue specimens from Rascher. Further embarrassment came in the shape of Rascher's wife, an athletic, doe-eyed woman fifteen years Rascher's senior, who claimed to have given birth to three children after her 48th birthday and, it transpired, after her menopause. Some irregularities in her family tree had prevented her from marrying her beloved Sigmund. Not only had Himmler sorted them out, but he foolishly agreed to be godfather to the three remarkable children. When they were arrested in 1944 for child abduction, she and her husband were kept securely at Dachau and the case against them dropped, before Rascher was shot on Himmler's orders just before the Americans entered the camp. Frau Rascher was hanged.

Georg Elser, who rigged up the bomb intended to kill Hitler in the Burgerbräu Hall in November 1939, was anything but the 'simple carpenter' he is often portrayed as. Treated surprisingly leniently by Himmler, after the explosion he was placed in a concentration camp in easy reach of a Himmler order. A fellow prisoner, the English agent Sigismund Payne Best, received a smuggled letter from Elser in which he claimed he had been working with the approval of the security services in a convoluted plot to get rid of Otto Strasser. This plot could only have emanated from Himmler and Schellenberg. The execution order came just before the camp was liberated; Elser was executed and another embarrassing loose end tied.

As the Reich imploded, a power vacuum was created which Himmler had every intention of filling. Still reluctant to be seen to seize power, he seemed to want to do it with the aura of legitimacy, unsullied by criticism and unclouded by dissenting rivals. He had ruthlessly eradicated telltale witnesses who might prevent a succession free of accusations of plotting and skulduggery, and made inadequate attempts at facilitating his acceptability to the Allies as post-war leader. Now the Third Reich was in its death throes, Himmler displayed his comprehensive lust for power in his venomous attempts to destroy any potential rival who might make deals with the West by selling secrets or using their position to make peace gestures.

Foreign Minister Ribbentrop had long considered making his own peace gestures, employing his Foreign Office associate Fritz Hesse in multiple talks with the British through Swedish intermediaries. At the last minute he made up his mind to try to convince the British of his concern for the fate of Jewish concentration camp inmates by offering to help save them from extinction. Himmler neatly aborted this proposal through a leak to the Western press. Himmler faced numerous rivals within his own ranks. Hans Kammler had something of the aristocratic bearing and hauteur that character-ised Himmler's early favourite, Reinhard Heydrich. A high-flying engineer who had been involved in designing Auschwitz, he was chosen by Himmler to take over the air research programme from Albert Speer. Rather like his boss, Kammler was a ruthless, opportun-istic schemer whose quiet, cold manner belied a vaulting ambition of which Himmler was well aware. Indeed, Speer related that Kammler's carping criticism unwisely included the Reichsführer himself.[32] In the naivety of vanity, he let his colleagues know that he believed his engineering and organisational talents would be well appreciated after the war, especially considering what he had to offer. For Kammler was also in charge of the V Rocket establishment at Peenemünde, and made a deal with the Americans in which he would supply them with all the scientists and engineers from Peene-münde. He was to assemble them at Oberjochim and himself join them later to lead them across the border as arranged. He never arrived, having been shot, it was later supposed, by his own aide,

helpfully supplied by Himmler. Ernst Kaltenbrunner tried to seek
sanctuary in south Germany, taking with him rather a large amount
of gold. Kaltenbrunner seems to have given little thought to trading
with the Americans, despite his powerful position in the SS hierarchy. Loose talk about any such intentions might also have cost
him his life had he done so; Himmler detailed Gottlob Berger to
follow Kaltenbrunner south to ensure that he did not attempt to
make any last-minute deal with the Allies.

SS Obergruppenführer Gottlob Berger was one of the earliest
recruits to the SA. He was known as Himmler's *éminence grise*,
nicknamed 'the Duke of Swabia' for his aristocratic behaviour, but
widely feared for his outrageous sycophancy. He came to Himmler's
attention by writing to tell him that staff at the Waffen SS bypassed
his orders, adding, 'I have witnessed this myself'.[33] He proved his
loyalty through constant tale-telling, explaining that he was such a
faithful follower because 'My Reichsführer confides in me and tells
me things personally, which he would never do unless he was completely at ease with me'.[34] It was a powerful echo of the behaviour
Himmler manifested in his own rise to power, but unlike his master,
Berger was a very physical man who could prove lethal to his or
Himmler's enemies. He rose to become the head of the SS's central
department, the *Hauptamt*.

Gottlob Berger was not the only weapon Himmler had against
his enemies. Himmler considered Albert Speer a rival to his economic
power, and briefly saw him as a threat to his succession after a
throwaway remark by Hitler. Speer revealed how, when he was
suffering from a grossly swollen knee, he was talked into having
an opinion at the clinic at Hohenlychen from Himmler's surgeon
Professor Gebhardt, supposedly an expert in knee injuries, whose
previous clients included King Leopold III of Belgium.[35] Speer was
kept in bed in a tight plaster that immediately felt painful. His toes
became numb and blue when his leg was elevated. He was forced
to lie uncomfortably in this position for some twenty days, before
the plaster was removed and he was allowed to try standing upright.
He immediately developed a near fatal pulmonary embolism, went
blue, had pains in his back and chest, and he was spitting up copious

blood. The diagnosis was obvious to the junior physicians but Professor Gebhardt diagnosed 'rheumatism', even after a second near-fatal attack. 'There was menace in his deliberate attitude and stubbornness which terrified me and even more so my wife, who immediately went to Dr Brandt, Hitler's physician, who suggested Dr Koch see me,' Speer recalled.

Dr Koch was an assistant to the eminent surgeon Professor Sauerbruch at the renowned Charité Hospital in Berlin. He was appalled at Speer's treatment, which he declared was 'designed for the morgue'. He reported back to Dr Brandt who put Dr Koch in charge. When Gebhardt refused to accept Koch's authority, Brandt then forbade Gebhardt from issuing any medical orders on Speer's case. Still the drama continued. 'Gebhardt had a nurse who always went with him on his rounds,' Speer recalled. 'After he had finished his visit, she would call in and start interfering in my case despite all that was said. My wife, who was awake all the time, then became near hysterical and once again saw Dr Brandt who made arrangements that Dr Koch, who I am sure had better things to do, was given a room next to mine and was to stay at my bedside day and night.' Unknown to Speer at the time, Gebhardt repeatedly recommended tying off the femoral vein under general anaesthetic, at a time when such an undertaking would have proved hazardous in the extreme.[36]

'Dr Koch was terrified,' remembered the luckless patient. 'He kept telling me not to say anything at all controversial and not to mention any opinion or conversation I had with him, as he kept hearing threats about the Gestapo. He told me that he'd been summoned for a very ugly dispute with Gebhardt, who had threateningly accused him of not being politically aware – that his duty was to the Reich and not his patient.'[37] In Speer's last conversation with Dr Koch the doctor unwillingly admitted that 'the kindest interpretation [of Gebhardt's behaviour] was that he was trying to keep you in hospital, the unkindest, the hospital morgue'. Speer later learnt from Walter Funk, the Minister of Economics, that Gebhardt had remarked to a circle of SS leaders that Himmler 'considered Speer dangerous and he would have to disappear'.[38]

Himmler's attempts at eliminating rivals to his potential dealings with the Allies now seem futile and vindictive because he was utterly unacceptable as a post-war figure. However, they do demonstrate an ability to consider every avenue and opportunity with an attention to detail illustrative of his unerring grasp of the need to plan for any eventuality. He did not give up easily, but nor did he overlook alternative options. It seems Himmler persisted in a last-ditch attempt at negotiation. When communications with Field-Marshal Montgomery were established in the first week of May through General Kinzl, the liaison officer, Himmler gave Kinzl a letter asking Montgomery for an interview under safe conduct. Should they wish to take him prisoner, he asserted his right to be treated as a high-ranking General, as he had been Commander in Chief of the Army Group Vistula.[39] The letter was never delivered, as General Jodl personally destroyed it before it left Flensburg, but Speer says that in essence, Himmler had wanted to use the 400,000 fresh troops in Norway and the remaining troops in Denmark and Germany as a bargaining tool to gain personal concessions.[40] At a time when Dönitz was handing out ministerial posts in his new government, this seemed the madness of a deluded man still convinced that he had the power to rule armies. Yet it is equally possible that it was a red herring, designed to give out the impression that he was desperate and throw people off the scent of alternative plans.

There is strong evidence to suggest that Himmler never envisaged anything other than being in supreme command at the time when it would be necessary to negotiate with the Allies. That presupposed Hitler's death to order. He seemed to lay great store by the date of the Führer's demise, as was conveniently predicted by the famous astrologer Wilhelm Wulff during a two-day meeting with Himmler in March 1944. Himmler habitually used Wulff to predict actions that fitted in well with his requirements and invariably happened. On this occasion Wulff told him Hitler's life would be in danger on or around 20 July, and that he would die before 7 May 1945. The cause of death – by alkaloid poisoning – would never be discovered.[41]

By May 1944 Himmler was toying with the idea of creating an independent Poland to act as a buffer against the Russians, and

Schellenberg raised the subject of acting 'positively' to help along Wulff's predictions. But Himmler did not do anything about it. A year later, shortly after visiting Hitler, at a meeting with Count Folke Bernadotte on 23 April 1945 at the Swedish Consulate in Lübeck, Himmler declared that Hitler would 'be dead in two days – three at the most'.[42]

On 26 April Schellenberg was told by Count Lewenhaupt, Counsellor at the Swedish Legation in Lübeck, that Himmler's grandiose peace gesture, offering to surrender troops to the Allies, had not been well received because Himmler was 'unacceptable to the Western powers as a person with whom discussions could be undertaken'.[43] Perhaps wisely, he did not pass on this information. Himmler was still hopeful that a formal offer of capitulation carried by a captured American General, Vannaman, former Air Attaché in Berlin, who had been released into Switzerland on 24 April, might bear fruit. Swedish Foreign Minister Gunther had backed Himmler's peace proposals, at least as far as Scandinavia was concerned. Schellenberg and Bernadotte, with whom Himmler breakfasted at Apenrade on 27 April, both hoped to achieve some limited accord with the Allies in which Himmler could still play a part.

By now the world press had got news of the peace offer. On 27 April Himmler learnt that his secret scheme had, for once, been exposed; worse still, the West's dismissal of his peace offer was made public. This was the first of two major blows, confirming his worst fears about the possibility of remaining in any sort of public office. When Himmler met with Schellenberg at 3 p.m. on 27 April at General Wünneberg's HQ with astrologer Wilhelm Wulff in tow, he was acting with resilience, as if the rebuff had never occurred. He officially designated Schellenberg as his *Sonderbevollmächtigter* – 'plenipotentiary extraordinary' empowered to deal all Himmler's cards at any future discussions – and gave him specific directions on how to conduct these affairs. In Himmler's opinion, the slight from the Allies did not shut off future discussions. Once again he reiterated his opinion that Hitler would, in any case, be dead within the next two days.[44]

At a later meeting Schellenberg felt 'that he was displeased with

the fact [. . .] he was not already successor to Hitler [. . .] I received
the impression that something had gone wrong with his plan to do
away with Hitler.'[45] Schellenberg, who knew Himmler better than
most, thought that he had tried to arrange for Hitler to be poisoned
in the Berlin bunker. Someone may have got wind of this, for back
at the bunker open warfare broke out between Hitler's chosen quack
Dr Theodor Morrell, the VD specialist, and Dr Ludwig Stumpfegger, Himmler's chief SS surgeon who was in charge. His remit
included all the poisons. Accusations flew about, increasing Hitler's
paranoia about poisoning. To poison Hitler when such suspicions
abounded was hardly practicable, even for Dr Stumpfegger, quartered
only yards away from the Führer. Nor was the choice of alkaloid
poisons particularly wise. To be effective, especially in such critical
circumstances, the poison had to be quick, certain in its effect, easily
administered and difficult to detect. Only alkaloids derived from the
skin of amphibians, such as the Columbian frogs whose poison is
used to coat the tips of arrows, their Ecuadorian cousins, or three
newts found in the western United States, are instant in their effects.
More commonly available plant alkaloids are not only slower, but
more uncertain in their action. Moreover, the prolonged death throes
these induce would only have served to draw attention to the probability of poisoning, even in the already severely unwell Führer.

  We now know from Russian archives that the undoubtedly genuine corpse of Hitler showed no evidence of any gunshot wound.
The detailed pathology report by two celebrated professors makes
interesting reading. Surprisingly, 'There was no trace of cyanide or
any other poison in the tissues.'[46] Moreover, the qualitative tests they
used in 1945 gave an easily discernible orange precipitate, and were
more than good enough to detect alkaloid poisoning. Moscow
archives of NKVD interrogations show that those SS men caught
escaping from the bunker were quite convinced that Hitler had been
strangled by his SS valet Heinz Linge. Linge's defensive statement
that if they had found his fingerprints around Hitler's neck, 'it was
because I carried him out that way from the bunker', did not allay
the NKVD's suspicions.

  Himmler's expectations had come to naught. Hitler had clung to life long enough to denounce Himmler as a traitor and appoint Admiral Karl Dönitz Führer, thwarting Himmler's expectations of legitimate succession. When Himmler learned of Dönitz's succession, he was with Schellenberg at his new HQ at Kalkhorst. Himmler was being pressed by his Waffen SS aides to take over Dönitz's new government by force, but that was not his mood. Schellenberg found him nervous, distraught, and indecisive. The *Sonderbevollmächtigter* had come of age; Himmler thrust him forward as the more acceptable face of the SS, asking him to negotiate with Eisenhower, the Swedes, and Dönitz and Von Krosigk who, at Himmler's suggestion, Dönitz had chosen to replace Ribbentrop as Foreign Minister. Through Schellenberg, Himmler advised the fledgling government to 'dissolve the Nazi Party and Gestapo forthwith'. This remarkably sane advice was ignored by Ministers who were beginning to enjoy their new-found importance.

By 2 May 1945, his ego badly bruised, Himmler had opted to take a back seat. He was finally in a position to appreciate the extent of his wishful thinking. In the course of only a few days, all his illusions about his acceptability to the Allies were shattered; romantic dreams of continuing in any legitimate role in public life were quashed. Himmler offered to meet Eisenhower. This is hard to credit. Speer was one of many who believe that Himmler was just too cautious to risk his own skin, and would have sent Schellenberg as his emissary, rather than risk placing himself in Allied hands. His earlier reluctance to meet Count Folke Bernadotte or Abraham Stevens Hewitt in Sweden supports this view. This suggests that Himmler's rather grandiose peace gestures were no more than an attempt to test the water. Much of what Himmler said was purely political posturing. When he talked to the SS Nazi leadership at Posen in October 1943 and assumed personal responsibility for the nation's guilt over the Holocaust, this was for the sympathetic consumption of the home audience. He had no intention of volunteering himself as scapegoat at the inevitable international war crimes commission.

Himmler was driven by a savage, determined desire for self-preservation. He had displayed this ruthlessly in his use of the conceptual weapon of *Sippenhaft* (the guilt of the family for any individual's actions) as an excuse to wipe out the entire families, grandparents and infants alike, of those deemed guilty in the 20 July plot. When we consider the sheer scale and prescience of Himmler's plans for personal wealth and a post-war empire and compare it with the apparent absence of preparations for his impending fate as fugitive war criminal, we face a strange anomaly. It was as if, despite his persistent, detailed secret negotiations, and financial arrangements based on Germany's total defeat, Himmler never really envisaged the personal implications of that defeat. He had been secretly dreading and even proclaiming this defeat as inevitable, for over two years, yet we are asked to believe he had made no provision for his own safety. It comes as no surprise that closer examination of other plans Himmler made reveals that despite this impression, the same methodical preparations had gone into providing for other options.

Himmler's chance of personally retaining some semblance of power or legitimate status within the Reich had gone for ever. For once out of the limelight, the Reichsführer SS was poised to take one of the other, more realistic options. Examination of the possibilities that remained open to him is long overdue.

9

Preparations for Survival

'I have no understanding of a person who throws away his life like a dirty shirt because he believes he will evade his difficulties.'

Heinrich Himmler, 1938

'The disappearance into civilian clothes and corresponding civilian professions, if necessary in an extreme way (clergymen, monks, etc), is the only thing we can advise.'

Amt advice to SS officers, 1945. Appendix VI, Schellenberg Papers

It was 11 a.m. on 12 April 1961, the twenty-fifth day of Nisan in the Hebrew year 5721. Adolf Eichmann stepped out of legend straight into a Jerusalem court that was merciless in its atmosphere. He slid shyly into the room, almost unnoticed, accompanied by three policemen in blue, British-style uniforms and peaked caps. He had almost made the safety of the bulletproof glass box before the courtroom, which was buzzing with excitement, fell deathly quiet. A barely audible 'There he is!' heralded the awed silence. Translators in their booths, notaries at their small tables, even the normally raucous gallimaufry of the press, just sat and stared.

Parallel strips of neon lighting gave the hearing a cold, clinical brilliance. The great menorah glittered like an unforgiving sun above the hapless figure. He was hardly cringeing. Wearing his best suit, Eichmann's horn-rimmed spectacles and severe countenance made him look capable and composed. In his transparent cubical, Eich-mann was sealed off and yet hideously exposed. It took those watching several minutes to realise that behind his stiff, awkward gestures, made with just a hint of defiance, Adolf Eichmann was trembling.

Any dignity that he strove to retain was eclipsed by the saturnine, bearded Procurator, complete with forbidding skullcap, his five eager juniors and the three sombre, bare-headed judges, Dr Moshe Landau, Dr Benjamin Haveli and Dr Yitsak Raveh – all Jews from Germany. Eichmann was represented by a German, Dr Servatius, previously one of the defence counsels at Nuremberg, who was too busy talking with his young assistant to catch his client's eye.

Eichmann quickly rose to his feet, self-consciously sucking in his paunch, to await the initial question from the President of the court with all the concentration he could muster. 'Are you Adolf Eichmann?' Reporters watching Eichmann in his tank, heavily festooned with microphones and wires, saw him incline his head and mouth the answer, but could only just make out the muted 'Yes, sir'. The sound, divorced from the movements of the prisoner's mouth, seemed to come from the past; the portable radio sets they had been given for simultaneous translation were not working. The widely publicised 'moment of truth for the Jewish nation' dissolved into a cacophony of clicks, muffled bangs and the noise of plastic tapping on wood, with loud mutterings of annoyance as people attempted to fix their headsets. The awe of the moment had gone and the first Jewish trial of a Nazi was underway. Yet the most interesting aspects of Eichmann's case had already been dealt with. Away from the eyes of reporters, Eichmann's Jewish interrogators had learned a great deal before the trial had started, and much that was to prove problematical.

So complex were the issues raised, and so different the needs of the Secret Service from those of the lawyers, that some twenty-six hours into the 275 hours of interrogation by ex-Berliner prosecutor Avner Less, a strict format for that questioning had to be agreed. A team of advisers, including members of the Israeli Secret Service and prosecution barristers, were always present in some form to witness the sessions and represent their respective interests.

The series of interrogations had begun on 29 May 1960, some nine days after Eichmann's arrival in Israel. In all some 3,564 pages of transcript were agreed, which were eventually matched with the contents of the accompanying tapes. Both judiciary and Secret Service listened to each tape and its contents were agreed and edited before Eichmann was able to listen to them again, with a rough transcript for cross-reference. He laboriously amended each transcript by hand, and it was once again matched with the tapes. When the task was over, he appended the phrase, 'I certify the accuracy of this report with my signature.' Eichmann was apparently allowed to exercise his right over the material he submitted, but the whole procedure compromised the completeness and accuracy of the tapes, lending them a spurious credibility. There were subjects discussed by Eichmann, deleted from the tapes and therefore absent from the transcripts, that were dutifully recorded in hand-written notes by the secret servicemen in attendance.

At the end of the trial, in its 120th session on 13 December, Eichmann was sentenced to death. He responded with a simple statement, reminiscent of the self-justifying defiance that had echoed around the cold halls of Nuremberg: 'My guiding principle in life has been the desire to strive for the realisation of ethical values.' His appeal for clemency to the President was refused on 29 May and he was hanged three days later. When Eichmann was interrogated he knew that no one had ever been executed in the State of Israel. Even in the most violent cases of terrorism, the death penalty had always been commuted. He lived to the last under the illusion that he too would be spared, and when he gave his testimony he had given it in the belief that co-operation, honesty and reasonableness would benefit his case.

The Israeli Secret Service was anxious to question Eichmann about the whereabouts of other Nazis wanted for war crimes. He was living proof that many had escaped Germany and justice. Eichmann was asked about the attempt by several Nazis at the Nuremberg trial to declare their absent colleagues dead, and newspaper reports falsely certifying them deceased. Eichmann had himself been declared dead by Kaltenbrunner, who gave the naive American psychologist at Nuremberg, Dr Gilbert, an extremely graphic account of his death that Gilbert helpfully published. The packed court at Eichmann's trial was treated to the sight of Dr Gilbert glaring accusingly at the defendant as if he could not quite believe he had been misled.

Eichmann's responses to questions about his former colleagues from the SS proved effusive and voluble; he was bitter about the mediocre job and scant assistance he had received from his compatriots during his time in Argentina. As a result, the Israeli Secret Service was able to amend its files considerably. It drew up a list in March 1961 of those war criminals touched upon by evidence submitted to the Eichmann trial.[1]

A copy of this four-page list was passed to the prosecuting counsel for guidance and was retained in counsel's papers. The hand-written list was divided into three categories: those war criminals who had disappeared entirely (headed 'Disappeared'), those war criminals arrested previously, under the heading ('Arrested'), and those war criminals free after arrest (listed as 'Free'). Examination of this list today gives us an interesting insight into what information the Israeli Secret Service already had at its disposal, and reveals actions already taken. SS Hauptsturmführer Theodor Dannecker is listed as 'disappeared', as is Dr Karl Klingenfuss, who had been sentenced with Franz Rademacher before they jumped bail in 1952. Dannecker and Klingenfuss had been responsible for a futuristic idea for a 'Jewish Paradise Lost', planning the creation of a giant Jewish ghetto of four million people on the island of Madagascar, where they could live out their lives under the paternalistic direction of the Sicherheits-polizei. Dr William Höttl, in charge of forgery for the SS, was also in the 'disappeared' category, as was Franz Rademacher, formerly head of the Jewish Desk at the Foreign Ministry's Home Department.

Interestingly, one of Eichmann's regional deputies, Eberhard von Thadden, who had been arrested by order of a Cologne court in 1952, is also listed as disappeared. A note states there was 'No trace of a sentence'. A red line that was added later on removes him from the list and the same hand, still using red ink, added the names of Hans Günther and his brother Rolf, Eichmann's second in command. These two had previously been reported by SS officer Franz Novar to have committed suicide in 1945. Following Eichmann's testimony there was renewed interest in pursuing their case, which had only been removed from the Israeli Secret Service list in January 1961.

The next two pages of the list of war criminals mentioned by Eichmann deal with those already arrested, naming twenty-three war
criminals, mostly captured in 1960 or 1961. By the time the secret
service had finished giving advice to counsel in December 1961, the
list had been updated to show progress in each case, sentencing
indicated by a large red tick.

The all-important fourth page, headed 'Free', names Eichmann's
henchman Franz Mürer, who had been sentenced to twenty-five
years' hard labour by the Russians, but was released to return to
Austria in 1955. Two more are named and then halfway down the
page is a critical entry. Under the title 'Anomalous' is the entry:
'Eichmann tps 3, 4 – Reichsführer Heinrich Himmler, alive Germany? c, Lorenz.' There is neither subsequent red mark not comment on this entry, presumably denoting indeterminate findings.
The 'c' does not really make sense. It could just be a personalised
shorthand. It could be an abbreviation for 'circa' (around), which is
usually, however, used for time, or it could be 'cum' (with), which
in England is usually abbreviated to 'w' or 'c' with a dash across the
top. It might be American or continental in origin, but it is not
possible to find a satisfactory explanation. However, the content of
the comment is obvious enough. Eichmann was raising the spectre
of a live Himmler, despite the apparently accepted historical record
of Himmler's suicide in British hands.

Eichmann, a pragmatic realist whose very life was at stake, was
trying hard to establish his credibility with his captors by co-operating
as fully and accurately as possible in order to ameliorate his circumstances and to save his life. He gave accurate information about the
whereabouts of Eduard Roschmann and Josef Schwammberger, both
living in Argentina. If his doubts about Himmler's demise had no
substance, why would he have raised them and risked derision that
would undermine his assiduous efforts at co-operation?

We cannot know if this comment resulted from Israeli Secret
Service knowledge of alleged sightings or reports of a live Himmler,
or from British rumours of uncertainty about how Himmler had
been identified that may have reached Israeli agents' ears. Perhaps
Eichmann himself raised the subject, for whatever reason. It must

be presumed that the Israelis took his comments seriously, as his discussion of the possibility that Himmler might be alive occupied at least part of two of the tapes before they were edited for the trial. More significantly, his remarks about Himmler later became known in intelligence circles.

The Israelis clearly took these comments seriously or Himmler's name would not have appeared on the list. But the first question is, who or what was Lorenz? The answer lies in Germany in 1945, when Himmler was on the brink of discovering that there was no possible future for him in public life.

At noon on 22 April 1945 Himmler and Schellenberg left Wüstrow outside Berlin, and headed for Hohenlychen. Their departure was hastened by reports that a spearhead of Russian tanks was operating nearby. Wehrmacht columns, heavy guns, tanks and low-flying aircraft delayed the journey, forcing them to drive north to Mecklenburg and thence to strike off eastwards to Hohenlychen.

The prospect of being killed or captured by the Russians had profoundly affected both men. After a very late lunch, Himmler asked Schellenberg to stay behind to discuss 'Berger's journey and Lorenz's affairs'.[2] When questioned by an American intelligence agent in Nuremberg, Schellenberg said the Lorenz in question was Obergruppenführer Werner Lorenz, head of the VOMI or Volksdeutsche Mittelstelle, a position that would not be liable for prosecution for war crimes. He forgot to mention that Werner Lorenz was in charge of the resettlement of Germans from the Baltic states, and at the end of the war had been appointed by Himmler as Commander of the north-west region of Germany. It was a critical position, leaving Lorenz in overall charge of Hamburg and the remaining rump of the Third Reich. He would be a useful man for someone looking for a place to hide.

Schellenberg told his interrogator that Himmler agreed with Schellenberg (about what, we do not know) and said, 'I must act in one way or another.'[3] Once again, we do not know if this refers to Berger or Lorenz. Gottlob Berger was, according to Schellenberg, about to depart for the south in Himmler's private plane, a luxury previously denied him. The purpose of this journey was to keep an eye on Ernst Kaltenbrunner, ensuring he did not attempt to negotiate with the Allies and steal Himmler's thunder. Berger's only other concern was to ensure the safe transfer of 'Prominenten', high-rank prisoners from other concentration camps, to his personal care in Austria. With British tanks vying with the Russians to capture the whole of Schleswig-Holstein, and the progress of the war rapidly closing down Himmler's options, Berger's jaunt to the south can hardly have warranted the undivided attention of both men, and certainly did not require an immediate decision. It seems far more likely that the discussion concerned Werner Lorenz.

Obergruppenführer Werner Lorenz was a *bon viveur* who had the air of a master of backstairs intrigue. Adroit and personable, he owned a house in Hamburg and a large estate in Danzig. He is not known to have played any role in covert negotiations. He was, however, Himmler's personal friend, and had been handpicked by him to head the VOMI. He had impressed Hitler and was often found attending critical conferences that seemed far removed from his official remit. Lorenz was blessed with that rare combination – wealth and intelligence. He had two very attractive daughters: Jutti, married to Count Kinkelbusch, who owned one of the biggest wine businesses in Germany, and Rosemarie, wed to publisher Axel Springer. Himmler could count on post-war support from the powerful Springer family, who kept faith with the Nazis throughout the war.[4]

It is quite possible that Lorenz's expertise in the complex requirements of resettlement, his widespread influence and his local knowledge of the Hamburg area, his own stomping ground, were considerations that occupied Himmler and Schellenberg at a time when their survival was uppermost in their minds. Lorenz received a 20-year sentence at Nuremberg, but served only eight. He was released on the grounds of ill health in 1955, amid a howl of protest, and lived to the ripe old age of 83. He enjoyed some very influential contacts in Germany, Sweden and the Baltic states. Lorenz was also linked with Himmler through a close neighbour, Hubert von Blücher, who held a Swedish passport and was, at the time of Himmler and Schellenberg's post-prandial discussion, busily engaged in stashing away some of Himmler's gold bullion. It is not hard to find reasons for thinking that this powerful man, who enjoyed such power and influence in the area that was to remain most loyal to the Nazis, might have been the Lorenz to whom Eichmann referred.

But there is another candidate. Erika Lorenz was Himmler's personal secretary, and had accompanied him into Poland in 1939. The importance and oddness of her relationship with Himmler has never been adequately explored. The recent discovery of Himmler's daily appointments book for 1942 reveals that at what was a critical time for the Reich, the Reichsführer SS set aside an extraordinary amount of time to spend on whatever pleasantries passed between them. At the height of the war, when his appointments book was full of meetings with generals, politicians and the like, we find that when Erika visited she would see Himmler for two hours at a time. Her visit would be officially recorded with the same gravitas as the entries for dignitaries, except for the somewhat bizarre purpose of each visit. Sometimes it is 'Presents for the Italians', at others 'Christmas presents', or 'Birthday lists', and sometimes just 'Private Talk', trivia that cannot explain the amount of time actually spent with Himmler. No evidence of an affair has ever been discovered. Her loyalty and influence were considerable. Before the war ended she alone was entrusted with the task of destroying the entire (unknown) contents of one filing cabinet at the SS castle at Fischorn, just after Hitler's demise. For this task she travelled by herself from Salzburg with Himmler's authority. It was a strange mission, and at first she denied it when questioned by American agents.

There remains the third possibility that Eichmann's 'Lorenz' was neither Werner nor Erika, but a company. In 1945 the American Secret Service was acting on the information in the Red House report, trying to cover hidden Nazi assets and identify the post-war influx of personnel into large scientific concerns in both the Americas and Europe. They became very concerned about the Spanish branch of Lorenz AG, and on 4 December 1945, Washington requested that Schellenberg, then in Nuremberg, be urgently questioned again.[5] After US intelligence officer Captain Horace Khan had questioned Schellenberg, the British arrested Schellenberg's secretaries and obtained useful comparative testimony.[6]

Lorenz AG was a German subsidiary of the giant American company ITT. Ownership was cloaked through a holding company, European Standard Electric, arranged by none other than the German firm Albert and Westrick in co-operation with their business partner Allen Dulles.[7] This was the same man who had a penchant for handing out forty blank American passports at a time to SS negotiators. Because Spain's leader, General Franco, encouraged talented Germans to move to his country, the Spanish branch of Lorenz AG was considered by the SS to be the most important German subsidiary abroad. It is not surprising to find secret American documents such as a letter from 11 January 1946 containing the request: 'Washington would be extremely interested [...] in finding out what personnel [...] may stay on with this Co [Lorenz AG] after the war.' Dr Schmidt, a Sturmbannführer from the SS Economic Section, sat on the board of directors of Lorenz AG as Himmler and Schellenberg's representative. He worked closely with an ITT representative, the cigar-chewing ex-US Army Colonel Bane, to literally get the best out of the company at the end of the war. Dr Schmidt had every reason to be loyal to Himmler, for he had married a Jewish wife. Himmler had got her 'aryanised' and supported Schmidt against constant calls from Amt IV for his dismissal.[8]

The American investigators were too late; the moment for urgent questioning and urgent action was past. Franco's government ensured the post-war security of the newly acquired German personnel in Spanish Lorenz, and the head of Spanish police was a friend of Himmler's. The belated American investigation petered out in March 1946.

Of the three options, Himmler's true intentions for post-war survival would most likely be shared, if at all, with Erika Lorenz. But in May 1945, with the Allies closing in, Werner Lorenz's empire in Hamburg and north-west Germany, and the attractive facilities, not least those abroad, afforded by the massive firm of Lorenz based in Hamburg, were surely now of greater relevance to the Reichsführer. Might the 'Lorenz' connection claimed by Eichmann have a direct link with Hamburg, and did it signify further planning by Himmler for his personal survival and the post-war perpetuation of the SS state? Whichever Lorenz Eichmann was referring to, each possibility points to Himmler planning for a life after the second world war. Himmler assiduously arranged the transfer of a huge chunk of Nazi Germany's assets abroad. As the Red House report emphasised, his long-term aim was to reinvest this capital and expertise in building a new Fourth Reich that would arise, phoenix-like, from the skeleton of the SS 'state within a state', to be governed by a hard core of the élite.

To mimic the previous SS takeover of power in the Third Reich, it would again prove necessary to have substantial influence in the police, the judiciary and the public administration, and among financiers. To hope for immediate large-scale success throughout post-war Germany would be unrealistic. But to gain control initially in a province was, as we shall see, a very different proposition.

In their post-war 'Brown Book' report on West Germany's fascists, East German Communists unmasked concealed Nazi assets and tracked down Nazi war criminals – activities that were often inextricably linked. Disturbingly often, they also uncovered links to Allied interests.[9] They studied individual *Länder* to see whether there was any substantial difference in the post-war concentration of such Nazi power and influence and discovered the state of Hamburg was unique, not only for its remarkable post-war prosperity. Several Nazi war criminals listed by the Nuremberg trial remained at large in Hamburg, many more than in any other *Land*. They were left unmolested by German authorities, and the selective indifference and inertia of the British military government ensured that most remained undisturbed. Their position was doubly secure thanks to the very right-wing Hamburg justice and police departments. In the 1950s the police alone contained thirty-one former SS men, many of them officially named as war criminals. They were employed as chief inspectors, chief superintendents, and one was even chief commissioner in charge of police training. Their appointments were made so soon after the end of hostilities that the East German investigators came to believe they had been prearranged in wartime. This view was supported by the fact that at the end of the war, most senior SS men and members of the Nazi hierarchy had gravitated to Hamburg.

Confirmation of this East German finding came independently from the American Secret Service in Germany who, in the immediate aftermath of war, concluded that Hamburg was the kernel and head-quarters of a well established SS network.[10] They found that within two years of the end of the war a conference had been arranged in Dortmund to teach the methodology evolved after May 1945 by senior SS personnel in Hamburg. The new organisation was struc-tured following the same sub-groups as the original SS. Hamburg was also the first German city to benefit from Himmler's carefully laid financial plans. Herman Abs, one of twelve directors of the Deutsche Bank, was appointed to the Hamburg branch after the Maison Rouge meeting as a guardian to thwart hostile Allied inten-tions and keep control of SS funds. However, the intentions of some of the British finance houses and merchant banks were to prove anything but hostile, even to a bank with such a tainted reputation. Worse still, a remarkably complacent British Military Governor failed to enforce American General Clay's orders that Abs be physically barred from entering any Deutsche Bank. Despite heated representations, the British did not put into effect any of the banking controls they had agreed with the Americans, which were essential to prevent the Deutsche Bank from resuming its all-powerful position. Thanks to such compliant inertia, Abs was the ex-Fascist mastermind at the heart of the German banking world, a position he could not have achieved without tacit approval from those who were supposed to prevent just such a scenario from hap-pening. It is quite possible that some of the last-minute financial negotiations carried out with the British in Stockholm may after all have paid dividends.

The State of Hamburg and the surrounding countryside of Schleswig-Holstein, with a population a considerable proportion of which was pro-Nazi, proved to be an almost magnetic destination for hundreds of fleeing SS men to go to ground. Rehabilitation was only a matter of time for some. Himmler, through his friendship with Werner Lorenz, had established a powerful position for himself in an area that offered a very real option of safely disappearing. Of course, a bolthole was only a short-term solution. Support was essential for long-term survival. Proof of the back-up provided by the right-wing population of the Hamburg area lies in the mere handful of resultant arrests. Even the notorious 'Dr Sawade', who was involved in euthanasia projects in the concentration camps, was supported by his loyal new patients. The SS had not overlooked this need, and support systems were arranged before war ended. Organisations such as the Brüderschaft (Brotherhood) or the aptly named Stille Hilfe (silent help) completed the arrangements behind this exodus. Stille Hilfe became a registered charity and successfully helped resettle many unfortunates. These charity cases included Anton Malloth, the most feared of all the guards at Theresienstadt concentration camp, who was sentenced to death *in absentia* in 1945 by the Czechs. There was also Hermine Ryan, the infamous 'Mare of Majdanek', whose equine reputation was painfully built up by her capacity for kicking inmates to death with steel-capped boots. Decades later, Stille Hilfe gave moral support to Klaus Barbie, the 'Butcher of Lyon', as he languished in a French prison. Just prior to his death, Klaus Barbie began making unsubstantiated but nevertheless interesting comments about Himmler's survival that rivalled those of Eichmann. His comments were generally ignored, but it is worth noting that they began after his supportive visits from Stille Hilfe.[11] An integral part of Stille Hilfe was Gudrun, Himmler's daughter, who became something of an icon and guest of honour at SS veterans' dinners. Dubbed the 'Angel of Mercy', she specialised in social visits to elderly SS officers. Obsessed with exorcising the spectre of a guilt-ridden Himmler shamefully committing suicide, might she have been indiscreet? Perhaps Barbie's contact with Stille Hilfe inspired his surprising claims.

There is every reason to believe that Himmler and Schellenberg planned their exodus from Berlin at least a few months beforehand, as early as March, with the object of going to Sweden and accepting the existing Anglo/Swedish agreement, managed by Ewan Butler, which meant no less than anonymity, sanctuary and immunity from prosecution. Key personnel chosen to accompany them were those that had previously been involved in the secret negotiations in Sweden.

On her return from Sweden in Autumn 1945, the British captured Frau Maria Luise Schienke, who had been Schellenberg's senior trusted secretary and described herself as his watchdog. She was secretly engaged to Hauptsturmführer Franz Göring of Amt VI wi, the economic section of the SS, whom Himmler trusted to accompany the released Swedes and Poles to Stockholm. Schienke and Göring had planned to go to Sweden with the group around Himmler and Schellenberg. According to her testimony this had been arranged months in advance of their May departure. Her initial questioning by Sergeant T. Newman on 25 November 1945 at BAOR HQ gives us a unique insight into the savage enmity felt by Müller's Gestapo towards Walter Schellenberg, a man they felt certain was a traitor about to benefit richly from his treachery.[12] In February 1945 Schellenberg, 'the best chief one could ever wish for', had been ordered by Himmler to relocate his office and sleeping quarters outside Berlin into a reinforced second-floor security suite. Schienke and another secretary moved in and cooked for him to 'prevent him being poisoned'.[13] Himmler also insisted that Schellenberg kept two large police dogs in permanent attendance at the office, and one of them accompanied him on all car journeys. His house in Babelsberg had been robbed; his car was kept under constant Gestapo surveillance – Schellenberg was literally under siege. Müller and Kaltenbrunner were waiting for any indication of flight, and in Amt II Amtchef Standartenführer Josef Spacil was waiting for any sign of financial irregularity that would indicate Schellenberg's imminent departure.

Preparations for the journey to Sweden were made in secret by Schienke, who had been drawing out moderate amounts of money on Schellenberg's behalf, amassing some 4,000 Reichsmark for Schellenberg's personal use and about double that amount for an emergency fund. She had also arranged the collection of a large amount of Swiss and American currency.[14] Free from suspicion, she had the monies 'sealed and then without let or hindrance secreted this money and took them to Sweden'.[15] Passports signalled desertion, and if found by the Gestapo they guaranteed a death sentence. The provisional government at Flensburg issued Schienke's passport, No 1703145, on 4 May 1945, just before she fled to Sweden.

On 21 March 1945 Schienke had left her home in Berlin with her fiancé and Schellenberg's younger secretary, Christel Erdmann, who had also worked for Himmler's economic section, to meet up with Schellenberg and later Himmler. No Allied investigator realised the significance of all this early preparation, carried out by what was, after all, a very small, select group in Himmler's large entourage. This long-term planning indicates that Himmler had given good thought to the need for an escape route well in advance of the last, desperate days of the war.

On 4 May, once Schienke, her fiancé and Erdmann had collected their passports, they were ideally positioned near Travemünde on the north coast of Germany, where Count Folke Bernadotte's motor launch was waiting to whisk them off to Sweden.[16] By 15 May Franz Göring and Schienke were moving from Bernadotte's Swedish home to the house of Rittmeister Ancarkrona, head of the Red Cross delegation at Saltjoe Duvnæs, where they joined other members of Himmler's staff.[17] They then moved to a boarding house in Trosa, some of the staff, however, staying in two sumptuous chalets at Bernadotte's summer residence, Trosa Castle.[18]

The evidently pre-arranged move of a select few of Himmler's staff to Sweden was complete. Received wisdom that Walter Schellenberg went over to Sweden with Count Bernadotte as a last-minute *ad hoc* attempt at peace is misguided; his journey, like that of others of Himmler's staff, had long been planned on both sides. When Himmler and Schellenberg left Berlin on 22 April the Swedish option must have been paramount in both their minds, but subordinate to the vain hope that they could still retain some official status in the rump of Germany, assisting the Allies against the Soviet hordes.

By 4 May 1945 the status of the two men and their relationship had radically changed. Schellenberg's ego was already bolstered by the fact that he had got on so well with the Swedish Count Bernadotte and seemed totally acceptable to Bernadotte as a negotiator. His self-esteem received another boost when Dönitz's provisional government appointed him Minister, with the personal backing of the influential new Foreign Minister, Count Schwerin von Krosigk. When Schellenberg crossed to Sweden on 5 May he was still under the illusion that he was acceptable as negotiator, not just to the Swedes, whose backing was automatic, but also to the Allies. His misguided self-confidence pushed him forward into the public arena.

On 4 May 1945, for Himmler to take up the still viable option of flight to Sweden and the Anglo-Swedish offer of sanctuary and immunity from prosecution, their previous offer of anonymity was more essential than ever. Himmler, essentially cautious, did not have to imagine the revulsion and hostility that would be unleashed by the exposure of his attempts to set himself up as a negotiator: Reuters and Pathé's horrifying reports from the concentration camps had seen to that. The cooling atmosphere surrounding Bernadotte at Lübeck should have completed the picture. News of Himmler's attempts to negotiate with Eisenhower by sending a letter through Bernadotte had travelled like wildfire, and he must have felt uneasy about entrusting himself to Swedish hands when international reaction was so mixed. Furthermore, he would have realised that the leak, which was swift, professional and specifically targeted, must have emanated from Allied Intelligence, indicating a certain ambivalence about the mooted deal among the people he would have had to trust.

The source of the leak designed to sabotage the immunity agreement was none other than the man who had dealt with Schellenberg in Stockholm. Ewan Butler, who could not stand his own part in the sleazy situation, was still on the verge of a nervous breakdown.[19] Receiving no support from Sir Victor Mallet, and little enough from his fellow intelligence officers, he had turned in despair to Jack Winocour, who was director of the British Information Service in Washington, and who also worked from room 8002 in the Palace Hotel in San Francisco where Princess Stefanie and her friends had done so much business. Winocour approached Paul Scott Rankin of Reuters who spread the story of Himmler's letter to Eisenhower simultaneously with Sefton Delmer's Atlantic Radio Station, of which Ewan Butler was the Stockholm correspondent. But Himmler had information to offer still of great interest to those involved in British Intelligence. Even for Himmler, the option of escape and immunity was still open.

On 4 May Himmler defiantly told Von Krosigk, 'They'll never find me'.[20] Yet at around the same time he asked Obergruppenführer Ernst Busch, commander-in-chief of German forces in Denmark, to advise him what to do. Were such contradictory statements empty posturing, or deliberately designed to mislead? His discussions with Busch gave the impression that no preparation had been made for him or his men, suggesting vacillation and panic. The same impression of a Himmler plagued by uncertainty and without a plan was given by the later testimony of Macher and Grothmann, two of his adjutants, and Admiral Dönitz. But all three men knew full well that Himmler had by that stage obtained at least one set of false documents for himself and his followers, giving them the identity of seamen returning home. These papers had been provided by Admiral Dönitz's office.

The widespread dissimulation that was so necessary in May 1945 continued after the war for many and disparate reasons. It has hampered attempts to ascertain the truth, which was simply that preparations were made in advance for SS men attempting to escape retribution, either by fleeing the country or dissolving into anonymity. These preparations had been surpassingly thorough and both short- and long-term.

Travel across Allied or Soviet-occupied Germany in May 1945 seemed suicidal and most did not even try. Himmler had hesitated before sending Berger south to keep an eye on Kaltenbrunner. Those that did use an escape route chose one thoughtfully set up by the SS, with guides, a northern control centre at Kassel, and southern control centres in Ingolstadt and Eichstadt. This axis had been designed for north/south or south/north journeys, the only realistic option left open to them as the Reich imploded from east and west under Soviet and Allied assault. Resting-places were provided at intervals of every 50 km or so, as well as a succession of safe houses. Similar routes were found throughout Switzerland, and in the Italian Alps, where guides were provided to take the SS men across the borders to safe houses by an organisation called 'Die Schleuse' (the lock gates).

In Hamburg, SS Hauptmann D. Assman was the chief organiser, and in Schleswig-Holstein SS Hauptmann Heinrich Müller controlled the guides. In south Germany and Austria the route forked at Kufstein, one way leading to Scharnitz, Innsbruck and Merano, the other through the Brenner Pass to Bolzano and Genoa. Josef Wolff, Kaltenbrunner's protégé, ran the organisation in the south from Merano. Most travellers were provided with false passports and work papers that had been printed by the Gestapo in their thousands and distributed to the chosen on 25 December 1944, as a welcome Christmas present. If Himmler had used the southern route he would have put himself in the hands of his fiercest enemies, Müller and Kaltenbrunner. Moreover, a list of safe houses in the south was also known to have accidentally fallen into the hands of the Russian 4th Bureau General Staff.

On 1 May 1945 Himmler was in position at his new HQ at Kalkhorst near Travemünde, right on the coastline, and paid a visit to Dönitz's new government, which had moved to the naval academy at Mürwick. They were right next to Denmark, and about as far north as it was possible to get from the mythical Nazi 'Alpine Redoubt' that so worried Eisenhower's staff, where some of the more gullible Nazi leaders were heading.

General Reinhard Gehlen came up with the idea of creating a post-war German resistance force in 'Operation Werewolf' along the lines of the Polish resistance forces, based at a redoubt that was supposed to have been engineered by General von Marcinkiewitz. In his memoirs Gehlen relates that Himmler dismissed the idea as 'total madness'.[21] Himmler also knew the redoubt had already been abandoned because of lack of building material and troops; for Himmler any reason for journeying south had evaporated with the fantasy of overt German resistance.

Nothing puts a contemplated journey to southern Germany into context better than Schellenberg's description of the carnage and chaos that he encountered on his relatively short trips back from his meetings with Bernadotte in Denmark. These 90-kilometre journeys took many exhausting hours, in conditions that Himmler had also experienced: 'Roads jammed with vehicles, retreating columns of motorised troops immobilised through damage and shortage of petrol, burnt-out lorries, corpse-strewn streets, exploding tanks and ammunition trucks, and sporadic machine gun fire, added to the confusion.'[22] Inured to such sights, Schellenberg forgot to mention the desperate misery of columns of refugees, or the spectacle of civilians hanging from trees and lamp-posts, summarily executed by the retreating SS, and Dönitz's men, the despised 'Kettenhunde', for alleged cowardice or defeatism.

Himmler could not ignore the danger of cross-country travel. He had no fortress in Southern Germany to go to. So what were the alternatives?

The escape of Nazis from the Reich is a subject that has long exercised the imaginations of writers and historians, and both have mixed fact with fiction. One product of this creative brew is the concept of the 'Flensburg Escape Hatch', referring to the romantic idea that Nazi leaders fled by submarine to South America. As hostilities came to a close, the coast of Flensburg, Kiel and Norway was peppered with U-boats. Military conditions proved too hazardous for most of them to sail. Despite preparations made well in advance for a special escape section under Submarine Commander Edmund Good's direction, according to Submarine Commander Peter Cremer only two boats actually made the hellish journey to South America.[23] For those leaders who were not claustrophobic and willing to take a gamble, it might have been a legitimate choice, but surely not for Himmler, who was always cautious not to act without a reasonable chance of success. Nor is there any evidence that he even contemplated making such a journey.

The Russians came to believe that many Nazi-stuffed submarines had been allowed to escape from German and Norwegian waters thanks to collaboration with the West. This suspicion seems to have arisen from the disparity between the actual strength of the submarine fleet and their strength according to records; on close inspection, this disparity appears to have been a genuine mistake of the type that was widespread on all sides. However, the Russians remained convinced.

At the time the Allies overlooked the possibility of Nazis escaping by boat to Sweden or the thousands of islands that surrounded Sweden. Fast launches abounded on the German coast and British naval control of the Baltic was patchy at best, increasing the chances of such a venture's success. After all, Bernadotte travelled to Lübeck by Swedish launch. But apart from the use of small launches and two brave submarines, the mass exodus of Nazis from Flensburg was largely a myth.

Escape from the Hamburg area by air was a far more realistic option. After hostilities were over, Allied Intelligence arrested the personnel of Air Squadron KG200, hours of interrogation leading to not one prosecution. Questioning was based on the Allied belief that this squadron had spirited away many high-ranking Nazis. Their planes included all the German types, specially marked American B17's and Flying Fortresses, as well as some French planes and the largest flying boats in the world. KG200 was a specialist squadron, the crews considered the best available. It carried out raids on bridges, and had a few *Totaleinsatz* personnel – suicide pilots. During the war it had been mainly engaged in dropping secret agents behind enemy lines. As part of their routine operations, this squadron also carried *'Goldfasanen'* (Golden pheasants), that is, Nazi bigwigs with their brown uniforms and colourful medals. The whole squadron was under the control of the RHSA under Himmler, not the Luftwaffe. 3KG200 is the unit that is of greatest interest. Under the orders of its commander, it moved from Rügen to Flensburg where Himmler was then at the seat of government. The most obvious difficulty facing Allied investigators at the end of the war was that, as with the submarine fleet, the operational strength of the squadron on paper bore little relation to the number of aircraft on the ground. They had to rely on the testimony of the commanders and crew, some of them fanatical Nazis, and all engaged in subterfuge of the highest order. By the time Allied investigators caught up with 3KG200, all the aircraft they would admit to were back at Flensburg. There was no way of knowing where they had been during the last few days of the Reich, although the Americans suspected most journeys had been to Spain.

Therefore it is fascinating to find that at the very end of April 1945, Squadron Leader Werner Baumbach was appointed 'Chef der Regierungsstaffel', in other words chief of the special section employed specifically to spirit away Nazi leaders. He was relieved from his crucial task of destroying bridges over the Oder, to hinder the Soviet advance. The removal of such a key figure at such a critical time was on Himmler's orders, revealing his ruthlessness and strong sense of priority. Baumbach went 'missing' for a critical period, his whereabouts unknown. Although he denied he was ever unobtainable, a letter exists stating the final position of aircraft from an irate Luftwaffe, impotent against Himmler's orders.[24] It sarcastically records that they had been unable to track Baumbach for more than two weeks. SS Sturmbannführer Josef Kiermaier claims to have suggested to Himmler that they fly south while they had the chance, as Himmler still had an aircraft at his disposal. He suggested that this would give them both time to see their 'womenfolk' before they left. He recalled that Himmler rejected this suggestion on the grounds that 'in times as adverse as these no man should indulge his personal desires'.[25] If such an exchange ever occurred, Himmler was lying. On 12 September 1944, Himmler had drawn up legal documents acknowledging that he was the father of his former secretary Hedwig's two illegitimate children, a young boy, Helge, aged 2 and Wannette Dorothea, his infant daughter. Far from not indulging his desires, he had brought them all with him as they withdrew to Schleswig-Holstein, Dr Brandt minding them at Hohenlychen, before Himmler arranged a house at Lübeck. His wife and daughter remained alone in the south.

Willi Frischauer, the first historian to research Himmler's last days, was quite convinced after questioning Hedwig and locals that Himmler had stayed with her at Lübeck until almost the end, contrary to all other later accounts. Himmler had indulged himself fully. He was also in a position to take advantage of the best specialist escape squadron available in the world, its leader personally available to serve his Reichsführer, ready and waiting at a critical time. At the sandy flat coast of Travemünde, overlooking the Baltic, having given up his illusions of acceptability, Himmler was faced with the fear of discovery and retribution. The preparations this obsessive man had made for himself and others left him the option of going to ground, an option that held a good prospect for success in both the short and the long term. On the other hand, he could opt for anonymity in Sweden, dependent on the gratitude of the Swedes and the strength of his bargaining position: the British fear of exposure. Or he still had time to flee the country and seek suitable, well-organised sanctuary – probably in Spain, using the unparalleled skills of Baumbach. He could even choose to rough it and face the uncertain but high risk of capture, trying to journey southwards to an uncertain destination. This option seems to go against his nature.

He might have had another option, one that gave him absolute certainty of survival, that avoided long-term reliance on others, did away with the uncertainty of deals with reluctant partners such as Ewan Butler, and removed the risks of travel. It was an alternative that could only succeed by being so outrageous that it was unthinkable. It relied on his powers of organisation and on the fear he inculcated. He could use his inhuman policy of *Sippenhaft*, the threat of eliminating an entire family to put pressure on one person to carry out actions that would otherwise be quite inconceivable. As Walter Schellenberg wrote in his autobiography, 'Never forget the alternative solution, make those words one of the basic principles of your life.' It was a principle his master had taught him well.

10

The Arrest of Heinrich Hitzinger

'I for one shall certainly not commit suicide.'

Heinrich Himmler, 5 May 1945

There are several conflicting accounts of Himmler's movements at the end of the war. One thing they all agree on is the impression of a depressed, confused and cowardly Himmler meekly visiting the newly appointed Führer, Admiral Dönitz, to beg for public office in the remnant of the Third Reich, only to be brusquely swept aside and cast out from Flensburg, a monster with nowhere else to go. This version of events stems mainly from the accounts of Admiral Dönitz himself, backed by the recollections of Dönitz's loyal assistant Peter Cremer, and Himmler's adjutant, Sturmbannführer Heinz Macher. These stories all serve to diminish Himmler's image and conveniently distance their proponents from his evil. History has been left with the pleasing image of a stern Admiral Dönitz, revolver hidden in his desk, treating the most feared man in Europe like an errant schoolboy. Himmler was dismissed and skulked off just before female air-ace Hanna Reitsch, the Hitler's fanatical disciple, arrived with Luftwaffe Oberstgruppenführer Ritter von Greim with orders to arrest the Reichsführer for his treasonable attempts to negotiate peace terms.

The truth was somewhat different. Himmler was put in charge of all the military in the Reich, apart from the troops in Denmark, Norway and Schleswig-Holstein, by an order issued by Dönitz after he had been officially declared Führer. Other orders clearly show that Himmler's command of the Army Group Vistula continued undisturbed. Indeed, only a week or so before his succession was announced, Dönitz had expressed his willingness to serve under Himmler's military command. Himmler and Dönitz had been in deep discussion about the imminent surrender of Hamburg at the very time that the message of Dönitz's succession arrived with instructions to arrest Himmler. Far from being dismissed, Himmler continued in conference with Dönitz over dinner while Reitsch and von Greim joined Peter Cremer and Heinz Macher in the basement to share a bottle of Black & White whisky. The next day Himmler returned to have lunch with Dönitz.[1]

Evidently much of the testimony relating to Himmler's actions during the Reich's last days cannot be believed. Other authors have come up against similar untruths, recording some at face value. Until now the accepted story has been that Himmler fled south from Flensburg. Two accounts that do not fit in with the received history are worth recording. The first is that of historian Willi Frischauer, who researched events only six years after the war. He took the trouble to visit Hedwig Potthast, Himmler's mistress, who recalled that Himmler came to stay in rooms he had taken for her at Lübeck, on the coast some fifty miles south-east of Flensburg – a time when history tells us that he was already travelling south. The second comes from Major Paul Odgers, who recorded in the British Army's *Tac Chronicle* that one of the British liaison officers visiting Flensburg on 12 May 1945, after peace had been declared, saw Himmler in the corridor at Dönitz's HQ, an impossibility if Himmler was travelling south at the time.[2] To add to the confusion, Foreign Minister Von Krosigk recalled a conversation he had with Himmler sometime in early May. 'They will never discover me,' he boasted. 'Political developments are going to be in my favour. I shall go into hiding to await them.'[3] Several contrary claims have Himmler leaving Flensburg on 5 or 6 May. However, we can state with certainty that the man who ended up in British custody on 22 May started his journey from Flensburg on 10 May, travelling under the name of Heinrich Hitzinger, a man whose identity card he carried. Hitzinger was a rural policeman who had been tried by a people's court for defeatism some months previously and condemned to death as a public enemy. There is no evidence that Hitzinger was actually executed. However, it is known that he was said to bear a remarkable resemblance to Heinrich Himmler.[4]

Himmler's interest in Hitzinger apparently sprang from a coincidence. One day, the story goes, the Reichsführer SS happened to see Hitzinger's identity papers on the desk of his arch enemy Heinrich Müller, and openly appropriated them 'for his later use.' To do so in front of Müller was a clear advertisement of his intentions, either a very rash or a very clever move. Certainly the option of quietly and discreetly acquiring such documentation without anyone's prior knowledge would seem infinitely preferable than drawing attention not only to his intention to change identity, but to whose identity he was going to assume. Unless, of course, this was the whole point of the exercise.

History relates that on 8 May Heinrich Himmler, Reichsführer SS, shaved off his moustache, changing his appearance considerably. Forty-eight hours later, a man claiming to be Heinrich Hitzinger set out on his final journey from Flensburg. According to Australian war correspondent Chester Wilmott, reporting from the new provisional Nazi government at Flensburg on 8 May 1945, this is what Himmler left behind:

In the streets civilians were going about their normal business with expressionless faces, but the crowds outside the foodshops were much larger than those gathered to read Dönitz's proclamation about the end of the war in the North West. Neither the civilians nor the ordinary troops any longer care [...] I did expect that somehow the atmosphere at High Command Headquarters would be different; but this was the scene. A rather dirty marine barracks housed the Headquarters and the Government; outside it eighteen scruffy sentries, as dirty and dishevelled as the troops in the town. In the car park beyond the gate there were a dozen big staff cars, replicas of those great black Mercedes in which the Nazi leaders have swaggered through the capitals of Europe. And now, here they were in the last bolt hole, their shining black surfaces hastily camouflaged with paint that had just been splashed on, and with the branches of trees tied on so that they looked like Macduff's men who carried Burnham Wood to Dunsinane [. . .] The only evidence that this was the High Command Headquarters was a small sign painted in black on the torn off bottom of a camouflaged boot box.

Germany was in chaos, its army and government smashed, communications and services shattered. The roads were choked with vehicles of every description, from farm carts to tanks. Endless groups of men were on the move, sleeping rough and carrying what food and clothing they could muster. Some were still armed, posing a hazard to both themselves and others, often using their weapons to bludgeon loose food from unwary travellers. The war-weary populace did not know what to believe any longer and suspected trouble at every step. The atmosphere of lawlessness was strongest in the open countryside, as opposed to the towns, where the British had established comparative law and order.

Progress across country was exasperatingly slow and extremely dangerous. Hitzinger travelled in a large and unwieldy group of fifteen men. The one factor uniting them was their allegiance to Himmler; almost all were members of his staff. If, therefore, a substitution had been effected, then several, if not all, were likely to have been privy to it, and briefed to maintain the deception. The most notable members of the party were SS Obergruppenführer Dr Karl Brandt, Hitler's personal physician; SS Obergruppenführer Karl Gebhardt, Himmler's surgeon; SS Obergruppenführer Otto Ohlendorf; SS Sturmbannführer Josef Kiermaier, Himmler's personal aide and secretary, and Himmler's adjutants, Waffen SS Obersturmbannführer Werner Grothmann and Sturmbannführer Heinz Macher. There were two more officers from the escort battalion of the Waffen SS, and seven non-commissioned officers from Himmler's personal staff. All carried papers claiming they were a newly demobilised detachment of the secret *Feldpolizei* (field police) who were ill and on their way to Munich under the supervision of Dr Gebhardt. They had removed all insignia from their uniforms, and in their assorted unmarked jackets and raincoats they were a memorably conspicuous bunch of cut-throats. In the words of Frischauer, several were 'strikingly crew-cut and objectionably Aryan'.[5] To complete the effect, the man calling himself Hitzinger sported a piratical black patch over his left eye.

The presence of almost all Himmler's entourage makes it seem unlikely that Hitzinger was anyone but Himmler, yet what better way to establish the identity of a leader than surround him with his customary crew? It is difficult to credit that a man of such cunning as Himmler could envisage behaving in such an obvious and dangerous fashion. However, such a view must be tempered by an awareness of the chaos of the time and the need for companionship and reassurance that even Himmler might have felt. Then again, Himmler of all people would have known that any Germans wearing the grey uniforms of the *Feldpolizei* would be pounced upon by the Allied Intelligence Services.

The group's progress south through Schleswig-Holstein was slow. Having left Flensburg in four large cars on 10 May, they took two whole days to cover the sixty-odd miles to Marne, in the south-west corner of the peninsula. At the north bank of the Elbe estuary, they then had to abandon their vehicles and take a ferry to the small town of Neuhaus on the southern shore. From there on they were obliged to proceed on foot.

In 1983, almost forty years after the event, a former intelligence officer revealed to newspapers that British Intelligence agents received information from Danish Intelligence, given out by Ewan Butler, that Himmler would be attempting a breakout towards the south, so the British were ready and waiting for him. But, thanks to the way the group travelled and behaved, the tip-off was to prove superfluous. By 18 May they had got no further than Bremervörde, a little town on the river Oste some 25 miles south-east of Marne, where they made a seemingly unaccountable decision. They could have forded the river upstream of the town, as hundreds of other refugees were doing, or they could have headed south across country, avoiding the river altogether. Instead of these simple options they chose to cross on one of the bridges guarded by the British army with its very visible checkpoints.

Of the two river bridges, the western was intact and passable to vehicles, but the eastern had been blown up and replaced by a temporary Bailey bridge. At the time, this was being used as an intelligence screening and security point by 45 Field Security Section of the Intelligence Corps, and guarded by Scottish infantry of the 51st Highland Division. Since 8 May the checkpoint had been manned by Staff-Sergeant John Hogg, assisted by Sergeants Arthur Britton and Ken Baisbrown who were based at the mill between the two bridges. All of them spoke good German. To help them carry out immediate checks, they had the wanted list of SD, Gestapo and SS personnel and known war criminals, compiled by CROWCASS, the Central Registry of War Criminals and Security Suspects (a copy of which had ended up on Himmler's desk).[6] They had no photographs for making comparisons, but if in doubt, they could consult the Allied Intelligence network by telephone or radio.

After arriving in Bremervörde, the refugees found shelter in the farmhouse of Herr Dangers at 165 Waldstrasse. His son Heinrich, only nine at the time, never forgot what he described as the odd 'tensions' between the various members, some of whom he felt certain were acting as 'guards' to prevent an escape as much as they were there to protect. Leaving the rest of the party in the house, Kiermaier set off to investigate. Twice he demanded passes to cross the bridge from the local mayor, Herr Dohrmann, whom the British had installed as a district counsellor. Dohrmann refused, later remarking to investigators and historians that these people were crazy to use the bridge at all, as they could easily have avoided the checkpoint by wading across the river like everyone else.

After Kiermaier returned, it was decided that the group should stick to their original plan. They would masquerade as ailing policemen and try to get through the British control point with their demobilisation passes. It was a baffling decision; if the district counsellor had already refused them, arrest looked certain. At about 3 p.m. on 20 May Kiermaier and Gebhardt set off to reconnoitre the checkpoint itself, with the intention of returning for the others if all seemed well. At 4 p.m. they were stopped on the bridge by Sergeant Baisbrown. Not wanting them to take fright and run off,

1. Reichsführer SS Heinrich Himmler.

2. Himmler visiting the Łódź ghetto in 1942.

3. Himmler with Rudolf Hess and Martin Bormann at Berlin's *Building and Planning in the East* exhibition of Nazi ambitions for places such as Łódź.

4. Ernst Kaltenbrunner in the witness stand at Nuremberg. He was hanged in October 1946.

5. A page from Himmler's diary in which he related how he was scarred in a duel.

6. Himmler stands at Hitler's side as they watch SS Stormtroopers put on a show.

7. British Ambassador Sir Victor Mallet (right) with Swedish Crown
Prince Gustav Adolf at a memorial service for the Duke of Kent in Stockholm,
1942.

8. Peter Falk, secret agent and schoolmaster.

9. President John F. Kennedy presents the National Security Award to Allen Dulles, retired Director of the CIA, in November 1961.

10. John Foster Dulles arrives in Frankfurt early in 1949 for crisis talks about the Berlin Blockade.

11. Kim Philby at a press conference after he was named in the House of Commons in connection with defected diplomats Burgess and Maclean, 8 November 1955.

12. Art adviser Sir Anthony Blunt accompanies Queen Elizabeth II during her visit to the Courtauld Institute of Art, February 1959.

13. Himmler's adjutants, Werner Grothmann (left) and Heinz Macher, photographed the day after the suicide.

14. Dr Carl Marcus, Mayor of Mönchengladbach.

15. The prisoner's last hours, captured by Captain Bryan de Grineau for the *Illustrated London News*, 2 June 1945.

THE DRAWING-ROOM OF THE GERMAN SUBURBAN VILLA IN WHICH WILLIAM JOYCE AND RIBBENTROP WERE QUESTIONED.

A TYPICAL EXAMINATION OF A WAR CRIMINAL AT 31a, UELLENERSTRASSE, LÜNEBURG: THE ROOM WHICH ALL IMPORTANT SUSPECTS CAPTURED IN THE BRITISH ZONE ARE INTERROGATED.

16. A typical interrogation scene in the room 'in which Himmler committed suicide', as represented to readers of the *Illustrated London News*. In fact it was bare, with only two people present when the suicide took place.

17. The dead prisoner as he was filmed by Pathé.

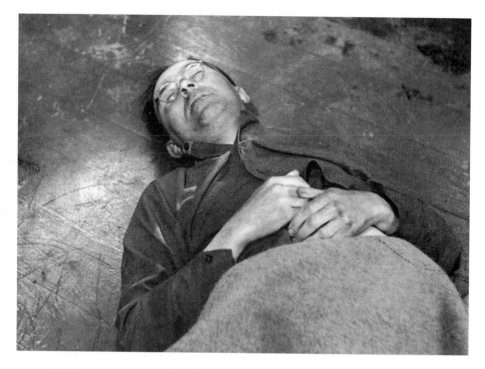

18. The dead prisoner. The disparity between his nostrils clearly shows the facial asymmetry recorded in the post-mortem.

19. Bill Carrotte's photograph of the dead prisoner, arranged in a peaceful position.

20. A wartime photograph of Himmler. The fencing wound described in his diary shows as a scar midway between his ear and eye.

CADAVER OF
REICHSMINISTER HEINRICH HIMMLER.

REPORT ON DENTITION.

[CADAVER examined at 11.00 hrs to 13.15 hrs on
25. May. 45 at 31.a. UELSENERSTRASSE,
LÜNEBERG.]

Sepia and
(Abbreviations employed are those authorized in
Regulations for the Medical Services of the army,
1938, appendix 13.)

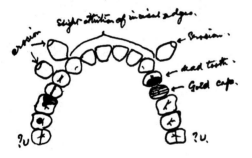

NOTES.
① Oral Hygiene - Good.
②. ⅃ missing.
③ all fillings are of Silver amalgam.
④. Teeth well-formed.
⑤. Shade of teeth. (incisors, upper) = Shade 7. (Ames Vita pr)

25. May. 45.   Lieut Col.
                    ADDS. Second army.
LÜNEBER'   (sd) G. R. ATTKINS. Major.
                    74 (Br.) General Hospital.

21. The dental record from the post-mortem report.

22. Smiling soldiers in the garden of 31a Ülzenerstrasse.

23. Sergeant Bill Ottery and Ray Weston return to the actual burial site on Lüneburg Heath.

24. Walter Schellenberg.

he gave the impression that all would be well, sending them back with two three-ton lorries and an escort to bring in the rest of their party.

As soon as the group arrived, their façade began to crack. Although Gebhardt claimed that all the men were in his care, some at first denied that they were members of the party. All carried release documents dated 1 May, but the papers bore the stamp of SD headquarters, an instant giveaway. Although carefully smudged, it did not fool Britton who, together with Baisbrown, grilled the youngest German. The man soon admitted that the party were indeed together, and all belonged to the SD, although he claimed that he only worked in a menial capacity. At about 6 p.m., the group was duly arrested and dispatched in lorries for the civilian internment camp at Westertinke, the 'Cage', near Zeven, some miles to the south.

From the British point of view, the success of their little operation was marred by the fact that three Germans were still missing. Before the main party went off, several expressed concern about the sick comrades they had left behind. Staff-Sergeant Hogg took Gebhardt, whom they had kept with them, back to the farm, but Macher, Grothmann and Hitzinger were nowhere to be seen. Once again, the Germans' motives are hard to fathom. There seems little doubt that they originally planned that the whole group should cross together. Yet when Kiermayer and Gebhardt returned from their reconnaissance of the checkpoint, with the impression that everyone would get through all right, their tactics seem to have changed; the three did not wait at the farm, but went off to another hiding place. Perhaps Macher and Grothmann wanted to make certain that they and their charge were arrested. Had they really been trying to slip through independently, they would surely have detached themselves from the large and noticeable group much sooner. As it was they did the very opposite, and detached themselves at a stage that, thanks to their talkative comrades, in the end served to focus attention on the three. The British soldiers certainly thought the group's behaviour very odd. If the first twelve men had been allowed through unhindered, it would have made sense for them to draw attention to their sick companions; after they had been arrested, it seemed crazy to mention the missing men. Baisbrown attributed their behaviour to misplaced loyalty: the main party, he thought, just did not want to leave the stragglers behind. This hardly seems sufficient reason; it could equally well have been well-placed disloyalty, or something more sinister. To compound the undercover party's apparent incompetence, on a later visit to the farm Britton discovered a valise in a loft, which contained pyjamas, slippers and a manicure set, helpfully engraved with the letters R.F.SS. What man seeking anonymity arms himself with possessions bearing inscriptions revealing his true identity?

The twelve were duly processed and only learned from rumours in the camps what had happened to their missing friends. Both Gebhardt and Brandt seemed to think that their title of 'Doctor' would automatically exclude them from intensive interrogation. Neither showed much concern about their war record, and both later professed amazement at the Allies' indignation about what they considered routine experiments, such as the sterilisation of women by X-rays. Grothmann and Macher had been ordinary soldiers as members of the Waffen SS and so thought they had little to fear from Allied questioning.[7] The one man who, if he had had any sense, would not have given himself up was Ohlendorf, head of the Einsatzgruppen (death squads). However, he thought his behaviour morally correct, and actually enjoyed debating his actions. While in prison in Nuremberg, Ohlendorf irritated the Allies by 'persistently claiming that Himmler had told him that he was going to seek refuge with Prince Waldeck at Arolsen in North Germany'.[8] As he had been part of the escort party, this claim was particularly odd; once Ohlendorf realised he faced the death sentence, perhaps he was seeking to buy his life with more than debate. Ohlendorf was suspected of starting prison rumours that Himmler was still alive, which were picked up by Göring, who in August 1945 wondered aloud to his interrogators at Nuremberg 'if he's really dead'.[9]

Allied intelligence personnel were told to keep their eyes peeled for three more SD-sponsored refugees in the area and the sentries were warned to keep an especial lookout. Macher and Grothmann must have realised that their colleagues had gone through the checkpoint, but had no means of knowing whether they had been arrested or allowed to go free. Whatever their suspicions, they hid for another twenty-four hours before attempting to cross the bridge. Finally, on the afternoon of 22 May, the bizarre trio walked openly through the town of Bremervörde along the straight, east–west high street. Himmler's adjutants, wearing long, dark green overcoats with felt collars, were clearly military men. They flanked a far less impressive figure wearing an odd collection of civilian clothes under a blue raincoat. They moved slowly, and the third man seemed especially reluctant to hurry. As soon as the British saw them, they got the impression that the two tall officers were *in charge of* the smaller man. They drew even more attention to themselves, one witness recorded, by the way the officers glanced around from time to time as if 'to ensure that their charge was still there'.[10] The trio did not even reach the bridge before they were stopped by a British army patrol and escorted to the guardroom in the mill. When they arrived, at some time around 5 p.m., they were met by Sergeant Britton, who immediately telephoned Staff-Sergeant Hogg to report 'the three men have come in'.[11]

Baisbrown went to the mill at once, where he found the two military characters standing up and their charge squatting miserably on his heels. All three claimed to be sergeants, but once again the smudged SD stamp was in evidence. Had the third man been Himmler, surely he would have arranged to equip himself with discharge papers of a decent calibre. According to Schellenberg, the forgers working for the SD were so skilled that nine times out of ten their notes fooled the Bank of England. The documents gave away their bearers instantly. Given the resources it had enjoyed until a few days before, the group could have furnished itself with any spurious identity it chose. But instead of assuming the name of some harmless unit, it opted to identify its members as belonging to the *Feldpolizei*, an organisation that would certainly appear on any Allied automatic arrest list.

'Hitzinger' carried an old and genuine identity card, but his demobilisation pass showed he had been discharged as a sergeant from the special armoured company attached to the *Feldpolizei* on 3 May. In fact all the group's papers had been made up between 1 and 3 May. All sources agreed that between these dates Himmler was still considering many different options; the papers prove that a plan for a group of his supporters to travel across country together had been laid at that time. Promptly arrested, the three men were confined to the mill for the night, sleeping in the corner on the first floor among the sacks of grain. None of the British recognised their weedy-looking third prisoner as anybody special, and his identity as 'Heinrich Hitzinger' survived preliminary questioning (although his impressive personal magnifying glass with its tell-tale eagle wings was confiscated). The prisoner was fast running out of personalised items that would serve to prove the identity he was so carelessly trying to conceal.

At 7 a.m. the next morning, Wednesday 23 May, they set off for the civil internment camp at Westertinke, and for the rest of the day they moved in fits and starts. The official British record of their journey gives precise timings for each arrival, but the whole account is riddled with anomalies and inconsistencies, both of times and other details. In one way these small points do not matter much; forty years later it makes little difference whether the prisoners reached a certain point at a certain time markedly different from that given. What does matter is that the differences strongly suggest that the entire account put out by the Army of the handling and death of the prisoner known as Heinrich Hitzinger was fudged from start to finish.

They stopped briefly at Zeven, where a report was made to Captain Excel of the 45th Field Security Station, who did not bother to come out and examine the prisoners. The driver, Sergeant Britton, was told to carry on to the Westertinke 'Cage' where the prisoners would be registered. According to Britton's report, he completed the 20 km journey in 1 hour and 10 minutes; therefore he should have reached Westertinke at 8.10 a.m., but the registration of the prisoners did not begin until 9 a.m. Again, 'Hitzinger' was not recognised as someone significant. As they were former members of the SD, the three men were moved almost immediately to the special interrogation camp at Kolkhagen, on the western edge of the village of Barnstedt, a further fifty miles to the south-east. This stage of their journey began at 9.40 a.m. It is no longer possible to be certain which route they took, as there were several options open. Nevertheless, official army routes had been established for trucks transporting suspects of this kind, and as there was a special check-point at Fallingbostel for vehicles proceeding east, it seems most likely that they travelled this way, rather than by the more direct route through Neuenkirchen and Soltau.

Allowing for the customary half-hour tea stop at Fallingbostel, the Bedford truck ought to have reached Kolkhagen at about 12.30 p.m. This does not fit the official booking-in time, given as 18.30 hours. But it is exactly the time stated by Karl Kaufmann, the former Gauleiter of Hamburg, who was standing with other prisoners inside the barbed wire fence of Camp 031, watching the lorries drive up. 'Among those who got out was Himmler, minus his moustache and with a patch over one eye,' he later recorded. 'He didn't recognise me, and suddenly disappeared behind rhododendron bushes, where he removed the eye patch. This was, in my opinion, the time when he decided to give himself up.'[12] A few minutes later, according to Kaufmann, a stir went through the camp as the news spread. Extra guards came on duty and extra sentries were posted on the gate. 'Soon the cause of the excitement was being passed over the grape-vine in the camp. The British soldiers seemed overjoyed that Himmler was among their prisoners.'[13]

It is hard to know what to make of the fact that the star prisoner did not recognise Kaufmann and his associates, whom Himmler had met many times. There is also no obvious reason why he should have chosen that moment to give up masquerading as Hitzinger; he had already survived several preliminary interrogations without discovery. Whatever the man's motives, he and his two companions soon began making a fuss and demanding an interview with the camp commandant, Captain Thomas Selvester. This was also strange. In general, former SS men were the quietest and most docile of the prisoners. Hoping to live down their reputations, they behaved as meekly as possible and strove to create a good impression. In contrast the three men were so boorish and abusive that they soon succeeded in getting themselves brought before the commandant. Here the anomalies of timing become most marked. According to the army's official version of the story, the men reached Kolkhagen at 18.30 hours, and came before Selvester at 19.00 hours. Yet Selvester told various historians that he was informed of their arrival at 16.00 hours, and claimed on another occasion, that 'Hitzinger' spent eight hours in his care, before being handed over at 21.45 hours – in other words that he had reached the camp at 1.45 p.m. From this and the journey described above it can be inferred that the prisoner reached Kolkhagen around lunchtime and spent the afternoon and evening there.

When the trio entered the commandant's office, the first man to come in, according to Selvester, was 'small, ill-looking and shabbily dressed',[14] and still wearing his eye patch (another contradiction). The other two were 'tall, soldierly looking, one slim and one well built. The well-built man walked with a limp.'[15] Sensing something a little unusual about the group, Selvester ordered a sergeant to place the two military prisoners under close custody and prevent anyone speaking to them without his authority. Grothmann and Macher were removed, whereupon the small man 'removed the eye patch over his left eye and put on a pair of spectacles. His identity was at once obvious, and he said "Heinrich Himmler" in a very quiet voice.'[16]

Selvester informed the headquarters of the British Second Army at Lüneburg of his captive, and Major Rice, an Intelligence staff officer, was dispatched to confirm the prisoner's identity. Meanwhile, Selvester carried out a body search. He ordered the man to strip and as each item of clothing came off he examined and handed it to a sergeant, who examined it again. In the jacket Selvester found a small brass case, 'similar to a cartridge case', containing a small glass phial that he immediately recognised as a suicide capsule. When asked what it contained, the prisoner replied, 'That is my medicine. It cures stomach cramp.'[17] Soon a second brass case came to light, but this time it was empty. Selvester assumed the prisoner had hidden the missing phial somewhere on his person. He had him completely stripped and closely searched.

> All the orifices of his body were searched, also his hair combed, and any likely hiding place examined [. . .] At this stage he was not asked to open his mouth, as I considered that if the phial were hidden in his mouth and we tried to remove it, it might precipitate some action that would be regretted.[18]

After the search, which revealed nothing, Selvester claimed to have sent for thick cheese sandwiches and tea and watched the prisoner closely while he was eating, but 'did not notice anything unusual'.[19] Altogether the man gave Selvester the impression that 'things had caught up with him'.

> He was quite prepared to talk, and indeed at times looked almost jovial. He looked ill when I first saw him but improved immensely after a meal and a wash (he was not allowed to shave). He was in my custody for approximately eight hours and, during that time, whilst not being interrogated asked repeatedly after the whereabouts of his adjutants, appearing genuinely worried over their welfare. I found it impossible to believe that he could be the arrogant man portrayed by the press before and during the war.[20]

Selvester's account is quite unacceptable for two reasons. First, the size of the Zyankali suicide phial that later killed the prisoner is clearly shown on a Pathé film. And there is accurate information from RKTH concentration camp at Sachsenshausen where they were manufactured. They measured 9mm in diameter, were 35mm long, had a blue annealed top, and contained 8mg of hydrogen cyanide in the form of anhydrous sodium cyanide stabilised with hydraulic acid. Three to four thousand such phials were made, of which 950 were ordered by Criminal Police Chief Artur Nebe for the use of senior officials of the Nazi leadership. If the prisoner had had one in his mouth he could not possibly have eaten bread and cheese without revealing its presence. Either he was not searched thoroughly, and had the suicide capsule hidden elsewhere on his body, or the 'thick cheese sandwich' episode was invented afterwards to give the impression that Selvester had taken all reasonable steps to prevent suicide.

It is worth noting Selvester's assertion that the prisoner was not allowed to shave. It is well known that hair continues to grow for a time even after death, but the photographs of the corpse taken the next morning show a relatively clean-shaven face. Selvester's mention of shaving itself suggests that the man had at least a day's growth of beard on May 23. If he had missed shaving altogether that day, which, considering the travelling, was highly likely, the stubble would have been pronounced by the following morning. But there is even better evidence in a report: 'One of the second party was Sgt Heinrich Hi[t]zinger, an unimpressive figure with several days' growth of beard, no glasses, and a patch over one eye. He was dressed in an odd collection of civilian garments, with a blue raincoat over the top.'[21] This document, signed by Captain John Excell and no fewer than twelve others, may not reflect the full truth, but it does suggest that Hitzinger was allowed to shave; Selvester probably later realised that this facility should have been denied to a potential suicide. As before, the official account contains an element of whitewash.

There is only one surviving record of the prisoner's interrogation, given by Colonel M. A. C. Osborne, and printed years later in *Ça Ira*, the journal of the West Yorkshire Regiment. In 1945 Osborne was GSO 1 (Military Intelligence Operations) at 2nd Army Headquarters, and for a few hours he became involved in the case. However, it seems likely that he was not present (as the *Ça Ira* report claimed) when the prisoner committed suicide. The investigation team led by Major Rice reached Kolkhagen at about 7.30 p.m. To help with his identification, Rice had the SHAEF index-card on Himmler, which contained a two-paragraph summary of his career, his Nazi Party number, his SS number, his date of birth, and a specimen signature. Clipped to the card was a photograph that showed Himmler, Reichsführer SS, resplendent in black uniform. Rice did not have any dental records or physical details such as weight, height, etc., nor a set of fingerprints. On the other hand, he came forearmed with the knowledge that the prisoner had already declared himself to be Himmler, and this must have influenced him strongly. Rice had not dealt with any other members of the Nazi hierarchy, so had nothing to compare with the prisoner's manner under interrogation.

According to Osborne, the team's brief was 'to establish the identity of Himmler beyond all reasonable doubt'.[22] They began by taking special care 'to compare the ear of the prisoner with the one [partly] visible in the photograph' and it was 'found to be identical'.[23] This was a shaky foundation on which to base all that followed. Ears have never been considered a reliable guide to identify, even if they can be viewed as a pair, and from all angles. The SHAEF snapshot of Himmler, showing one ear, only partially visible from an angle, was completely inadequate evidence.

What followed was still less satisfactory. When asked to give his Nazi Party number, the prisoner replied that 'it was in the 14,000 series'.[24] The number given on the SHAEF card was 14,303, so the reply was not, strictly speaking, inaccurate. But it is unusual to answer such a specific question by quoting 'in the so-and-so series'. It is almost as if the prisoner were discussing someone else's number. It was certainly inexplicably vague for one of the old faithfuls. Every army officer, sergeant, corporal or private you are likely to come across knows his number by heart and can reel it off instantly: it is a fundamental part of his life. Moreover, army personnel do this without being obsessive about personal details or possessing a phenomenal memory, unlike Himmler. It is hard to believe that the real Reichsführer would not have given his number correctly.

When asked his SS number, the prisoner gave an equally loose answer, replying that 'it was 169 or thereabouts'. The number on the SHAEF card was 168. Not only was the prisoner's reply wrong: it was, as before, oddly vague. The next question concerned his date of birth, and once more his answer produced a discrepancy. He replied 7 October 1900. Here, for once, the mistake was the SHAEF officials'. The real Himmler was indeed born on 7 October 1900, whereas the card showed 7 November 1900. If Osborne's account is to be trusted, as before the investigating team accepted a near miss as good enough. To complete his examination, Rice asked the man for a signature, and the prisoner gave one, only on condition that it was instantly destroyed. They agreed, and he duly signed his name. Rice, going on common sense rather than any expert analytical technique, decided that the new signature corresponded well enough with the one on the card. This clinched it. 'Heinrich Hitzinger' was, Rice concluded, Heinrich Himmler.

This trying inquisition over, the prisoner asked to see Rice's photograph. The moment he looked at it, he said that it must have been taken before the war, as he had not worn black uniform since the outbreak of hostilities. This was not true, although Rice was in no position to know it. At the Eichman trial alone, reference was made to Himmler wearing his black uniform for its terrifying effect when he visited concentration camps, on one occasion as late as 1945. This was confirmed by a photograph of a 2 August 1943 visit to Sobibor produced for the court.

According to Osborne, the prisoner 'required no encouragement to speak'. He claimed that on 8 May he had written a letter to Field-Marshal Montgomery asking for an interview, which he had given to General Kinsel for delivery. His intention as he made his way to Bremervörde had been to 'roam about the country for a few weeks until the tumult of victory had died down and circumstances were more favourable for an interview'.[25] He wanted to discuss future events with Montgomery because the Russian menace was growing daily, and 'sooner or later there would be another war to stop the intrusion of Asiatic hordes into Western Europe'. The prisoner went on to mention some recent episodes in Himmler's career, including his command of an army group on the eastern front, and defended the role of the SS, as well as that of the concentration camps. Himmler had, however, already given a frank talk to a horrified audience of senior military witnesses, including Admiral Dönitz, at the Posen conference in October 1943, taking a perverse pleasure in assuming responsibility for all extermination programmes. The contrast between the sentiments of Himmler and the prisoner could be explained by the differing attitudes of their respective audiences. History does not record what impression these lengthy statements made on his captors. Perfunctory though it had been, the team at Kolkhagen were satisfied with their identification.

In retrospect, it seems amazing that they felt as confident as they did. To recapitulate, the suspect had made close but woolly guesses at Himmler's Party and SS numbers. The date he gave as his birthday was a month out from that shown on the SHAEF card. Comparison of ear-shape was carried out by an individual with no medical qualifications, using a wholly inadequate photograph. Their prisoner's statements contained generalised information about Himmler and the war that would have been known to large numbers of German officers. He made no reference to the areas of special knowledge which one would have expected the real Himmler to use as bargaining tools, such as the secrets of the rocket establishment at Peenemünde or details of the huge spy organisation that Obergruppenführer Gehlen had built up in the east. Nothing can be gleaned from the fact that the prisoner gave a passable signature. Signatures are relatively easy to forge, especially after practice, and even expert graphologists admit they can often be deceived. Why did the man insist on his signature being destroyed as soon as he had given it, and why did his captors comply with such a wish? It has been suggested that he was afraid it might be used as a souvenir. Would such trivia really worry a man clearly bent on self-destruction in the near future? Perhaps they never actually asked him to provide one.

Superficial as his interrogation was, it raised a worrying number of discrepancies. It is important not to underestimate the effect of stress on a prisoner. One particular form of prisoner psychosis is worth examining in this context: the Ganzer syndrome, named after the man who discovered it in prisoners of war in 1898. The syndrome's main feature is a tendency to avoid giving a direct answer and waffle about ancillary features of the question. It might be contended that the prisoner did just this, missing the dates and party numbers by a small margin, as a result of stress. But this explanation will not suffice, for an essential part of the Ganzer syndrome is that the answers are not merely approximate but ridiculous.[26] Moreover, a sufferer fails to identify objects presented to him and to correlate them with their function – for instance, he might state that a spoon is used for cutting meat. In effect, it is an hysterical attempt to avoid responsibility. The real Himmler would have had every reason for doing this, but there is no evidence that the prisoner behaved in any such way. He remained calm and rational, and never feigned amnesia. There is no psychological explanation for the mistakes he made.

As soon as the question of identity seemed settled, another message was sent to the headquarters in Lüneburg, whence Colonel Michael Murphy, Chief of Intelligence in the Second Army, set off to take charge of the prisoner. That Murphy was an able man there is no doubt. His commander-in-chief, Montgomery, had the highest opinion of him, and once wrote, 'He is first class and what he does not know about intelligence in the field is not worth knowing'. Among his equals and subordinates Murphy was inclined to be officious and not much liked. One of the officers concerned in the traumatic events of 23 May described him as 'a young full colonel, looking brand new' – not a vote of confidence.[27] That evening he was unwell, suffering from a severe stomach upset thanks to the excessive celebrations for the end of the war. When his own car broke down it must have seemed the final straw. He got a lift in Colonel M. A. C. Osborne's car, reaching Kolkhagen at 9.45 p.m.

Presented with Rice's findings, Murphy ordered the prisoner to strip for a second search and put on fresh clothes. Initially, the man refused to do either, on the grounds that he had already undressed once and the only alternative clothing – British army battledress – was not his uniform and he would not wear it. Threatened with forcible stripping, he did eventually undress, but still refused the battledress, and after the search dressed himself again in a grey shirt, underpants and socks. His uniform was taken away, and he was given an army blanket to wrap around his shoulders.

Although this search also failed to reveal the missing phial, Murphy felt it was still possible for the man to have a poison capsule hidden about him, 'the most obvious places being the mouth and buttocks'.[28] He decided to conduct a medical search. While the man was dressing, he telephoned his aide-de-camp, Lieutenant Jack Ashworth, back at headquarters, telling him to get a doctor to stand by at a house that had just been taken over. 31a Ülzenerstrasse in Lüneburg, a semi-detached villa set back a few yards from the road, one of several houses requisitioned by the British, was still being prepared for the reception of important captives. At 10.40 p.m. the prisoner, still shivering under his blanket, was bundled into the back seat of Murphy's car between his second in command Lieutenant-Colonel Bernard Stapleton and a guard, and driven off across Lüneburg Heath with Murphy in the front. At one point Murphy began to suspect that they had lost the way, but when he turned and asked Stapleton what he thought, to their great amusement the prisoner interjected 'You are on the road to Lüneburg'. Stapleton later confided to a colleague that he heard the man moving something in his mouth, and saw him fiddle with his teeth, using his right hand.

Meanwhile a doctor had been recruited, and was standing by. Captain Clement Wells was a former general practitioner who, by his own account, enjoyed regimental soldiering, but greatly disliked the size and bureaucracy of army headquarters. It was sheer bad luck that he was caught for the unpleasant task ahead, for he was not the unit's regular doctor, who was away on leave. That evening, as it happened, Wells was out of camp trying to make arrangements to fly home for his own leave. So he did not hear the loudspeakers blare out a sudden demand for the duty medical officer to report to police headquarters, and when he got back he was greatly surprised by the urgency of his reception. Police headquarters had also been set up in Ülzenerstrasse in another of the requisitioned houses, next to 31a. It was, Wells recalled, a 'blisteringly cold evening' with an unseasonably sharp east wind, 'which would have taken the varnish off the mantelpiece'.[29] His temper was by no means improved as he waited in the road with Sergeant Austin, who teased him by making him guess who was the prisoner they were waiting for.

For a while they walked up and down, with the wind roaring in the pine trees; then they withdrew to the relative calm of Sergeant Austin's office, posting a corporal outside to watch for the arrival of the VIP. Captain Wells was puzzled about what he was supposed to be doing. Austin told him that Second Army headquarters wanted the prisoner medically examined to see whether he was fit to continue the journey to Montgomery's headquarters, utter non-sense as they were only a few miles away. When the convoy eventually drew up outside, there was an instant personality clash. Murphy got out first. 'Taking hardly any notice of Austin', Wells later wrote, 'he turned to me and said arrogantly, "Are you the doctor?"'[30] Whether or not Wells answered is unclear, but his badges were sufficient proof, and Murphy quickly instructed, 'Then you will examine this prisoner for poison.' Both the order and the manner of its delivery greatly offended Wells. It was, he felt, a 'monstrous request', delivered with unwarranted arrogance. Why should he, a doctor, be better qualified than anyone else to discover poison? Surely, he thought, Austin should make the search. Wells replied firmly, 'I am a doctor not a detective.' Looking back later he realised that his remark had not been well received:

> It may have been the way I said it. It may have been that in the semi-darkness he could not see that I was an older man than he, or it may have been that he could not realise quickly enough that I was not speaking as an officer to a superior officer but as a man with a professional training to a layman.

Whatever Murphy's interpretation, he turned to Wells and said curtly, 'You will do as you are told.' As Wells, who would later torment himself about what followed, ruefully explained, 'the whole thing was starting on the wrong foot'. The scene was set for the disaster that quickly followed.

As animosity crackled between the two men, the prisoner was brought out and hustled towards the house by two guards. To Wells he looked 'a deplorable object'. The army blanket around his waist became entangled in his feet, and he was half-dragged into number 31a. It must be emphasised that the official account of what followed bears little resemblance to the truth. Carefully fashioned by the Army, and lent veracity by two feature articles complete with drawings and photographs in the *Illustrated London News*, Selvester, Murphy and Austin's version of events was a whitewash.

Company Sergeant-Major Edwin Austin claimed to have instantly recognised the prisoner as Himmler. As the headquarters had already lost one important Nazi prisoner – General Pruetzmann, who had committed suicide – Austin looked to Murphy for permission to sandbag the man and render him unconscious. Murphy refused with a slight shake of the head, and warned Wells *sotto voce* that he feared a phial of poison was concealed. The prisoner was ushered into a well-furnished room, which had at least one plush armchair and a chandelier with an elaborate shade suspended over an ornate, circular wooden table. Thick brocade curtains framed the windows, and a still life of sunflowers hung on one wall. A dresser full of china, with a clock on top of it, lent further warmth to the room. In these cosy surroundings a formidable collection of officers assembled for the search. One perched on the back of an armchair with a revolver in his hand. Another sat at the round table taking notes, and two more looked on with their backs to the windows. A security guard with a tommy gun stood immediately behind the prisoner, and a sergeant assisted the doctor by shining a fierce electric lamp into the prisoner's face. Altogether, there were eight people in the room. As the doctor looked into the suspect's mouth for the first time, he thought he saw a gleam of a dark, silvery object. The sergeant held the light higher so that he could see better into the back of the mouth. 'Open your mouth,' he ordered. Instead of complying, the prisoner panicked, bit down hard, and instantly keeled over. At once Murphy shouted for a needle and cotton, with which he transfixed the prisoner's tongue, pulling it forward while the doctor sloshed a basin of water into the moribund man's mouth. Already he had turned pale green, and despite attempts at artificial respiration he died at 11.14 p.m.

Such was the gospel according to the Army. Here is the truth. The key factors which enabled me to establish what really happened were Dr Wells' testimony and the presence in the house of a further witness whose role in the affair has not been revealed in any account published so far. Captain Norman Rimmer was an intelligence officer, not stationed at Lüneburg, who happened to have dropped in for a meal on the way back to his own unit.[31] Officially he should not have been in 31a Ülzenerstrasse at all; he had just come to visit his fellow Lancastrian intelligence officer and friend Major Norman

Whittaker, then quartered in the house. Unlike other witnesses, Rimmer had neither personal motive nor was subjected to SIS or any pressure to massage the facts. When Whittaker was called to the telephone to receive news that an important prisoner was on his way, he and Rimmer were carefully stewing a Lancashire hot-pot in the kitchen on the first floor. Rimmer took charge while Whittaker went down to brief CSM Austin about the impending arrival, but Whittaker was soon able to resume control at the stove, for he was not present during the examination of the prisoner.

The setting where the suicide took place was quite different from the one portrayed in the *Illustrated London News'* account of the interviewing of important Nazi suspects. It was a large, unfurnished room at the front of the house. The bay windows stood wide open, letting in the icy wind. As Dr Wells entered, 'the prisoner was ordered to strip, and he stood there shivering more from physical exposure than fear'.[32] This, the doctor decided, was exactly the way not to go about the delicate task; they needed to give the captive 'the confidence that at any rate for the moment he would be treated generously'. Wells told Murphy that he wanted to examine the man alone. Murphy left the room, as did the two armed men standing guard. Wells ordered the windows shut and a blanket thrown over the prisoner's shoulders.

When the final examination took place, it was made before an audience of two, CSM Austin and Wells, rather than the large and impressive quorum portrayed in the *Illustrated London News*. Murphy, who had been taken short, retired to the lavatory across the hall and locked himself in. When the suicide occurred, he was grappling with internal problems rather than with the prisoner's tongue. The doctor asked Austin under his breath why poison was suspected. He replied that some had been found with poison in their clothes, but that he did not know what form it might take. Afterwards, Wells justly complained that Murphy had not told him specifically to look out for a phial of cyanide. Murphy should have told him exactly what had been found, and shown him the glass phial taken from the patient's clothing, for Wells had never seen a suicide capsule. Wells could only imagine two places where the prisoner might be harbouring poison undetected. In his own words, he decided to 'examine his mouth last and his rectum not at all'. Here too he was quite correct. He had the requisite instrument for rectal examination, but he could not have carried it out without the prisoner's co-operation. Besides, if the prisoner did have the poison concealed in his rectum, there was no way that he could suddenly transfer the poison to his mouth without them noticing. In a somewhat naive attempt to camouflage his own intentions, Wells searched all the least likely areas first and shook his head lugubriously when he drew a blank. He was, he claimed, polite and gentle, in an attempt to lull the prisoner into a false sense of security. The man was 'quiet and co-operative'. Finally Wells came to the mouth and 'casually asked him to open it'.

> In doing this he threw his head a little backwards and away, but only in the same way that many other people do when asked to show their teeth. There was nothing exaggerated in the movement. I can see the mouth now. They were goodish teeth. But what I did see was a small blue tit-like object sticking out of the lower sulcus of his left cheek [the space between the jaw bone and the inner cheek]. That was something abnormal. That more than likely was it. What on earth was I going to do now?

The real question, the doctor realised, was whether or not the prisoner knew what he had seen. Hoping for the best, Wells shook his head again, turned to Austin and said that, to satisfy everyone, he had better repeat the examination. Wells went through the motions of searching the whole body again, but this time, when he asked the prisoner to open his mouth, without waiting he slipped a finger into the prisoner's mouth to sweep out what he had seen. The man, who had been watching him acutely, immediately clamped his jaws on the finger.

> We struggled for a moment. He wrenched my hand out of his mouth, swung his head away and then with almost deliberate disdain faced me, crushed the glass capsule between his teeth

and took a deep inhalation. His face immediately became deeply suffused and contorted with pain. His neck veins stood out, and his eyes stared glassily, and he crashed to the ground.[33]

According to Whittaker, who was not in the room but later described the event in his diary, Wells shouted out, 'My God, it's in his mouth! He's done it on me!'[34] The words were quite uncharacteristic of Wells' essentially middle-class manner; whatever he did say, there was certainly a shout, perhaps from one of the guards outside. The noise of the scuffle brought people on to the landing and Whittaker ran downstairs. Meanwhile, Wells had snatched a bowl of water, soaked his handkerchief and started mopping out the prisoner's mouth. He also administered a burst of artificial respiration, but he knew that it was useless. He described his actions as 'a kind of automatic reflex'; he knew full well that there was no way he could prevent 'the dramatic rapidity of death'.

> There was a slowing series of stertorous breaths, which may have continued for half a minute, and the pulse for another minute after that. To anyone who has owned a killing bottle, to anyone who has dispensed medicine, the smell of hydrocyanic acid which exuded from his mouth would have been unmistakable.

During his brief struggle Wells called for someone to fetch a cardiac stimulant. Another officer tried to reach Headquarters by telephone but could not get through, so Whittaker yelled up the stairs to Rimmer to take a jeep. As Rimmer came down past the open door of the examination room, he saw Whittaker still grappling with the body, hoisting it up by the heels in a vain attempt to make the poison drain out, but Wells was standing back with an air of resignation. Afterwards Whittaker remarked that the doctor had been 'wet' in the way he had reacted to the emergency; he did not appreciate the speed or finality of cyanide poisoning.

Rimmer scorched off in a jeep with Osborn, but his journey was a waste of time. When he reached the hospital he found most of the doctors having a terrific party, and his request for a cardiac stimulant was met by a roar of laughter. 'There's your cardiac stimulant old boy,' somebody cried, handing him a large shot of whisky. By the time he got back to Ülzenerstrasse the drama was over.

When the prisoner keeled over in the examination room and crashed backwards to the floor, his glasses skidded off across the bare boards. As soon as the doctor had declared him dead, Austin, a dustman with an astute eye, walked over and pocketed them, triumphantly shouting 'Souvenir!' They covered the body with a blanket, and as Austin was about to go out and report to Murphy, Wells suggested acidly that, next time they wanted a German VIP searched, it might be better to sandbag him first and examine him afterwards.

The room quickly filled with people. Wells went off to find Colonel Murphy, who was still painfully hungover. 'He looked round, and with an assumed and awful dignity said, "This prisoner-of-war came into the room wearing glasses. Where are they now?" He looked suspiciously at me, then at Austin. Poor Austin, his conscience pricking him disagreeably, disgorged them before the assembled company like a naughty schoolboy.'[35] (It is interesting to note that the glasses bore a Munich optician's name, but were rimmed and not the glasses that Himmler usually wore.)

News of the suicide quickly spread. At about 1 a.m., having at last done justice to the cherished hot-pot, Rimmer slipped out to return to his unit. On the way he looked into a padre's mess, and there too, found victory celebrations underway. 'All the dodgers were there,' he reported, 'and they'd got a very nice place.' A game of whisky-bridge was in progress when Rimmer, the son of a clergyman, brought the players up short by asking if they proposed to give Himmler a decent Christian burial. One of the guests at the part was Brigadier Glyn Hughes, a fiery Welshman who was then senior medical officer in the division. He immediately telephoned Colonel Murphy who asked him to send a doctor who could certify the cause of death: he wanted a report confirming it had been suicide, and that no charge of brutality could possibly be levied against his section. Hughes brushed aside this request with typical brusqueness, remarking that cyanide poisoning was obvious to anyone and

irreversible; what they really needed was a medical identification.[36]
He did not have the facilities for a full post-mortem, he said, but in
due course he would send round a pathologist who would take
measurements and compile a report that would serve as an identification document. Not long after Hughes' call other brigadiers arrived
at the house to look at the body but, according to Whittaker, no
one seemed much concerned about what had happened, and
everyone started drinking whisky and water.

When Whittaker later came to record the evening's events in his
diary, he loyally stuck to most details of the official account. Elsewhere in his journal there are hints that he itched to tell the truth,
but he was all too aware that his words might be read by someone
in authority, and he toed the army line. According to his diary, both
he and Murphy were in the examination room at the time of the
suicide, even though he was to tell his friends that Murphy was
'soldered to the toilet'.[37] He also gave a graphic account of the needle
and thread episode:

> I smelt cyanide and knew it must be a very strong dose. We
> immediately up-ended the old bastard and got his mouth into
> the bowl of water which was there to wash the poison out.
> There were terrible groans and grunts coming from the swine.
> Colonel Murphy and I were taking it in turns to get hold of
> his tongue. All this time the Doc was working on artificial
> respiration [. . .] We had now procured a needle and cotton
> to fix his tongue. The first thing we did was to get a needle
> through his lips and we had to get it out again. Finally we got
> his tongue fixed but it was a losing battle and the evil thing
> breathed his last at 23.14 hours.[38]

Vivid though Whittaker's narrative was, most of it was fiction. No
needle or thread was passed through the dying man's tongue. If it
had been, the marks would certainly have been recorded in the
course of the thorough post-mortem examination carried out the
next day. All this was invented to make it look as if the British had
been more resourceful than they really were, and, of course, in no
way culpable.

In retrospect it is easy to criticise. The fact remains that, no doubt unsettled by his row with Murphy, Wells found himself unprepared at the critical moment. If, after he first saw the phial, Wells had given the prisoner a reassuring pat and told him to get dressed, said everything was all right, and then gone out to confer with other officers, they could at least have formed a proper plan of campaign. Then they could have tried to knock the prisoner out, or gagged him to prevent him crunching the capsule, or even resorted to subterfuge and upgraded his status, according him the deference that he would have craved – had he been Himmler.

Evidently Wells realised his errors. As soon as the crisis was over, he felt a great weight of frustration and exhaustion settle upon him. He was furious at the 'ham-fisted' manner in which the whole affair had been conducted, and the way he had been put in a false position by his inadequate briefing. He wondered bitterly why he had ever allowed himself to 'give up the best practice in the Midlands for this sort of sordid beastliness'. Some comfort arrived in the form of a general who robustly declared it an excellent thing; the country had been spared the expense of a long legal investigation into the crimes of at least one leading Nazi. But after Wells crept away to bed at 1 a.m., unable to sleep, he lay wondering what he could have done to frustrate the prisoner's intentions: 'If I had placed him against a wall so that he could not have drawn away [. . .] If I had hit him hard in the solar plexus or delivered a fierce uppercut à la Jack Johnson . . .' Sleep did not come to release him and as dawn broke he got up and went for a walk.[39] Dr Wells was excluded from all further involvement with the prisoner's death. Twice he was warned about the Official Secrets Act, and realised that he was in danger of being blamed for the débâcle. Nevertheless he had nowhere else to go, so hung about and watched the way that the photographs were being taken, or rather, as he suggested, not being taken. In his account to the Oxford Medical Society years later, he was to suggestively recall his disquiet with extraordinary prescience: 'Of what interest was it to me whether they took photographs of the incident or not and from what positions – if any – [or] whether the information should be fully released or reserved for the favourable few.'[40]

This was the first hint that something was wrong with the photographs of the corpse. Can the British Army's peculiarly oblique approach to identification photographs explain the immediate reaction of several of Himmler's acquaintances, such as his friend's wife Henriette von Schirach, who when first shown the pictures in an American news sheet failed to recognise the corpse?[41] Or might it be that inadequate photographs were what they were after?

All that night the corpse lay on the floor, naked except for the blanket thrown over it. An armed sentry stood guard. The following day, 24 May, a succession of sightseers came to visit, some on official business, some not. As before, the army's version of what took place bore little relation to the true sequence of events.

The first party to arrive at 9.30 a.m. were a mixed bunch, among them some padres from the mess Rimmer had dropped into on his way home. They had come to look at the body, but the guards on the door allowed them only a brief glimpse from the hall. Some women ATS officers followed, and the blanket over the corpse's lower half was lifted as a chorus of lads of the Defence Company gave a suitably ribald commentary. It is not possible to establish why the post-mortem was not carried out that morning. The reason may be simply that after a tremendous spate of parties, no one had been in a fit state earlier to make the necessary arrangements.

A short conference was called at 1.30 p.m. by a partially rejuvenated Colonel Murphy. He wanted to work out a party line to present to the world. This task was hardly made easier by a rumour that had reached the press the night before, that the Reichsführer had been captured as a result of a carefully planned operation and was alive in British hands. Murphy had clearly been shaken by the suicide and the fact that he had not been in effective charge of the prisoner at the critical moment.

Among those summoned to the meeting was Dr Wells, who received his first warning: strict orders not to discuss the affair with anyone. Even if people started pointing out what they saw as discrepancies in the official account, they were not to be answered.[42] Also present were Lieutenant-Colonel Stapleton, Colonel Murphy's second-in-command, Lieutenant-Colonel Joe Ewart, and two other unidentified officers. Murphy set out the agenda. They must curtail exposure as far as possible, and get the body buried. At 1.40 p.m. an unwell Colonel Murphy once again retired.

Meanwhile, Whittaker and Austin were in charge of the body and helping Lieutenant Jack Ashworth organise photography by Sergeant Carl Sutton of the Photography Unit and Sergeant McCandle and Ken Gordon of Pathé. Sutton propped up the corpse into a position of calm repose after Whittaker had re-dressed it in a shirt, flinging a brown army blanket over the lower body. Ashworth had already sent out messages to the Americans and the Russians confirming that Himmler was indeed in British hands – stone cold dead. As usual, the Americans had reacted promptly. The first to arrive was a liaison officer, at about 2 p.m., just as the filming was finishing. The delightful raconteur Normal Whittaker had an armchair and side tables brought in along with the mandatory whisky. Carl Sutton captured the moment on film.[43] Later the same photograph was to be used to show Americans 'identifying the body'. Then a Soviet liaison officer came to view the body from the Russians' military mission at Flensburg. When Captain Kutchin reached 31a Ülzenerstrasse soon after 4 p.m., he found Colonel Murphy still strictly unavailable, and Ashworth had left for Flensburg, so the Russian visitor saw the corpse in the presence of only Major Whittaker.[44] A later drawing in the *Illustrated London News* depicted three Soviet officers standing over the corpse, 'commissioned by Marshal Zhukhov to inspect the body of Himmler'. Captions identified the visitors as Colonel Gorbuschin, Lieutenant-Colonel Levley and Captain Kutchin. This whole episode was invented, a story conflating this and a later event. Captain Kutchin was in no sense an expert and carried no photographs or records which he might have used to make an identification. Nor did any Russian, as the news story claimed, 'grudgingly agree that the corpse might be Himmler's'. All Kutchin said to Whittaker was that he would return with his superiors.[45] He went back to Flensburg, where he sent a message to Soviet headquarters in Berlin for the formidable Colonel Vasili Ivanovich Gorbuschin, Marshal Zhukhov's poetry-loving chief Nazi hunter.

That evening, two or three other reporters, and Chester Wilmott visited. Wilmott's BBC broadcast went out at 8 p.m. The next morning the post-mortem was carried out. At 9.30 a.m. Brigadier Hughes, the senior medical officer, telephoned his counterpart in the Royal Army Dental Corps, the jovial and astute Colonel Browne, asking him to take medical and dental records of the corpse for the purposes of identification.[46] This was a normal request and did not indicate that anyone had doubts about who the corpse might be. At that stage it seemed everyone firmly believed it was Himmler. Making records was purely a matter of routine. At 10.15 a.m. Browne collected materials from the Lüneburg Military Hospital, including rubber and plaster of Paris, and brought along his enthusiastic assistant, Major George Attkins. At 31a Ülzenerstrasse they were met by Captain M. C. Bond, the young army pathologist sent to do the post-mortem, commanded by Hughes to 'identify the bastard carefully and record everything including needle marks.' With no disrespect to Bond, who did an excellent job, it must be said that the choice of pathologist was strange. Right on his own doorstep he had a leading forensic pathologist, who had for the past few months specialised in the gruesome task of gleaning information from war victims' remains. Dr Ian Morris was at the time attached to Unit No 2 of the War Crimes Commission, and had recently spent much of his time in Belsen concentration camp, that had been liberated by the Allies in April.[47] On 25 May he happened to be in Lüneburg, along with the two large caravans that housed his mobile forensic unit, only two hundred yards from the house. The presence of this eminent pathologist with all his equipment was hardly a military secret, indeed there had been much talk in the mess about the unpleasant specimens the unit had handled. But no attempt was made to contact him or solicit his advice.

Browne, Attkins and Bond set to work in Ülzenerstrasse at 11.00 a.m., with two guards still posted outside the room. First they pulled the corpse to the window to get better light. Bond then measured the body recording every minute detail. The examination was meticulous; he even recorded the amount of hair in the man's ears, but he did not have any data with which to compare his findings. He did not even have the SHAEF card, with its photograph. Browne and Attkins then recorded the state of the corpse's dentition. As there was no furniture in the room, Whittaker's unofficial hospitality suite now dismantled, Bond had to write his findings on sheets of paper laid against the parquet floor.[48] Browne and Attkins proceeded to make a death mask in latex rubber. (The purpose of this seems obscure, other than to provide a souvenir. One copy of this mask was sent to General Eisenhower's headquarters and another to this day resides in the Royal Army Dental Corps Museum at Aldershot, donated by Colonel Browne.) The examiners completed their work and left the house at about 1.15 p.m.

After conducting such a meticulous post-mortem, the curiosity of Browne, Bond and Attkins about the result was aroused to varying degrees. Captain Bond died long before his views could be canvassed, and it is not known whether he raised the issue of identity with anyone. Attkins was a different matter. His wife recalled that he wrote repeatedly, if sporadically, to the Ministry, and at one time even went to Germany to see if he could find any comparative dental data on Himmler.[49] He remained curious for the rest of his life. Although Browne never thought the identity was really in question, he was full of enthusiasm 'for being involved in a piece of history'.[50] He was irked that no one seemed to share his enthusiasm and surprised by Colonel Murphy's lack of interest. He recalled that when Attkins had suggested they take fingerprints, he was told that the Royal Military Police would complete that job, only to find out several days later that the RMPs had never been asked. No fingerprints were ever taken from the body.

Later that afternoon on 25 May, Colonel Murphy held an eccentric form of press conference from 16.30 to 17.00 hours. Instead of meeting the assembled reporters in an appropriate room, he walked them up and down a nearby lane, talking rapidly on the move. Anyone might have thought he wanted to avoid a face-to-face confrontation. His task was awkward, for half the press men that had arrived had not heard the BBC news reporting the prisoner's death. At five o'clock they eventually got a chance to glimpse the body, fighting like animals to get to the door to look across at the corpse, which was now dressed. Nobody was allowed into the room. In the scramble Rex North of the *Daily Express* and Neil McDermott fought over the black eye patch and glasses which were lying on a chair near the door, just within reach, but the glasses were retained by the guards.

At 6 p.m. CSM Austin was telling reporters his all too believable tale of how he had had the idea of sandbagging the prisoner before the final examination began. Whether he had picked up that idea from Dr Wells we shall never know. In any event, his story laid the foundations for many of the falsehoods that were to follow. Austin, being a warrant officer, and a former dustman, carried salt-of-the-earth credibility. He was the ideal person to put over the official Army version of events. But the story was already beginning to invite sardonic remarks in the mess about Austin, Murphy's pet. Whatever Murphy's suspicions and motives, he became extremely keen to dispose of the evidence. 'Put the body under the earth,' he told Whittaker. 'As few people to know the location as possible.'[51]

Accordingly, in the early hours of 26 May, a 15cwt Bedford truck backed up from inside the park behind the houses in which the Defence Company was quartered, getting right behind number 29, the house next to 31a Ülzenerstrasse. The body, which had been wrapped in camouflage netting and bound with wire, was taken out of the back of the house, down the steps, shielded from prying eyes. With Sergeant Weston driving and Ottery in the back of the lorry, they then drove behind the back of Ülzenerstrasse, and through the park gates. Their hooded lights dipped, they followed the jeep driven by Norman Whittaker, the large figure of Austin filling the passenger seat, and set off to find a burial site.

Whittaker's macho diary entry read, 'Took the body out in a truck for its last ride. Hell of a job to find a lonely spot. Anyway we did find one and threw the old basket into the hole which we had dug. We had wrapped the thing in a camouflage net, the press are still asking as to when we are going to have the funeral!' The more moderate and reasoned version he later gave his friend Norman Rimmer was far more specific and made much more sense. According to this account, having unwrapped the corpse and tipped it out of the camouflage netting, which Whittaker thought 'would only help serve identify the corpse if found', they rolled it into the grave. Then they had to 'reposition the damn thing because the legs stuck out'[52] before filling in the grave, and tamping it down firmly. The excess earth was scattered around before the whole area was covered with leaves and sticks to disguise the site.

Later that day Whittaker compiled a report on the night's activities, which he handed in with a map, giving a set of co-ordinates and directions to the site of the grave. Colonel Murphy was rid of his body, but he was far from the end of his difficulties; the hasty, premature burial now brought down the wrath of the Allies upon him. The first wave of trouble came at 10.30 a.m. on 26 May with the arrival of a three-man Russian delegation. Its leader was Colonel Gorbuschin who had come hotfoot from Berlin via the Soviet mission in Flensburg, alerted by the summons from Captain Kutchin. Zhukhov sent him to establish beyond doubt that Himmler was dead. At 31a Ülzenerstrasse he was met by Jack Ashworth, who had the unenviable task of telling him that the body he had come to inspect had already been buried. Gorbuschin demanded to see Colonel Murphy, who though available, once again declined to meet with his, this time senior, Russian colleague. Gorbuschin's demands for immediate exhumation were ignored. At 12.30 p.m. Norman Whittaker returned and 'walked right into it'. At least he had the sense to realise that the Russians had no idea that he had been actively engaged in burying the evidence. After a futile further hour's wait the Soviet officers departed in thoroughly bad humour.[53]

The great irony of this wasted visit was that Gorbuschin almost certainly had some of Himmler's actual dental records in his possession. They had been picked up from Berlin on 9 May with those of other Nazi leaders. Having come specifically to identify the body, it seems certain that he must have brought these documents and X-rays along with him. If anyone was qualified to decide with certainty whether or not it was Himmler, then Gorbuschin, with his team of Soviet pathologists back in Berlin, was the one person in a position to provide a conclusive answer. As things transpired, he was not even allowed a copy of the dental chart drawn by Attkins, even though it is most likely he demanded to see all such evidence whilst awaiting a decision on exhumation.

For ten years after the war, through the medium of *Izvestia*, the Russians propagated the fiction that Himmler had in fact been captured by two Soviet Intelligence officers, Vasili Gubarev and Ivan Siderov, who had then handed him over to the British. Perhaps this story was put out in pique at the treatment meted out to Gorbuschin's team. More than thirty years after the event, the *Lüneburger Heide Landeszeitung* ran a story claiming that two Kripo (criminal police) agents had also viewed the body, and taken fingerprints and a death mask. It would have required Colonel Murphy's permission for the Royal Military Police to have contacted the Kripo (a force not recognised at the time) before any such procedure could have been carried out; it is difficult to believe Murphy would have allowed this. Because of the total dissolution of the SS state, the local police would have had no way of corroborating any fingerprints with SS records. No such fingerprints have ever surfaced and Colonel Browne was adamant that the Kripo were not involved when he made the face masks. No evidence of such a visit appears in any other records, and this story seems certain to be fiction.

Nearly an hour after the Russians' departure two Americans arrived at 31a Ülzenerstrasse, just before 3 p.m. They brought all their documentation about Himmler and the news that they held his brother Gebhard and mistress Hedwig Potthast, who were available for identification.[54] They were dumbfounded to learn the body had been buried, but proved more difficult to shake off than the Russians. Unable to hide behind the language barrier, Colonel Murphy was forced to meet them. After a heated exchange they eventually left, seething with resentment. At 6.15 p.m., Whittaker was telephoned that he 'might have to dig up the body as the Americans had caught Himmler's brother Gebhard who might have to identify the corpse'. Needless to say, no such action was taken and the grieving brother and mistress were never given the chance to see the body.

Norman Whittaker was, for all his bawdy sense of humour, a fundamentally quiet man sometimes lacking in confidence. He would often become serious and suddenly embarrassed when made the centre of attention, and display a nostalgic tendency that seemed out of place in the earthy Lancastrian. When back in London after the war he confided to his friend Norman Rimmer that he had been 'ashamedly close to tears' at his demob party in Bünde in August 45.[55] He had loved the excitement of the war, and adored the sheer difference of life in post-war Germany. Peace was proving to be a miserable anticlimax. So he was delighted when War Ministry officials approached him and asked him to give his time again for king and country. They needed him to guide people to the exact site of the grave. Excited, he told his closest associates in 'C' mess (the band of officers in military intelligence who landed at Crouilly together). Most were too happily employed in civilian life to be particularly impressed or interested. Eventually, he found his best 'C' mess friend Norman Rimmer (who had been in hospital), who became Whittaker's confidant for years to come. Their meetings in pubs in South Kensington, London, continued until two years before Whittaker's early death in 1958.

Whittaker told Rimmer about his summons to the War Office where he was briefed on his expected role, and how he was then flown out overnight at the beginning of 1946 to Bückeburg airport with some 'Foreign Office wallahs'. He recounted the story of his miserable, icy journey to the gravesite on the Lüneburg Heath, and the astonishing appearance of Himmler's right-hand man, Walter Schellenberg. Any hopes of being included in the drama were quickly dashed. Excluded from Schellenberg's remarks at the graveside, remarks which the corporal assisting him had obviously shared, he had been glad when he and his men were left to take the body back to Hannover. Cold and disgruntled, he did not need to be told, as various officials were later so keen to stress, that he had just witnessed another 'non-event'.

It was early evening by the time Whittaker got back to his mess, still unfed. He had had another hour's wait after dropping off the body at the morgue. After dinner he retired to his room and carefully marked the actual site of the grave on a large-scale map that one of the corporals had given him. Later that evening he was told by someone, probably an SIS officer, that he should prepare for a Board of Inquiry to be held at Hannover. He seized the opportunity to ask for more salubrious quarters and to his astonishment, the request was granted. But there was a stern reminder; he was responsible for the secrecy of the grave site.

Early next morning he attended another interview with the same, but now far less friendly individual. When he raised concerns about the empty grave's security, he was told that if the Germans found the site the Foreign Office would put out an official denial. That evening Whittaker was taken to the British Military Hospital in Hannover where another tight-lipped man asked him a few simple questions about the suicide. After dinner in the mess he was presented with his passes and told that he would be leaving for Bückeburg airport at mid-morning the next day. He would not be needed for the Board of Inquiry after all, and would be notified if required in the future. The chance of reliving the most exciting moments of his life, and giving evidence to a full-blown Board, was rapidly diminishing. Whittaker flew back to Britain where he recounted his bathetic tale to his friend.

Rimmer sympathised with Whittaker's disappointment. All the same, he had a cushy job in the War Crimes Commission, so it was not all that bad. A later meeting in a South Kensington pub yielded a few more surprises. The Germans *had* supposedly found the grave site on Lüneburg Heath. Whittaker had been bemused to read that they had removed a body from the grave, claiming the corpse was Himmler's. The British Foreign Office put out a statement in Germany decrying the discovery, but to Whittaker's consternation they confirmed to him, as unofficial guardian of the gravesite, that the site had indeed been uncovered. The civil servant he spoke to evaded any comments that would acknowledge that he knew Himmler's body could not have been found, as of course it was no longer buried there. Rimmer and Whittaker decided that someone had helpfully supplied the extra ingredients for this miraculous discovery. Corpses were, tragically, readily available in Germany at that time.

Their conclusions may not have been pure fantasy. In the course of my research into the peculiarities of Himmler's death, I wrote to the Foreign Office to request permission, as a qualified surgeon, to disinter Himmler's corpse. Of course they refused, referring in their letter to the discovery of the grave by the Germans; clearly their files did not record that this was contrary to their official statements at the time. Permission was denied on the grounds that 'We have no record of his identity having previously been questioned.'[56] As I had not actually posed the question of identity, it seemed odd that they should presume, albeit correctly, that this was my motive. The Foreign Office helpfully added that Himmler's brother Gebhard had identified the body. Yet when another author questioned Gebhard Himmler, he denied he was ever shown his brother's body.[57]

After the war persistent rumours circulated in army and intelligence circles which claimed that, due to official disquiet about the circumstances of the death, some kind of secret tribunal had been held. Willi Frischauer caught wind of the inquiry in the course of his research soon after the war for his biography of Himmler. Because he did not understand British Army procedure, he presumed this to mean that there had been a secret court martial, a contradiction in terms. When he asked the Ministry of Defence if such an event had occurred, oddly they replied that nobody had doubted the body was Himmler's, adding that Gebhard Himmler had identified it as his brother. It is a suggestive echo.

When I started my investigation I picked up the same rumours and thought they had no basis, until an old Foreign Office source confirmed that he knew of two people who claimed to have been notified that they would be required to attend exactly such an event. The Military Board of Inquiry is tailor-made for circumstances such as unnatural deaths abroad, deaths other than by military action and deaths of prisoners of war. It is attractive to the government because the public are excluded and its findings are never published. In short, it is the perfect instrument for asking difficult questions when the answers are potentially embarrassing. Strictly speaking, in the case of Heinrich Himmler such an inquiry ought to have automatically taken place immediately after the suicide. We do not know why there was a delay. Colonel Murphy would not have welcomed further scrutiny and he was clearly a favourite of Montgomery's, but there is no evidence for that being the reason it took so long for them to plan the inquiry.

According to the regulations for a board of inquiry, 'The inquiry is to ensure that the medical officer of the Unit concerned is asked to give his opinion.' Dr Wells had returned to his medical practice when preliminary arrangements were made. He was apparently contacted only once in person, by a young captain who told him to hold himself in readiness for a summons in the New Year.[58] Wells was highly suspicious about appearing at the inquiry, believing he would be made a scapegoat for the disastrous suicide. He was so sure of this that he immediately wrote a detailed account of his involvement, which later became the subject of his talk at Oxford. Hearing nothing more about the inquiry, he remained convinced to the end of his days that somewhere lay a report blaming him for the prisoner's death.

According to Mrs Attkins, wife of the dentist who compiled the report with Colonel Browne, the young officer who came around to deliver notification of a board of inquiry said a Colonel Scott was the convening officer, from whom they would soon hear more. Unfortunately, Attkins was not about at the time of the visit and heard no more about it despite attempts to find out further details. Colonel Browne had been the senior officer at the post-mortem and should have been involved.[59] Although he heard rumours, he was never contacted. He felt this was entirely in keeping, declaring that the 'whole suicide was a botched affair'. The only officer to deny any knowledge of the inquiry was Colonel M. A. C. Osborne, who had also claimed in the journal *Ça Ira* that he had been present at the burial, contrary to the accounts given by the burial party.[60]

Brigadier J. S. K. Boyd, who became Chief of Army Pathological Services in 1945, had known nothing of Captain Bond's involvement in the suicide, and was rather surprised as the Army Pathological Service was a relatively small and communicative section.[61] Since Boyd was an extremely well-regarded pathologist even outside army circles, it is doubly surprising that he was bypassed when one of his men was involved at such a level. He was somewhat taken aback to be asked, in early December 1945, about Captain Bond's competence.

Although fully supportive of his junior, he was concerned to learn that it was Bond who had given the definitive pathological report on Heinrich Himmler. Boyd was given a copy of the report and asked whether he felt anything further could be done. He suggested that the teeth seemed in good order and would still be in a reasonable state of preservation. He did not hesitate to recommend the best forensic expert for checking on the accuracy of the post-mortem, Dr Ian Morris, with whom he had worked closely. Moreover, Boyd knew his irascible colleague, who did not suffer fools gladly, was the last person that any secret service could bend; Captain Bond's reputation was assured.

Although Dr Morris was recommended in December, he was given very little notice and irritated to be summoned to Hannover at a time when he was busy compiling his extensive data from the concentration camps for the Nuremberg trial.[62] He was told that a report on the corpse of Heinrich Himmler was needed to assess an officer's competence, and surmised it was for a court martial. He was to stay in Hannover for two days, during which time he would have no chance to involve other colleagues in the nearby War Crimes Commission, which he only left in November 1945. Dr Morris recalled that two civilians were present when he had conducted his post-mortem examination, one of whom he thought, but could not be sure, had been in contact with him previously, and the other a morgue attendant. His clearest memory of the corpse was that the skin and outer tissues were in a reasonably good condition, in keeping, he said, with whatever he was told. He remembered that 'no one seemed to know what they wanted'. He was asked to find scars somewhere on the head but 'The skin was slimy and swollen everywhere and there were limits to what I could say'. Dr Morris had not been given Dr Bond's medical report, nor the dental drawing by Browne and Attkins. What he had been given were dental X-rays of German origin, which simply served to anger him. There were very few teeth left in the corpse: 'There may have been some at the back but that's all.' Perhaps someone had wanted some ghoulish souvenirs.

The thought of souvenirs had certainly been in the minds of those in charge at the time of the suicide. 'What a good thing I didn't let Jimmy take out those teeth,' wrote Major Whittaker in his diary.[63] He makes no further reference to souvenirs or to deliberate destruction of the dental evidence. Colonel Browne knew nothing of missing teeth either. It is one of many insoluble mysteries. Identification by comparing X-rays of any remaining teeth, such as wisdom teeth, and the architecture of the jaw and skull was still possible. This was exactly what Dr Morris's two-page report had suggested. But Dr Morris had his trial to get back to, and had tolerated more fools than he could bear. When he was told that he was not wanted in person for the inquiry, he left clearcut instructions on how they might resolve their doubts and whom to ask to do the necessary: anyone but him. It seems no board of inquiry ever happened – another muddle to add to the confusion and incompetence surrounding the death of Heinrich Himmler.

II

Operation Globetrotter

It was not until long after the aborted Board of Inquiry and the secret visit to the grave site by SS Brigadeführer Walter Schellenberg that anyone had a clue about who in MI6 had been so interested in Himmler's death. The matter was resurrected when I met Dr Carl Marcus in Mönchengladbach-Rheydt.[1] Marcus was a man of exceptional intelligence. He had been second-in-command to the very best intelligence agent in Germany. Even in the maelstrom of the war, Wilhelm Jahnke had managed to run his own private intelligence agency, the Jahnke Büro, based in Berlin, the heart of authoritarian Nazi Germany. Moreover, this agency fed highly select titbits of information, personally chosen according to Jahnke's designs, to Himmler, Heydrich, Göring, Hess and Ribbentrop. They were delivered in person, so Jahnke could carefully monitor their digestion and nanny any unpleasant wind they produced.

Before the war Jahnke had made a fortune in California, shipping back the bodies of dead Chinese to their grieving relatives in China at a high price. In Nazi Germany he kept chocolates in his impressive safe, where they could be raided by Müller's ever suspicious Gestapo, while sensitive papers were deliberately included in his routine junk, scattered about his desk.

Marcus learnt much from his master. He had impeccable credentials to be a British agent. He was arrested during Müller's investigation of the 20 July plot against Hitler, and had the distinction of being the first officer held in prison in his SS Sturmbannführer uniform. Himmler immediately countermanded his arrest, personally dismissed the charges and ordered his release. As many of the others involved in the plot ended up dangling on meat hooks in the

Plötensee prison in Berlin, Dr Marcus had every reason to be eternally grateful to Himmler. It was a debt of gratitude that understandably he would have preferred to live without.

Marcus's work as a British agent had long been known to his boss. He was, in essence, only continuing Jahnke's own work. Himmler, Brigadeführer Walter Schellenberg and Admiral Canaris had tolerated Jahnke's eccentricities and encouraged his contacts with foreign intelligence services to assist their own ends. When Himmler obtained Marcus' release he hardly did so in ignorance. Marcus was well aware when he fled to France later in 1944 that his escape was permitted. Before he left he had been encouraged, in a cat-and-mouse conversation with Walter Schellenberg, to take with him the 'goodwill of the SS towards achieving a rapid effective understanding with the Allies'.[2] Schellenberg hinted at his own important role in negotiations with the Allies; Marcus, refusing to be drawn, did not question Schellenberg on this remarkable admission and had no intention of mentioning it to the Allies and being tainted by association.[3] Marcus presented startled Allied intelligence in Paris with a personal letter from Lord Vansittart. He was whisked away to London for a haircut in 'Toppers', before meeting the head of MI5, Sir Stewart Menzies, in the basement of the Reform Club. A learned snob, taught a love for the good life as a student at Cambridge University, Marcus' eccentricities and understanding of the British ensured his position as head of his own intelligence section in the British zone of post-war Germany. So dubious were some of the actions of his section, so peculiar and specific some of its requirements, and so high Dr Marcus' alleged connections, such as Vansittart and Menzies, that there is a hardly surprising lack of corroborative documentation. His main concern was counter-espionage against the Soviets, building a network of agents, including many former Nazis who would also help him to monitor, and if necessary eliminate, resurgent groups. Given the sensitivity of his anti-Soviet activities in particular, which the British would deny any knowledge of should he ever be exposed, it is understandable that powerful men who would not wish to be implicated should make sure Marcus did not appear in any records. Despite the importance of Marcus' post-war position, neither MI6 Chief Sir Dick White, to whom I spoke at length about Marcus' exploits, nor indeed British Secret Service adviser Robert Cecil, had apparently ever heard of him. This disquieting lack of recognition extended to the German Federal Republic, which refused Dr Marcus a state pension. Anyone who knows how meagre is MI6's recognition of past services can readily appreciate Marcus' later financial circumstances.

When I first met Dr Marcus in the late 1970s he mentioned Adrian Liddell Hart, whose work in charge of an intelligence section in Berlin had been affected by Marcus' activities. Liddell Hart had long known of and wished to meet the German spymaster, and I arranged a meeting. The two eccentrics got on famously. Marcus loved the fact that Liddell Hart lived in 'The Castle, Stroud', and his card later enjoyed a prominent position on the mantelpiece (little did he realise that it was a flat near the town centre). They discussed Kim Philby's unannounced visit to Marcus at the end of 1946, a visit that laid the foundation for a costly exercise within an exercise that Marcus and Philby intended the American Secret Service would unwittingly pay for.

The British ran their own Intelligence network based at the Bad Oeynhausen Divisional HQ in north Germany. Dr Marcus was left in splendid isolation as Mayor of Mönchengladbach-Rheydt in the British-controlled zone near Düsseldorf, in charge of a civil service staffed almost exclusively by his own men. This independent power base in the heart of West Germany gave Marcus a tremendous advantage, one he milked to the full. Marcus' rationale was simple. He felt that anyone who was anyone in the Third Reich would have made provisions for early retirement. He felt that his men were best occupied in trying to identify and assess wealthy newcomers to the banking, financial and industrial chaos that was post-war Germany. There were obviously those who were profiteering from black-market activities who attracted his attention, but he felt they were less important, and less potentially threatening, than those who moved in legitimate circles. He claimed to have had an agent in every bank of significance in the British sector. By concentrating on the newly registered wealth and activities he hoped to find out who were the most powerful figures. He emphasised his isolation by insisting that official British presence be kept at an absolute minimum, so as not to scare off interested parties from a series of meetings that he hosted. It was a dangerous game. Marcus would identify his targets, wealthy former Nazis, and work hard at turning them into his agents. He would introduce them to one another, creating tame clusters of anti-Allied resistance that he would monitor carefully to identify where the money and power was coming from, and who were the strongest leaders. This information helped him to neutralise the threat they might pose. Marcus was always careful not to become personally involved, maintaining the low profile that has hidden him from history.

Dr Lörner, one of his contacts in Hamburg, who was trying to trace the monies emanating from businesses associated with the giant SS concern, Deutsche Ausrüstungswerke GmbH, told Marcus of substantial amounts of money being sent to Zurich. Apparently they stemmed from the sale of paintings, jewellery and a collection of Persian carpets that allegedly belonged to the legendary Léon Degrelle, handsome Belgian Waffen SS hero. Oddly, according to Marcus, Degrelle was not known to be interested in carpets; Himmler, on the other hand, had a substantial collection. When Hansen, a contact in Madrid, checked on Degrelle Marcus discovered he was at the centre of a neo-Nazi organisation. He was in contact with ex-Nazis in South America and openly bragged about the number of leaders who had survived the funeral pyre of the Third Reich and who were going to rise again to glory.

What interested Marcus most was that Degrelle claimed he was working to Himmler's master plan. These extravagant boasts made Degrelle both a cult figure and the focus of attention of several intelligence agencies. One of Dr Marcus' agents, posing as a wealthy Hamburg businessman, made contact with a banker codenamed Drexel, whose own SS background was being investigated. Drexel took him to a house on Lüneburg Heath, where he was offered more than a dozen Persian carpets. Drexel confirmed the carpets had belonged to Degrelle. The agent overdid it. His avid interest in further acquisitions of this sort frightened off Drexel. Nevertheless, enquiries revealed that the house belonged to the Ahlers family, at whose home Klaus Barbie's mother was later found to be living.[4] According to Dr Marcus, it did not take long to discover that Klaus Barbie was seen visiting a home for the blind near Marburg. He was in the company of Christoff Naumann SD who, we now know, first met up with Barbie in August 1945 at Bad Pyrmont, a beautiful spa town in the hills near Detmold.

A few months later, Marcus discovered that Barbie was staying in a house at 35 Baerfüstrasse in Marburg. He noted with interest that Barbie was often seen with an SS Captain Schaeffer, who had also previously worked in the SD, and was a former adjutant of Léon Degrelle. They were seen together with a man eventually identified as Dr Wilkenning, an Oberscharführer (Quartermaster Sergeant) SS who was quickly picked up and interrogated by Dr Marcus' agents.[5] This was always Marcus' strategy; find the weak link and exploit it, leaving the stronger party to go about their business unawares to lead to further important connections.

Wilkenning co-operated fully and quickly admitted to being in contact with Ludolf Alversleben-Schochwitz, a former SS adjutant to Himmler, who was himself promptly arrested. Questioning revealed that Alversleben-Schochwitz reported on a regular basis to a lakeside villa in Zurich, and often stayed in a house on the slopes of Zürichsberg. His early post-war visits to a Swiss banker known as 'Braun' were guaranteed trouble-free thanks to a contact in the Swiss police in Zurich. He would be met on the border by a high-ranking Swiss officer named Saby, and shepherded to the Grossmünster cathedral, where Annie Zwingli would meet him and escort him to the villa. He proudly claimed to have bought a fourth-floor apartment in a block directly opposite the Grossmünster and had finally been granted Swiss citizenship.

Marcus decided to organise the escape of Alversleben-Schochwitz from custody with a message that he sought co-operation with the leaders of his group in Switzerland in the creation of an efficient anti-Soviet intelligence net. However, Alversleben-Schochwitz immediately headed off for the region of Davos and, as far as Marcus knew, he never returned, nor did he ever hear from him again. Dr

Wilkenning was the next to be picked up, and he and Schaeffer agreed to become British agents. However, neither thought that they were suitable to recruit Klaus Barbie, of whom they seemed rather afraid. Klaus Barbie was the major prize, so Marcus decided to use his best former SS agent, Hoffmann. This highly intelligent man had worked for the propaganda department of Radio Bratislava and was a particularly smooth talker. Naumann, by that time also a British agent, accompanied Hoffmann to Berleburg in August 1946 where they met with Schaeffer and Wilkenning. Hoffmann's outstanding contacts with the British were promoted to Schaeffer by Wilkenning and Naumann in an attempt to get Schaeffer to persuade Barbie to join the group. Their activities under the mantle of British protection were aimed at communists in Germany, mirroring Barbie's wartime role. Hoffmann had been given civilian status, thanks to Marcus, and carried a handwritten letter from Marcus certifying that Hoffmann had been one of Jahnke's outstanding agents.

Barbie was persuaded to meet Hoffmann, who showed him another letter from Major Cook of British Intelligence in Bad Godesberg near Bonn. This was designed to reassure Barbie that working for the British would be financially beneficial as well as protecting him from arrest for his actions in the war, and any future neo-Nazi activities. Barbie fell for it and enrolled as a British agent. Unfortunately this carried its own problems for Marcus. It was not his habit ever to get personally involved with his agents, so Barbie was run by Hoffmann. As a result, Hoffmann's importance to Marcus, and visits to his home, had increased greatly. When Marcus came home one day to find his wife disporting himself with his key agent, it was too much to bear. Hoffmann's visits ceased and, claimed Marcus, the affair more or less finished his interest in Klaus Barbie. Marcus had become suspicious of Barbie's influence on Hoffmann, and determined to foist Barbie on to the unsuspecting Americans, removing him from the British zone entirely.[6] Even as he deliberated on this issue, Major Cook informed him that two women had been found passing messages to a warder at the Allied internment camp at Neuengamme. They were intercepted by a British agent, an ex-Hitler Youth official, before they reached their intended target –

Heinrich Springer, Himmler's adjutant and a prisoner in the camp. The two women turned out to be the wife and niece of a Hamburg banker, at whose house they found a young woman called Juliana, Alversleben-Schochwitz's daughter.

Major Cook encouraged sufficient openness at the camp to allow for a regular flow of information that might be diverted in this way. They discovered authoritative messages from Zurich exhorting Springer to establish contact with SS Brigadeführer Erhardt Müller, who was a member of a neo-Nazi group in Hamburg. He was also to contact other groups in Dortmund, Fulda and Kassel. The messages gave clear instructions about what he should do when sprung from the camp. Although the messages were from Alversleben-Schochwitz, what seized Marcus's attention most was the presence of tell-tale additions in the margin of one note. Although not signed, they 'were either written by Himmler, or someone who knew what effects those marginal additions would have on those accustomed to seeing them'.[7] Marcus was more than familiar with Himmler's marginal additions from his days with Jahnke. Coupled with the contemptuous self-confident tone of the orders, these strange marginalia prompted Dr Marcus to send a report to London. He warned that neo-Nazi groups in the British zone of post-war Germany were showing signs of greater organisation and receiving messages from Switzerland that suggested the resurrection of the Third Reich and its most frightening ghost, Heinrich Himmler.

Thanks to the messages sent to Springer, Marcus was able to entrap several of the groups mentioned by Alversleben-Schochwitz. One of the most effective informants, the sickly-looking 38-year-old Kreisamtleiter (district branch officer), Heinz Clöde, did the honours. Clöde gave the appearance of zany fanaticism, complete with all the accompanying jargon, and easily broke into the Müller group. By the end of December he had supplied Marcus with two other useful agents from the group, and told him the whereabouts of another fourteen members.

In the bitterly cold winter of late 1946, Kim Philby paid Dr Marcus a visit. It was an unprecedented occurrence.[8] Philby claimed to be on an official visit to Germany, yet he spent an entire afternoon and evening with Marcus in a Düsseldorf hotel. It was clear that Philby had studied Marcus' report. During the first hour he was extremely offhand, initially even keeping on his raincoat as if to impart a sense of haste and impermanence to the meeting. Marcus recalled, 'We didn't make any pretence about the dislike – it was mutual.'[9] Philby began to mellow as the hotel cognac did its work. He started off by decrying the possibility that Himmler might still be alive. While 'anything was possible', Himmler was, he assured Marcus, 'certainly dead'. Raising the very idea was 'werewolf mentality'. Marcus was rather surprised by these protestations, for as he told Liddell Hart and me, 'I had never thought otherwise; it was all *Quatsch* [non-sense]'. Philby then brought up Walter Schellenberg, Brigadeführer SS, who he said was playing an opportunistic game to try and split his prosecutors and who, though incarcerated, might well have been the source of these rumours. He confided that the British might have foolishly afforded Walter Schellenberg the necessary ammunition on which to base the myth. As Marcus understood it, 'some sadist had shown the body to Schellenberg, who saw his opportunity to create trouble'.[10] Philby dismissed Schellenberg as a smooth-talking self-aggrandiser. 'He had', said Marcus, 'nothing but contempt for him.'

As Marcus recalled, Philby's main concern was the existence of a neo-Nazi network that threatened to organise itself so thoroughly that it would soon be beyond British control. An attempt to release Springer seemed imminent, and Philby suggested instituting lax security to facilitate the escape, laying on a surveillance team to monitor Springer's subsequent actions. This would also, perhaps, lead them to a definitive answer about the question of Himmler's survival (though Philby was keen throughout not to let this appear a serious concern). Marcus suggested that they would need the superior resources of the Americans to enable them to observe Springer properly and to thoroughly investigate his contacts. Moreover, Springer's trail to Zurich might well lead into the American zone. Philby was not keen and decided the Americans were not in any circumstances to learn of the true nature of the exercise. Marcus, somewhat taken aback by his vehemence, suggested that if the British and Americans were co-operating in a larger intelligence exercise, then covert British surveillance in the American zone by a British team would pass unnoticed. That was what they eventually agreed to do.

Philby was also very touchy about operations in Switzerland, particularly Zurich, where the Americans had so many more agents in the field. He instructed Marcus to liaise with a 'Mr Cruickshank' in Zurich, who would be solely responsible for dealing with the Zurich aspects of this neo-Nazi organisation because, Philby claimed, of possible political repercussions. Switzerland apart, Marcus was to get untrammelled British assistance for their bold new venture, 'Operation Globetrotter'. The meeting ended, the bottle of Asbach empty, with the two men agreeing on 'the importance of destroying the myth before it caught hold, as Himmler's survival was [by now] highly improbable'.[11] In the space of an hour Himmler's death had moved from being a certainty to a probability.

Operation Globetrotter fitted in well with Marcus' own plans to pass Klaus Barbie on to the Americans. To scotch rumours that Barbie was working for Hoffmann and the British, Marcus arranged for Clöde to meet with Barbie in Hamburg where he introduced him to a neo-Nazi called Acker. By prior agreement with Barbie, after the meeting Marcus' team swooped in and arrested him, throwing him in jail.[12] He was allowed to escape shortly afterwards and it was so easy that it later attracted considerable interest from American Intelligence. When eventually confronted by their suspicions, Barbie cleverly said that he too suspected that someone had let him go free.[13]

Marcus now prepared to join with the Americans in a far wider exercise, Operation Selectionboard, which he had hoped for some time would allow him some laxity in the Frankfurt area, part of the American zone. American co-operation would make it much easier for him to have a greater intelligence presence there, enabling him to pursue his own agenda with less fear of scrutiny. Operation Selectionboard had been brewing for about nine months. In May 1946 a key German agent working for the Americans reported there was an underground movement in Bavaria made up of former SS officers, fugitives from the internment camps. This agent, a Swiss national, infiltrated this network's Munich branch and discovered they were attempting to find arms and money to set up a terrorist organisation.[14] Marcus was notified of his findings and responded with his own report of a similar grouping operating in the British zone at that time. Working together, the British and American Intelligence services discovered that there were essentially five separate groups. The first was headed by SS Brigadeführer Erhardt Müller, whose HQ Marcus found in Rosenheim near Bad Aibling. The second group seemed to be subordinate to the leadership of the first; its leader, SS Oberführer Kurt Ellersiek, had an HQ in Dortmund, and further contacts in Kassel, Marburg and Munich. Marcus claimed they had established safe houses as far south as Augsburg and Bad Eichstadt, and that he had managed to penetrate the group effectively.

Klaus Barbie was presented to the Americans as head of the third group, which was supposedly in charge of the procurement of supplies and weapons for an underground army. In fact, these weapons came from Marcus, emanating from confiscated weaponry of German army arsenals in the Kiel area. Marcus had also infiltrated a fourth group of special commandos, Skorzeny Jagdverbände, that was made up of men from the disbanded SS Brandenburg Division. This group had formed to break into internment camps and release select prisoners, or, as Marcus put it, to 'decant' the internment camps in Operation Brandy. Their targets included people like Himmler's adjutant, Springer. Marcus wanted to capture and disperse Skorzeny Jagdverbände – known as Operation Brandy personalities – before they became too successful, and the brandy too intoxicating.[15] The fifth group was, in essence, Marcus' fabrication.[16] He lumped together various former SS members, including Springer, who he wished to trace for his and Philby's secret Operation Globetrotter. In this way Marcus availed himself of American help to find Springer without drawing attention to his interest. In the first week of February 1947, Marcus met with several Americans in Düsseldorf to finalise arrangements for the massive Operation Selectionboard (1525831) which was to start on 22 February. His proposals are reflected in American records. Even within their own zone, the Americans would be limited in their activities and the way they would approach suspect personalities, even the way they could question them. The Americans agreed to 'Point 11 – All prisoners will be assigned to the British zone for detailed questioning.' On 17 February it was recommended that triple star suspects should not be questioned at all by the Americans, only by the British.

The operation was performed with commendable care. Almost all targets were identified and discreetly monitored. Reports of each target's location were handed by 19 February to the Americans, either Colonel Inskeep or Colonel Garvey, at the HQ of 970 CIC Detachment.[17] Initially over fifty suspects were successfully rounded up, with the exception of Klaus Barbie, with whom the Americans were now to become obsessed. But the American agents soon realised that the SS men they were picking up from the British zone, who were to be handed over to the British, were of a far higher quality and rank. Significantly, many seemed to claim legitimate status within the community, a legitimacy that had been bestowed by the British. Some claimed to have been addressed by a British brigadier-general in a wide-ranging welcome speech, while the civilian administrative status of some was only too evident from their papers.

American irritation was magnified – indeed evident early on – by the reluctance of the British to release any further information on several people who had been caught and were awaiting questioning. In a report of 8 March, American Intelligence Captain Frazier bitterly recorded that, in the case of several suspects thought to have worked in bacteriological warfare (listed by the British under the code name 'Mayfly'): 'Investigation of these personalities [. . .] has been limited to brief preliminaries, since little material is available to brief interrogators. Early transfer to British Authorities is contemplated.'[18] He noted that of those arrested members of the Barbie group, 'British Authorities are known to have considerable information on this group. This information is being requested and should aid materially in this investigation.' Further scepticism about the quality and quantity of the information the British had provided shows up in other American agents' reports, who suspected they were being used for political purposes.[19]

After Klaus Barbie had been captured, he told his American interrogator that, 'the swoop operations [were] of no great significance – that no actual underground net had existed and that the action taken to apprehend known personalities was dictated by British politics.' The Americans were inclined to believe him. US special agent Charles R. Hayes recorded on 3 June 1947, 'It seems highly probable that personalities in Operation Selectionboard were in contact with the British Intelligence Service. It is requested that this be verified or denied.'[20]

The Americans vented their frustration by taking counter measures to turn most of those SS men they suspected to be British plants so they would work for the Americans instead. On 18 March Deputy Infantry Commander Lieutenant-Colonel George R. Eckman instructed, 'It is desired that the subject be interviewed in such a manner as to dissuade him from working for the British.' American special agent Taylor, who was to run Klaus Barbie, promoted the anti-British bias. As a result of information from Barbie, American Intelligence effectively ceased co-operation with the British on combined operations (although, superficially, such operations continued for many years). At the time this suited Marcus' purposes, for the Americans had started asking difficult questions about the behaviour of several of his agents in their zone. Marcus arrested Dr Trestedt, who worked for his Büro, in order to allay suspicion that Trestedt's activities planting British agents on the Americans were initiated on his orders. Marcus added more names of people who were not British agents to the list of those wanted for pick-up in Operation Selectionboard, including Dr Priess, a certain Josef Lang, and Juliana Alversleben-Schochwitz.

By now, the reason for British co-operation in Operation Selectionboard, which was to mask the true purpose of Operation Globetrotter, had disappeared. The tailing of Springer had come to an abrupt, unsatisfactory end, and not at all as anticipated. Springer seemed to have been aware from early on that he was under surveillance. His contacts were with minor figures of no particular consequence, figures that were mostly already known to the Allied Intelligence services. This was surprising as the people who wrote to him in prison were far more significant. Nor did Springer make an immediate break for the Swiss border as anticipated, but instead stayed at the house of an Ebart Erlinger – later found to be A. Kohl, who was believed to have been in the SS legal section. Eight of Springer's contacts were photographed by Marcus' agents before Springer headed south. It ended after Springer visited Gefolgschafts-führer Werner Stender, an agent on the escape route watched by the Americans. Stender seemed to be indiscriminately supplying anyone who asked with all kinds of documentation, including identification (or D2 forms).

At this stage American interest in Springer became apparent. One of Marcus' best agents, Gunther Radek, a Swiss-born Pole based in Zurich who had been recruited by Marcus after being caught smugg-ling jewellery, reported that it now seemed certain that the Americans knew of Springer's Zurich link. This was surprising news as Springer had not and never did reach Zurich. The information emanated from Radek's father-in-law, a retired Zurich policeman, who Radek had used to keep an eye on the comings and goings around the Zürichsberg house. He sent Radek photographs of these visitors, one of whom Radek recognised as an American agent. The Americans had not fallen for the rubbish they were landed with in Operation Selectionboard. Captain Frazier, the main American organiser, was most vocal in his criticism, but even his superior officer, Lieutenant-Colonel Dale M. Garvey, recorded in a brief, 'It has never been proved that a well-organised escape route exists [. . .] Actually the operation only concerned the escape of Himmler's adjutant.'[21] They had worked out the extent of the British subterfuge without, it seems realising the plan was based on anxiety about Himmler's survival. As Springer was visiting Werner Stender, so Marcus sent a telegram to Philby, then in Turkey, reporting that Springer did not seem too keen to go to Zurich, where the Americans were also waiting.

Marcus was surprised by the rapidity of Philby's reaction. The mission was immediately aborted. Eight of Springer's contacts in the British zone were picked up, and the Americans notified about Stender, as if they did not already know. From one of these contacts Marcus learnt that the Zurich mystery figure to whom Ludolf

Alversleben-Schochwitz was reporting at the lakeside villa in Zurich was called 'Jesus'. When the Americans asked one of the British officers working with Marcus about 'Jesus' during the debriefing held after the exercise, he claimed he was Josef Lang, a wanted man whom Marcus had rated a lowly two-star suspect. The British officer identified Lang as a carpenter from Oberammergau, who had once played Christ in one of the nativity plays the little town holds every ten years to commemorate deliverance from the plague. Marcus gave this explanation full credit for quick-thinking originality. In fact, there was no evidence that Lang had ever been associated with any of the personnel involved in Operation Globetrotter, and certainly not with Springer.

Marcus' involvement in Operation Selectionboard was officially over. But Philby had not counted on the thoroughness of Radek's father-in-law. Marcus was not supposed to have any substantive contact with Cruickshank in Zurich, other than to inform him of the whereabouts of Springer. However, Radek's reports to Marcus indicated that Cruickshank and his small, four-man section had taken no discernible action against the occupants of the house Alversleben-Schochwitz used to stay in on the slopes of the Zürichsberg by the time his energetic father-in-law abandoned his watch. Marcus could find out no more about Cruickshank's activities from either Radek or Philby, with whom he renewed contact for guidance on further action later that autumn. Neither has it been possible to identify any 'Cruickshank', even as a pseudonym, among those serving in intelligence at the time.

Dr Marcus made another telling point when Liddell Hart and I asked his opinion about Operation Globetrotter, which had apparently been a total failure as far as Springer was concerned:

Philby must have had powerful proof to justify setting up this uniquely costly operation, and some very cogent problem to justify his own personal involvement [. . .] I never, at any other time, remembered him bothering to become personally involved in anything whatsoever [. . .] Philby liked to pressure you by what he didn't say, but in this case, admittedly after

the event, I realised that he must have been the one under
pressure.[22]

On another occasion Marcus stated, 'As far as the pseudo Himmler
was concerned, nothing really explained why he should care so much
whether the Americans were involved.'[23] In his opinion, Himmler,
if indeed alive, was required by Philby for far more than his value
as a war criminal.

The net result of the combined Allied operations was effectively
to eradicate the kernel of resistance groups in Germany and dampen
enthusiasm for overt demonstrations of neo-Nazi power and influence in the occupied zones. The arrest of resistance leaders precipitated gloom and despondency in the main, ill-formed body of the
movement. It also served as a stark warning to overseas groups,
particularly the most powerful ones in Spain and South America,
that the time was not yet ripe to return too conspicuously. It was
some time before those arrested were, in the main, released to take
up more discreet employment.

As Marcus looked back on it all, his final view was one of irritated
amusement. He had, he declared, never again heard rumours that
Himmler was still alive. 'In the case of Himmler, I just file it in my
miscellaneous file. I still don't know why such rubbish interested
Philby so much.' But he agreed that Philby seemed plagued by
some doubt. Anthony Blunt obviously shared Philby's concern.
One-time SIS chief Sir Dick White had more information about
what he called 'the Himmler fiasco', information that came from
Blunt himself. I was questioning White about the fate of the X-rays
and dental records from Professor Hugo Blaschke, Hitler's dentist,
which were given to White when he was serving as a Brigadier by
his deputy, Colonel John McCowan. At first he denied all knowledge
of them, but soon regained his memory when he realised that
McCowan was still alive. He said that all Hitler's records had sub-
sequently been given to Hugh Trevor-Roper to assist his investigation into Hitler's death. When I insisted that it was not Hitler's
but Himmler's records and X-rays that interested me, this triggered
an unexpected response. White said that the death of Himmler had

been disastrously handled. 'He should have been kept alive. He should never have been bullied. It should never have occurred.' It seems that in 1945 Blunt had told White that, 'Possibly understandably, the men took liberties [with Himmler].' However, the post-mortem findings clearly show that no bruises whatsoever were recorded. Bruising begins to become discernible within hours, even in a corpse, and it is highly unlikely that the first post-mortem, so meticulously performed, would have missed any bruising. According to White, 'Philby had to go out to Germany to clear up the mess' – not, it seemed, to establish identity, but 'obviously to counter any allegations that he hadn't committed suicide'. White made another surprising observation for a layman that revealed detailed, if partial, knowledge of the case and the importance that must have been attributed to it for him to recall specifics so many years later. 'Anthony', he told me 'was most concerned to ensure that he [had] died of cyanide.' When questioned further, he commented, 'Well, that was the story, wasn't it?' I pointed out that the post-mortem had not estimated the cyanide level in the blood, and nobody had expressed any concern to do so, and White seemed genuinely astonished. Despite a close friendship with Blunt, White had not known, he claimed, that there had been one, let alone two post-mortems. Neither, apparently, did he know anything about a Board of Inquiry or Operation Globetrotter.

After my conversation with White, he alluded to problems about Himmler's death to various other writers, curiously without any prompting from them. These later remarks may have been made out of genuine curiosity, or efforts at dissimulation. If White was to be believed, then he was under the impression that the story of the Zyankali suicide phial was untrue. He thought it was part of a cover-up by senior officers to conceal their failure to prevent their men's excessive behaviour that had led to the prisoner's death. I did not tell him that there had been no physical evidence of violence found at the post-mortem. He was left with an increased, apparently unshakeable conviction that Himmler had, somewhat understandably, been helped on his way. We know this is untrue; it can only mean that Philby and Blunt were engaged in deliberate disinformation in order to justify their interest in the corpse without arousing the suspicions of their fellow officers that they were concerned about its identity. After all, the remit of their jobs in no way justified their involvement in the case. Why were Philby and, by implication, Blunt plagued by such doubts and, as importantly, why was it necessary to conceal them from their colleagues?

12

Doubt

Evidence now available sheds light on the reasons for the doubts of Anthony Blunt and Kim Philby about Himmler's suicide. As the British authorities will not release any documents pertaining to Himmler's death until 2045, aspects of the story of the arrest, identification and suicide of the man accepted to be Himmler cannot be told in full. However, compelling new material reveals a pattern of ineptitude and misinformation that defies received wisdom about the Reichsführer's demise.

The confusion at 31a Ülzenerstrasse after the suicide presented Montgomery's Chief Intelligence Officer Colonel Murphy with a dilemma. Murphy was celebrated for his efficiency, but it seems that the sheer speed of events surrounding the suicide overwhelmed him as he tried to recover from the excesses of the celebrations for the Allied victory. Although Murphy was known to be irascible, to deny the Americans and Russians the chance to identify the corpse and hastily dispose of the evidence cannot be explained by irritation or fear of criticism alone. He refused the Russians access to the body or any evidence relating to it, missing the opportunity to match the dental chart of the corpse's teeth with Himmler's dental records, which Gorbuschin almost certainly had in his possession. Murphy even refused to let Himmler's mistress Hedwig Potthast and his brother Gebhard, who were in American hands, see the body, and both Ashworth and Whittaker felt obliged to apologise to the Americans for Murphy's behaviour.[1] All in all, Murphy seemed extremely reluctant to put the identification of the corpse to the test.

There is no reason to suppose that Murphy did not think the body was Himmler's. However, this highly regarded intelligence officer would have known from experience that the basis of the identification, without any accurate comparative data, was wholly inadequate. Once the news was out that the British had captured such an important figure, it would be difficult to backtrack. What is more, the press were initially under the impression that Himmler was still alive. Admitting to have lost a senior Nazi to suicide looked bad enough – Murphy knew that his absence from the room when Himmler died would not reflect well on him. He was on the defensive, hungover and needed to cover his back. The last thing he would have wanted to know about was any evidence that could conflict with the identification, and he would have been horrified at the prospect that the identification's inadequacy could become public, heaping further humiliation on the unit and its leader. For Murphy, the leap from cock-up to cover-up was impossible to resist.

Murphy did not prevent all efforts at confirming the corpse's identity. Brigadier Hughes railroaded him into having an immediate post-mortem to establish identity and counter any allegations of torture. There was no way Murphy would wish to come into conflict with a senior officer, particularly such a forceful and outspoken man as Hughes. The procedure went ahead. Murphy did not secure all copies of this secret report, and he was not aware that Colonel Browne had made a commemorative death mask. Nevertheless, the post-mortem has remained a secret for many years. Fortunately for Murphy, the press demonstrated little curiosity about the procedure that had led to identification. All the same, he stifled any possibility that they might be tempted to investigate, snapping at Lieutenant Ashworth before he took the reporters for a roving press conference that their visit to view the body was 'strictly and only commemorative'.[2] When the press were taken to view the body, their cameras were confiscated and they were only allowed to look at it from the doorway. Murphy did not realise that the *Illustrated London News* reporter Captain Bryan de Grineaux had been and gone before Murphy had surfaced that morning. Grineaux was an exceptionally talented artist and his sketches of the body, taken from a closer position, are a great tribute to his expertise.

Murphy was livid when he found out that under Ashworth's

instruction unit photographer Carl Sutton had already taken official photographs of the corpse.[3] Sutton was ordered to report to Murphy with all copies, which were seized from him. These pictures included the only two direct photographs of the corpse's face. Most of them have never been seen again. The only images that have been made available to the public are those taken at disadvantageous angles and from a distance, limited tools for identification. Yet again, Murphy was not in complete command of the situation. Understandably, Sutton did not tell his irate Colonel that he had already given some photographs to his mates.[4] Captain Taffy Davies, who had been with Sutton when he took the photographs, was given one as a souvenir (this picture has never surfaced), and Corporal Bill Carrotte, a guard on duty, produced another photograph that was published in the *Daily Mirror* on 6 May 1985.[5] Claimed as a world exclusive, it was the first photograph to show most of the face of the corpse, taken at an angle approximately twenty degrees from the left of the body. Unbeknown to Murphy, Ken Gordon of Pathé News had also been allowed on site and filmed a newsreel of the event, taking close-up shots of the body. This was only mentioned to Murphy long after Gordon and his film were on their way back to Pathé. The short clip of this film, shown in May 1945, included the villa where the suicide took place, the cyanide capsule, its carrying case and two oblique shots of the face seen from the right side.

In May 1945 the world's media had enough to report as war continued in the Far East, and Soviet forces occupied Eastern Europe. Nobody seemed to have the energy or the inclination to question Himmler's death. The *Illustrated London News* article was published, the Pathé News clip hit the screens, and with dustman Austin's account of 'good riddance to bad rubbish', these were all the exhausted British populace would ever hear of the matter. The British Army escaped censure for their clumsy handling of the prisoner and international coverage did not dissent from British reports.

It is obvious that the British SIS took an unprecedented interest in the death of Himmler very early on – even though such matters were outside their usual sphere of responsibility. They too seemed ignorant of the death mask, but they could and did do something about the photographs. The publication of Willi Frischauer's book *Himmler* in Britain in 1953, which contained an official photograph of the body released from the Imperial War Museum, precipitated a spate of visits from British Special Branch police officers to ensure that no one involved in the death had retained any appropriate 'souvenirs'.[6] Several factors may have prompted SIS concern. Frischauer, a thorough and persistent researcher, had been given information, derived from an unknown source, about British investigations into Himmler's death. This related to the aborted Board of Inquiry, but Frischauer misconstrued it as a court martial. In April 1951 he asked a British War Office official about this investigation, and the official unwisely admitted that there had been an 'exhaustive investigation' and the matter 'was now out of War Office hands'.[7] The SIS might have been worried because the first British publisher of Frischauer's book, Odhams, received complaints about mistakes in the account of Himmler's death. Sergeants Ottery and Weston of the burial party attempted to contact Odhams but received no acknowledgement. The SIS may also have heard that some people who had known Himmler did not recognise him from the photograph, as had Henriette von Schirach when she saw another of Sutton's photographs in an American newspaper.

In spite of the SIS's efforts, they could not or did not recover all souvenirs of the suicide. The Pathé News footage was not destroyed, Grineaux's sketches can be seen in any archive of the *Illustrated London News* and several of Carl Sutton's photographs have remained available. Examination of this visual material in conjunction with the post-mortem report suggests that embarrassment and incompetence were not the only possible motives for the furtive way the army and SIS dealt with the unlikely death of Heinrich Himmler. Grineaux's sketches for the *Illustrated London News* article published on 2 June 1945 include a drawing of the prisoner in a khaki shirt and grey army blanket, still alive, standing facing the viewer. Grineaux had seen the corpse face on and this sketch reflects how he drew directly from the evidence rather than preconceptions of what Himmler looked like. The prisoner's face is skewed: the left side is bigger than the right and there appears to be more tissue on the left cheek. The eyes are level, and the hard bridge of the nose is straight, but the tissue of the lower third of the nose deviates to the right and the nose tilts at its tip to form a little flattened plateau. It was not a nose that anyone who knew Himmler would recognise. Grineaux drew the exposed pinna (the fleshy rim) of the right ear far more crudely than the left, a brilliant observation.

Another sketch shows the prostrate corpse, from a perspective slightly to the right with the feet in the foreground. This confirms the skew of the nose to the right, revealing that the shape of the nostrils differs markedly, the right much larger than the left. Grineaux' expert pen faithfully described physical details that are at odds with what we know of Himmler's features; the photographic evidence and the secret post-mortem report support these troubling observations. The photograph published in the *Daily Mirror* shows the corpse sitting almost upright, as it had been left after the Pathé film was shot. Taken from an angle, it shows the whole of the right side of the face and the left side as far as the outward attachment of the glasses and the lateral angle of the left eyebrow. Due to the ravages of time this picture is in a poor condition and no meaningful scientific analysis can be made of either cheek contours or nostrils. However, it does show the face is unbruised with the nose skewed to the right, somewhat overemphasised because of the angle from which the picture was taken.

After a delay of some years, the War Office supplied Sutton's authorised photographs to the Imperial War Museum. Copies of these photographs were obtained before some were withdrawn from display during the 1980s. They are all taken either from the side or below the corpse, mainly to the left of centre, clearly showing the right of the face and most, but not all, of the left. However, they are of reasonable quality and, with comparison against the Pathé News film, allow us to assess the exact nature of the disparity in the nostrils, and the significance of the flat plateau at the tip of the skewed nose. The Pathé film shows the corpse's face from above from two angles, one about twenty degrees to the right of the corpse, the other at a slight angle to the right of centre. The latter perspective reveals an unmistakable rightward skew in the nose's soft tissue, this time not overemphasised by the camera angle. Taken together, this evidence confirms the facial asymmetry recorded by Grineaux. The left side of the face below the eyes is larger than the right, and the disparity in size appears to include the underlying cheekbone (the zygoma). Grineaux also drew a much larger, D-shaped right nostril, which is shown in the photographs. The flat area over the nose's skewed tip lies mainly over the area of this enlarged nostril, lying just above the septum.

The drawings, photographs and film powerfully illustrate a classic congenital abnormality, the reason for the deviation of the nose. Such cases of facial asymmetry are very common. They result from an unequal amount of tissue on the sides of the face in late embryonic development before those tissues fuse to create nose and lips. Consequently, the developing child shows a discernible facial imbalance that is obvious in early childhood, usually getting less, but sometimes more obvious as they age. A deviation of the nose dating from childhood causes a disparity in the nostrils, and exactly such a flattened area on top of the larger nostril, as nature tries in vain to correctly align the tissues. All the evidence agrees that the man who lay dead in 31a Ülzenerstrasse had a noticeably asymmetrical face with a skewed nose. The film and photographs did not show any evidence of a fracture, bruising, or swelling. The nose was not discoloured; its bridge, which is clearly visible, was regular and undisturbed; the tip displayed no swelling, and the flat plateau, a sensitive indicator of gravitational or traumatic oedema (that is, swelling due to a thump), was undisturbed. The corpse's facial architecture from forehead down to chin was entirely intact and undamaged, so the face's asymmetry cannot be explained as a result of violence. The photographs and film do not suggest that a spasm caused the nasal deviation or facial asymmetry; the major and even minor facial creases were entirely normal, there were no additional creases, and the mouth was central and even.

The photographs alone clear Murphy and his men of any suspicion of causing the sort of facial damage that Dick White wrongly believed had been inflicted. The extraordinary findings of the first postmortem tell us more. As it was designed to determine the corpse's identity, there was no internal examination and no tissue specimens were excised for pathology. Notwithstanding this, it must rank as one of the most meticulous post-mortem examinations ever carried out on a historical figure. Brigadier Hughes was not a man you would wish to cross. His orders to 'Identify the bastard carefully and record everything, including needle marks,' rang in the ears of Captain Bond, pathologist to the 74th British Military General Hospital, as he set out to compile his report.[8] The 'Post-mortem Examination to Establish Identification, carried out at 11-00 hrs, 25-5-45' was extremely detailed and precise, recording the thoroughness of the pathologist, backed by two corroborative professional witnesses, Lieutenant-Colonel Browne and Major Attkins, dentists who had both received medical training to cope with the demands of war. They worked in good conditions. Light flooded in from the bay window beside the body, and Bond received well-informed assistance from the dentists, who made their own dental report as well as their commemorative latex death mask. Most important of all, they were given as much time as they needed.

Aware of the political implications that would result from accusations of torture, particular as this was not the first such suicide in British hands, they were determined not to miss anything. The report started by identifying all bruises, including marks of pressure applied after death. Then it dealt carefully with all abrasions, scratches and scars. Bond was so keen that he even examined the scalp minutely and looked closely at all other places on the body where needle marks might have been concealed. He also recorded all accentuated skin creases, even the two small abrasions on the sides of the achilles tendon on both heels left by Whittaker's fingers and thumbs when he held up the prisoner's body in a futile attempt at revival. Bond noted a four-inch-long scratch over the left shoulder blade, and three small, fresh scratches across the back of the right hand. There was a slightly raised, pigmented mole, two centimetres in diameter in the midline over the seventh thoracic vertebra. The report then gives bony measurements of the skull, abdomen and extremities, all within one eighth of an inch in accuracy. Even the lie of the hairs in the eyebrows and inside the ears was recorded, as well as the actual size

of the spectacles' lenses and their optical strength, recording a disparity of 25mm in the lenses' diameter. (The glasses were anomalous,
as they were rimmed yet Himmler had not been photographed
wearing such glasses for several years since his mistress had persuaded
him he looked more handsome in rimless.)

They found only one scar on the body, oval-shaped and one inch
by half an inch, on the upper inner border of the right kneecap.
The description places it slightly too high for the customary surgical
scar that accompanied removal of knee joint cartilage. The scar could
feasibly have resulted from such an operation, although it is more
probable it was caused by trauma. Himmler was never recorded as
having sustained any trauma to his knee. Indeed, the only time
Himmler was hospitalised other than when he had paratyphoid fever
as a student, was after he took over the Army Group Vistula at the
end of the war when Berlin was under threat and he failed to dent
the Soviet advance. It is not known what treatment he underwent
but stress was his only known problem. Lieutenant-Colonel Browne
disagreed with this assessment; he thought the scar had looked 'surgical and neat, the type you see from removal of a medial cartilage'.[9]
Describing the post-mortem, Browne said that as well as looking
for skin pricks Bond ran his hand over the whole body to pick up
any subcutaneous collections of fluid that might otherwise have been
missed. He also examined the back of the corpse in great detail and
separated the legs widely to inspect the inner thighs, the anus and
rectum.[10]

Browne recalled how Attkins had come hot foot from Brigadier
Hughes equipped with the senior officer's latest and favourite post-
mortem tool, a Woods light used to show up and differentiate old
scarring. The light was deployed with great care and the detailed
report makes it seem inconceivable that any lesion, scar or even
needle prick could have been missed. Bond's observations were far
more accurate and explicit than any photograph; he could feel the
underlying bones, take bony measurements, and was able to feel and
assess the soft tissues. He found the head to be completely symmetrical, measuring the antero-posterior skull measurement (from front
to back over the dome of the skull), the circumference, and, with

his unusual attention to detail, even the coronal measurement (from ear to ear). The asymmetry was not discernible in the skull or upper face, and both eyebrows and eyes were absolutely level, but Bond discovered 'The face is asymmetrical, the left malar bone [cheekbone] is higher than the right, the left cheek slightly fuller'. Moreover, the orbit of the left eye was discernibly larger than the right, a disparity that explains the unequal size of the glasses' lenses and provides further proof of a developmental abnormality dating from child-hood.[11] If Himmler had had this skeletal imbalance it may well have shown up if his sinuses had been captured on the dental X-ray that later fell into SIS hands. Unfortunately, we do not know whether any comparison has been made; the X-rays have never been released.

Bond's examination of the nose recorded that the 'nasal bridge is moderately high and well shaped'. In other words, the bony structure of the nose, the upper two-thirds, was not skewed, yet the soft tissues below this widened out markedly. 'The nose increases in breadth acutely to the anterior nares [nostrils] which are wide, the right being larger than the left,' he wrote. 'The tip of the nose is slightly flattened and deviates towards the right, there is a faint cleft at the tip.' He also noted that the two facial creases, from the side of the nostril to the corners of the mouth, were pronounced but equal. The mouth was central and entirely normal, whereas the ears displayed a further slight anomaly. 'The right ear protrudes more from the head than the left and the upper border of the pinna [rim] is somewhat bigger and broader,' he wrote, echoing Grineaux's observation. It was further evidence of congenital asymmetry.

In summary, the post-mortem found that the facial bones were skewed; the nose deviated to the right, its nostrils uneven in shape and size; the left side of the face was slightly bigger than the right, and the right ear's rim was larger and more florid than the left. According to Browne, he, Attkins and Bond were all satisfied that they were looking at long-standing developmental asymmetry.[12] It is clear that Anthony Blunt's intimation to Dick White that the prisoner had been beaten up had no basis.

However, somebody was not satisfied that displaced features such as the corpse displayed should have such a long-term cause. In

January 1946 forensic pathologist Professor Keith Mant, who by that time had replaced Dr Ian Morris at the War Crimes Commission in Germany, had an interesting encounter upon his return to Hannover from holiday. An unidentified visitor asked him whether he could tell from looking at a corpse's face the likelihood of force having damaged or displaced any features without there being bruising.[13] His answer, of course, was no. If the body at 31a Ülzenerstrasse had died due to brutality, the post-mortem findings would have been quite different. There would certainly have been bruising, swelling and discoloration somewhere on the corpse, probably including the face. When trauma occurs, swelling results from increased fluid in the tissues (oedema). Bruising happens after blood leaks from broken capillaries. As anyone who has watched a boxing match will know, facial bruises and swelling are rapid and obvious, as the soft tissues are well supplied with blood. When the facial tissues are trapped between the fist and the underlying facial bones, the swelling is almost instant, and blue or red discoloration occurs shortly after. It takes at least eighteen hours, usually longer, for the bruise to turn yellow. If violent trauma had been inflicted before the prisoner's death, the effects would have been almost immediately apparent. Even if the prisoner had died just after impact, swelling and bruising would still occur, and certainly be evident by the time the post-mortem was carried out. Dr Wells, present at the time of the death, saw no such bruise, and neither did Bond, Attkins or Browne.

Another possibility is that the prisoner's upturned nose, with its flattened tip and hint of a cleft, are evidence of brutality. The lower third of the nose has no hard bony bridge, comprising purely of soft tissue stiffened by a little cartilage. A blow can dislocate this cartilage and the result is unmistakable; it often looks more like a broken nose than a true fracture. The concomitant swelling and discoloration are unmistakable, as is the lateral step to the side. No such signs are shown on the photographs or film, let alone recorded by the post-mortem report. When the tip itself is deviated by trauma, it only occurs as a result of a severe blow. As this part of the nose is tethered from above and below by muscles and soft tissue and inherently elastic, with a built-in programme to recover its master's good looks, such deviation is only temporary. The flattened plateau at the tip and differently shaped and sized nostrils separated by an undisplaced, straight septum prove that the prisoner's nose had not been distorted by violent impact. Trauma played no part in causing any aspect of the prisoner's facial asymmetry.

If the cheekbones' unequal size and the larger left side of the face are taken into account, could poisoning explain the nasal skew? During the death throes from respiratory poisons such as cyanide people exhibit convulsions, temporarily arching their spines, before the body usually becomes flaccid. The prisoner followed this pattern exactly: Browne vividly remembered turning over the limp body to examine its back. The lower third of the nose is attached to the musculature of the lips and moves from side to side with exaggerated movements of the mouth. Downward movement of the mouth tends to narrow the nostrils, and upward movement of the mouth tends to widen them. A small muscle (dilator nares) attached to the muscle ring around the eye lies on both sides of each nostril. When it is contracted the nostrils flare, causing visible creases over the bridge of the nose. Apart from violent impact, deviation of the nose can only occur if the larger facial muscles go into a spasm, in turn accentuating the facial creases. The corpse's mouth was central and the corners even, the nostrils of unequal shape and the labial folds and creases normal. In any case, according to Dr Richard Bogle of Guy's Hospital Medical Toxicology Unit, there have been no reports in the world literature mentioning oro-facial or muscular spasms persisting after death.[14] In short, cyanide poisoning did not cause the deviation of the corpse's nose.

Unlike the corpse, Heinrich Himmler had an unusually even face, with no evidence of any facial skew. A photograph taken of Himmler as a very young child with his elder brother Gebhard and their parents shows Himmler with a symmetrical face. In every one of the family photographs taken of the Himmler family when he was in his teens his even features are unspoilt. Another picture shows him as an adult standing on a wooden dais with SA leader Ernst Röhm. Typical of the dramatic photography favoured by the Nazis, the camera looks up at the Reichsführer from a slight angle, resulting in a three-quarters view of the face. Both nostrils have an even contour, with no evidence of deviation, and there seems to be no measurable difference in their size. Only two close-up full-face photographs of Himmler in the Imperial War Museum allow reasonable opportunity for comparison, but by far the best photograph for our purposes lies in the Koblenz Archives.[15] It shows Himmler at the exhibition *Aufbau und Planung im Osten* on 20 March 1941. His nose is shown from above down its full length. It is straight to its tip. Myriad other photographs taken obliquely, or in profile, are not perfect, but deviation and asymmetry would be visible to an extent, yet no such abnormalities are visible in any of the hundreds of photographs I have examined.

The photographs are troubling but it would be wrong to draw conclusions from visual evidence alone. Very high standards must be employed in the interpretation of photographs, especially when attempting to make comparisons. It is far better to rely on the concrete details of the post-mortem, carried out with ultraviolet light and a magnifying glass. Not only did Bond measure every anatomical detail that might be of use to identification – the lie of the hairs in eyebrows and nose, and a difference between the lenses of the strange rimmed glasses – but he recorded several other minor anomalies and one that was major. Himmler was supposed to have shaved off his moustache prior to heading off south on or around 10 May. When a moustache is shaved off after years it leaves a paler area of skin. No such patch is visible on the photographs of the corpse and neither was it recorded in the post-mortem report, nor recalled by Browne who should have noticed it during his dental examination.

The corpse was 5 feet 8½ inches tall, which accords reasonably with Himmler's height of at least 5 feet 10 inches as estimated from photographs. As we cannot discount the possibility that he wore built-up shoes or sought advantageous positions in posed photographs, little can be made of this discrepancy. The corpse's legs were muscular, which contrasts with the supposedly frail physique of the Reichsführer. Schellenberg described his master as a 'stork in a lily pond' because of his spindly legs. Speer laughed when I asked him whether Himmler's legs were muscular, replying with confidence 'Not at all – the very opposite'.[16] But how many people actually see a casual acquaintance undressed, let alone a figure of such exalted importance as the Reichsführer SS? On reflection, Speer admitted that he had presumed they were spindly. Such subjective opinion is of no value.

Another widely publicised feature of Himmler's known medical history ought to have been made known to the forensic examiners when they carried out the post-mortem. On 20 June 1943 Hitler and Himmler were driving to Scharfheide, Göring's estate north of Berlin. When they arrived, a young girl offering a bouquet of roses greeted Hitler, who was still in the car. At that moment a shot rang out from the crowd, fired at close range from a revolver, and the would-be assassin disappeared into the crowd. Himmler had sustained a superficial flesh wound in his upper right arm which was treated immediately by a local doctor. No exact details of the wound's characteristics are available. The only record is of Himmler's sentiments: 'How grateful I am to destiny, my Führer,' he gushed, 'that I was allowed to spill my blood to save your life.' For bleeding to occur from a gunshot wound at least the deeper layer of the skin must have been injured, so some kind of scar was inevitable. The tiniest such wound would have resulted in a shallow trough about half to three-quarters of an inch long. Only the firm application of pressure would be necessary to staunch such a haemorrhage, not sutures, but even so, a scar would result. Captain Bond's report mentions no such scar, which he should have found in the area he was carefully searching for needle pricks (the deltoid muscle was the usual site for intra-muscular injection in 1940s British practice). However, this discrepancy should be regarded with caution. Although it was a well-publicised injury, the truth of the account cannot be verified to my satisfaction.

As we have seen, Heinrich Himmler sustained a facial wound during his university days, a duelling scar that was the essential badge of courage for members of the fencing fraternity. The surgical apprentices paid to attend fencing bouts at the university were quite adept at their work, if not fully qualified. Their slightly imperfect technique was, in any case, just what the doctor ordered to obtain a more prominent scar. Indeed, sometimes powder was used to act as an irritant to ensure a visible sign of virility, but by the early nineteen hundreds this barbaric technique had more or less died out. Cuts sustained using the épée or foil were mainly Y shaped, due to the forward thrust of the weapon. They were nearly always sustained high on the lateral side of the cheek. The materials used to treat such wounds were not sterile, and the suturing far cruder than nowadays, with less than perfect apposition of the skin edges. Himmler's diary states that he required five stitches and one ligature or tie. Stitches are designed to hold a wound together and in Himmler's day they were spaced half an inch apart, further than is customary today because they were put in without anaesthetic and extremely painful. The use of five stitches would indicate that the three legs of the Y would be almost an inch long. Such a cut would usually need only one ligature, the rest of the bleeding controlled by pressure from the five-layered tierce cloths designed to staunch wounds. Interestingly, the amount of blood loss you would expect to lose from a Y-shaped wound of about three inches in the upper cheek area accords almost exactly with the description given in Himmler's diary. The inclusion of a non-sterile foreign body such as the ligature in the bottom of a wound would eventually result in an inflamed wound with somewhat raised edges. Surgical probability, the description in Himmler's diary, and a photograph dating from the 1930s all agree that Himmler's duelling scar would have been a slightly raised, reddened Y in the cheek bone area. Himmler never again mentioned the wound in his diary, nor has it been the subject of any comment apart from one book by a non-medical expert that misread Himmler's diary and described five separate cuts.[17] Yet the diary account of his wounding accords in every detail with a classic trefoil injury and would be hard for a person to invent.

I sought confirmation of Himmler's scar with people who knew him. Albert Speer had good reason to remember Himmler; he claimed to have a sense of dread when they met and avoided meeting Himmler's eyes, usually fixing his gaze just below his glasses.[18] Maybe because of this he noticed how Himmler used to rub the scar contemplatively with the index finger of his right hand, a gesture Speer came to recognise as a sign of annoyance. Dr Marcus remembered an occasion when Himmler was enraged at a message he had just received about Ribbentrop and went white with fury.[19] It was the first time he had noticed the scar, which became livid as Himmler paled, but Marcus was unable to give an exact description. When I questioned Himmler's adjutants Heinz Macher and Werner Grothmann separately neither would comment on the scar. They did admit that they had both been previously asked about this identifying mark, although they could not or would not remember by whom or when.[20] Each wanted to know what the other had said and discussing my questions together, they refused to make any further comment. Fortunately there is a photograph that shows Heinrich Himmler with a trefoil scar on his left cheek, over the left cheekbone, the stem of the Y pointing downwards. The scar is slightly reddened, raised and clearly visible outside the six o'clock shadow he frequently wore.

The exacting post-mortem that aimed to discover identifying marks on the corpse does not record Himmler's duelling scar. I asked Lieutenant-Colonel Browne whether he had seen any facial scar.[21] 'Absolutely not,' he replied. 'I can absolutely guarantee that there was *no* facial scar, we were looking very carefully for anything like that.' Then I showed him the photograph of the scar on Himmler's cheek. His reaction was one of shocked disbelief and he was very reluctant to accept the evidence. Once he had satisfied himself that the photo was genuine, he pointed out that the trefoil mark was deep and obvious, moreover exactly in the area they were comparing for bony disparity. 'It's laughable,' he said. 'That's *exactly* where we were measuring, are you saying that we could possibly have missed it?' Browne also revealed that he, like Whittaker and others, had been visited by two Special Branch policemen in 1947 and asked if he had kept any photos from the period of Himmler's death. Annoyed by the officers' rudeness and the peremptoriness of their weekend visit, he clammed up, not bothering to mention the death mask, then on display at Aldershot Museum. He felt certain the underside would not show any such mark. It did not, although the labial creases were clearly visible. There was no facial scar on the corpse of 'Heinrich Hitzinger'.

The anomalies revealed by the medical examination during the post-mortem are a developmental facial skew, an absent facial scar, an absent deltoid scar (of dubious provenance), surprisingly muscular legs and an absent halo for the moustache. They spent two hours and fifteen minutes on the external post-mortem, indicating unusual thoroughness. Although data derived from an external examination constitutes scientific proof, it has long been regarded as less conclusive than skeletal evidence, notably that produced by forensic examination of dental records. Dentition is now accepted as a means to establish a subject's identity by most courts of law because whereas soft tissues putrefy, teeth are relatively durable and allow questions of identity to be settled long after death.

Once Bond had finished his examination, Attkins and Browne took over to produce their dental report on the 'Cadaver of Reichsminister Heinrich Himmler'. There were 27 teeth, the incisors noted as shade seven, 'aurora vitype', a light greyish white. They found one premolar with a gold cap, a few fillings of silver amalgam, a dead tooth and no gap where an object such as a cyanide capsule could have been hidden. A diagram of the dentition was added to the post-mortem report. One copy was given to Colonel Murphy, Browne kept a personal copy and passed another to Brigadier Glyn Hughes. Then the SIS took over the evidence and retrieved Murphy's copy.

Soon afterwards the SIS secured some of Himmler's dental X-rays, although they did not make this known. Professor Hugo Blaschke, a brilliant University of Pennsylvania graduate, rose to the rank of Brigadeführer SS and became dentist to many Nazi leaders, including Himmler and Hitler. At the end of the war, a British team of Nazi hunters discovered Blaschke when a German relative to one of the team, a doctor in the Wohlfahrtsverein (the Nazi Party charity), took them to him.[22] The doctor stayed to make sure that Blaschke co-operated, but there was little need; Blaschke proved very willing to assist. Before he fled the Chancellery dental field station, he had stashed up-to-date cards and records of many Nazi leaders and over a dozen sets of small dental X-rays, including some of Hitler and Himmler, in a small brown leather satchel. The leader of the British team, Colonel John McCowan, spent most of the afternoon going over the records, listing them carefully before sending the satchel on to his boss, the then Brigadier Dick White. They reached the SIS office within days of the suicide.[23]

Blaschke was in British hands for little more than a day before one of the American teams seeking Nazi expertise kidnapped him. According to McCowan, the British were to blame as they treated Blaschke with great coldness and suspicion, and he must have feared his fate. When his American rescuers offered 'a full belly of wine and friendship!' he did not hesitate to go.[24] On 28 May he was interned and not questioned by American dental experts until November and December. Unsurprisingly, the official record of his interrogation does not refer to his previous capture or kidnap, nor does it appear he was asked about Himmler's dentition. Of course, by that time Himmler had been officially pronounced dead so they may have seen no reason to question Blaschke about him.

McCowan said that while with the British Blaschke was not questioned properly by the Intelligence Section let alone by any dentist, so little information was attached to the dental records when they were sent to Allied Intelligence. However, these up-to-date records would certainly have been in SIS hands when the second postmortem took place, and could readily have been compared with Attkins' and Browne's dental record. Dr Morris confirmed that he was shown German dental X-rays, which must have emanated from Blaschke, but he was never given anything, not even the first postmortem report, to compare them with.[25] If the SIS had followed Morris's advice, X-rayed the corpse's skull and asked his opinion, then at least he would have had some evidence from which he could draw a conclusion.

The irritable manner of Dr Morris's recollections and his wife's description of his impetuous character when young help explain why the SIS might have been reluctant to share any further concerns with him, risking an unwelcome opinion about the corpse's identity that he could not be trusted to keep secret. Perhaps this is why they waited until after Morris had left before attempting to X-ray the body. That they bothered to X-ray it at all suggests anxiety about the corpse's identity, but without Morris they lost the opportunity of an expert opinion that might have answered their doubts. Instead the SIS chose to rely on Corporal D. W. Williams, who had been a mortuary attendant in Putney before the war, who assisted Morris at the second Himmler port-mortem at Hannover Military Hospital.[26] Williams had been warned about the Official Secrets Act and in his late sixties he was still reluctant to talk about his work there.

Not a lot phased a mortuary attendant in the days before effective refrigeration, but he remembered being none too pleased at having to clean off the corpse before Dr Morris would come near it. Nevertheless, he thought Morris was 'all right', the highest commendation a pathologist could hope for. After the examination, Williams played cards with a Corporal Skudmore while Dr Morris and two other men discussed the body. When Morris left he started to take the body over to the crematorium as ordered, but was called back and asked to fetch a radiographer from the main hospital block, two hundred yards away, to help use an antiquated X-ray machine. Williams' memory was heightened by the macabre comedy of the situation. He had to supply a thin wooden wedge that was normally used as a door stop to jam open what remained of the jaw so the radiographer could take pictures of the head. The procedure must have gone well, for when asked how they had coped with the X-rays, he said it was 'all right'.

The resultant X-rays were top secret and it is not known what became of them. As they were made without the supervision of Morris or a dentist, using unsatisfactory equipment, and improvisation, they must have been of little value unless a sinus was accidentally included. Not only had the British missed the opportunity to verify the corpse's dentition when Murphy refused the Russians after the first post-mortem, but now the Blaschke X-rays were redundant because there were no reliable X-rays with which to compare them. However, they still had Blaschke's dental cards to compare with Browne and Attkins' diagrams, cards that the British government does not admit it has, which seems odd when it acknowledges possession of Blaschke's X-rays of Hitler that were part of the same package.

Even without these records it is still possible to ascertain that the SIS had real cause for concern about the corpse's teeth. Previous recollections of Professor Blaschke's dental assistant, Kathé Heusermann, about Hitler's teeth have proved to be remarkably accurate when Russian archives released original documentation in the 1990s. When I interviewed her about Himmler's teeth she confirmed that his pre-1943 treatment files were among those removed by Soviet Nazi-hunter Gorbuschin when he visited her at Blaschke's private dental office in Berlin just after the city's fall. She also said that when Dr Blaschke had left precipitately to seek refuge in the West, he had taken a few records with him but did not know which (these would have been the up-to-date files that fell into SIS hands). Heusermann did not reveal that Blaschke had removed these records in her first interviews with the Russians, who held her in captivity without charge for many years after the war. Gorbuschin took Heusermann to Vosstrasse shelter of the Reichschancellery Dental Station where she helped identify all the material that remained. Himmler's solitary X-ray was absent, as were all of Hitler's. It seems clear that when Gorbuschin came to Lüneburg to identify the corpse he did have slightly out-of-date dental treatment cards. Nevertheless, these would certainly have contained sufficient evidence for identification. The Russians also had Heusermann in custody, though she was not taken to Lüneburg. She claimed that she had never been asked about Himmler's teeth by anyone other than me.

She answered all questions clearly and if she did not know something she did not hedge, but immediately declared her ignorance. I could well understand why the American forensic odontologist, Professor Sognnaes, who has also interviewed her, had been so impressed. Himmler's file was 'very small and only routine', she told me. 'We only twice did any work on the Reichsführer – some fillings in the lower and upper left molar, otherwise only check-ups [. . .] I would certainly have remembered it if we had [done anything else].' The last visit she remembered had been about November 1944. She denied that Himmler would have received treatment elsewhere: unless he had had an accident 'it would have been most unusual for him not to have attended the Professor'. Her general impression was that 'Himmler had very, very good teeth, very white. He was very proud of them. Their whiteness, it was quite unusual [. . .] He only had two fillings, and you couldn't see those when he smiled.' When asked about any bridgework she replied, 'He had no teeth lost; we didn't often get that, I remember it well. His teeth were almost perfect.' Yet the corpse at Ülzenerstrasse had only 27 teeth. I asked her about gold caps: 'Many of our patients, I would say most, used to have them – but not Himmler, he had no such thing at all, not any discoloration, no fillings in the front, certainly not a gold cap.' I queried how she could be so certain when, by her own account, Himmler had only been an occasional visitor. She replied that Himmler was not a man you would ever forget.

I showed Hausermann a photocopy of Attkins' and Browne's dental diagram and scribbled comments, from which I had removed all official marks that might identify it as part of the Reichsführer's post-mortem report. When I asked whether this could possibly have been Himmler's dentition, she immediately replied with great certainty, 'No.' Asked to explain, she pointed at the gold cap, dead tooth and fillings – which she stated were definitely incorrect. 'It's just not right,' she said. Then I showed her the same diagram, this time as part of the official post-mortem report on 'Himmler', and awaited her response. Heusermann went completely silent. She refused to discuss anything further, and was obviously badly shaken. No attempts at reassurance were of any avail. In contrast to her customary professional courtesy, she would not comment on this issue ever again, refusing to answer any more questions on this subject. It might be that she feared that she would become embroiled in a dispute, understandable reluctance after her painful years imprisoned in Russia.

Heusermann did not comment on the colour of the corpse's teeth, mainly, I believe, because she did not understand the British colour chart definitions. Those described by Attkins and Browne do not sound like the sparkling white teeth she and others have described.

But their condition was good and, allowing for the vagaries of recollection, this discrepancy is acceptable. The slight variation between
the number of fillings is also minor. A more worrying anomaly is
the corpse's dead tooth, which was extremely discoloured and should
have been obvious to Heusermann when she attended Himmler.
The main problem is the corpse's old premolar crown. This would
have been visible to all who knew Himmler, yet has never been
mentioned and was categorically denied by Heusermann. I believe
that crowns and bridgework are remembered by professionals, and
tend to accept her word. If Heusermann's testimony is to be believed,
Himmler would have had to gain a dead tooth, a gold crown and
a few extra fillings between his last visit to the dentist in November
1944 and the suicide in May 1945 in order to match the dentition
of the corpse. Unfortunately, this evidence is based on informed
opinion, not proven fact. We do not have the full comparative
forensic data on Himmler's teeth which was supplied to Anthony
Blunt's SIS friend Dick White. The most that can be made of this
is that there is reasonable cause, judging from dental evidence alone,
to doubt that the corpse of 'Heinrich Hitzinger' belonged to
Himmler.

The conflict between the rigours of science and the need for
obfuscation is part of the dilemma that faced the SIS over the death
of Himmler. Professional scientists did not rank in their numbers,
which did not help. They did not understand the science, they did
not know how much they could trust the scientists' reports, and in
the interests of secrecy rather than accuracy, they limited the experts'
knowledge on a 'need to know' basis. Himmler's death is only one
example of the way the SIS would cling on to evidence and then
bury it without a thought. In the case of Blaschke's dental X-rays
of Hitler, received by Dick White at the same time as the Himmler
material, beyond British Intelligence circles they were considered lost
until Professor Sognnaes, the UCLA forensic odontologist, came to
a conference in Oxford in the 1980s. There he learnt to his utter
astonishment that these X-rays, for which the world had been searching for decades, had been quietly kept in British possession since
1945.

The hundred-year ban on documentation relating to Himmler's death makes it impossible to know what went through the minds of the SIS to make them demand a second post-mortem, only to miss the opportunity to take a decent X-ray. There is no evidence that the second post-mortem was instigated as the result of any pressure from the Americans, so the compulsion must have come from within the SIS. We do know that immediately after the second post-mortem they aborted the Board of Inquiry, robbing Whittaker of his moment of glory. Some months later Kim Philby, working under the direction of Anthony Blunt, launched a secret operation within Operation Globetrotter to pursue Himmler's adjutant Springer, again hastily abandoning it when the Americans started suspecting there was a hidden agenda. Every aspect of the SIS investigations into Himmler's possible survival was inconclusive and, apparently, abandoned.

There is no question that Philby's relationship with the Americans was reasonably good at the time of the second post-mortem. Had the SIS wished, they could have X-rayed the skull properly before final cremation, received unhurried professional opinion, asked Professor Blaschke, who they knew was in American hands, to certify the provenance of the dental X-rays they possessed, and Philby could have finished the operation to pursue Springer. We can only wonder why he did not follow this course. Had the SIS been more open they might have resolved an issue that seemed in everyone's interests to clear up. As it stands, we are left with Philby's legacy of secrecy. There is compelling, cumulative medical and dental evidence that the man who committed suicide at 31a Ülzenerstrasse was not Himmler. But no forensic surgeon feels totally at ease with mainly soft tissue evidence or the written and verbal accounts of other experts, however skilled and honest they might be. The testimony of Bond, Browne, Attkins and Heusermann is inconclusive, even though meticulous, professional and signally unchallenged by comparative data, all of which is hidden somewhere. Such is the extent and nature of the proof currently available on the death of Heinrich Himmler, that the two-paragraph descriptions of his demise in previous histories now seem derisory. No longer can Himmler be declared dead on the basis of evidence that would not satisfy a county coroner's court. More than half a century later that doubt leaves an unacceptable historical void.

There must have been compelling reasons for the SIS to keep their anxiety about the identity of the corpse from their American allies. Blunt's allegations to Dick White of violence causing the death do not withstand scrutiny. Himmler's death was regarded as an uniquely British affair. Years after the suicide at 31a Ülzenerstrasse, Blunt and Philby's dilemma about Himmler remained unresolved. They were haunted by the possibility of Himmler's continued survival, and someone very much alive who was attempting to deal some of Himmler's cards.

13

Sonderbevollmächtigter – the 'plenipotentiary extraordinary'

The British cover-up of the facts of the suicide at 31a Ülzenerstrasse means that Heinrich Himmler's true fate will never be known. However, the progress of his protégé, Walter Schellenberg, after the Reich's fall reveals the extent to which Himmler's hand continued to guide events long after he was declared dead. As the Allies trudged through the ruined streets of Berlin, a very different scene was opening in Stockholm.

In the first week of May 1945, orders were given three weeks ahead of schedule for the royal palace of Tullgarn on the Tosa archipelago near Stockholm to be opened for summer residence. Beech leaves were cleared from the steps leading down to the landing stage and the Dutch tiles in the entrance hall were polished to a shine, because Tullgarn was expecting special guests. Walter Schellenberg and his entourage were due to arrive from Germany. The head of the SD foreign intelligence section had been promoted to Minister in Dönitz's provisional government and was on his way to Sweden with plenary powers to act for the new Führer. It was less well known that Himmler had also promoted his trusted deputy, making him *Sonderbevollmächtigter*. Schellenberg was a 'plenipotentiary extraordinary' empowered to act in any way on Himmler's behalf.

Stockholm was suffused with an air of expectation. As war drew to a close in the rest of Europe there was little indication that intrigues as contorted as the streets leading down to the water's edge were about to break the calm. The little white steamers that plied their summer trade between the city and the red wooden holiday homes on the islands still lay tied up in the harbour.

To most Swedes living their ordered existence, Stockholm exuded confidence; to visitors from war-torn Europe it seemed smug. Nevertheless, there were signs the times were changing. The pro-Nazi owner of the Regenbågen restaurant in Stureplan had started selling cocktails to his growing American clientele. As British Naval Attaché Captain Henry Denham remarked to the new British Secret Service men, 'Once you had to order in German; this year you'd better order in American.'[1] The fashionable city centre was packed with well-stocked department stores a stone's throw from the foreign legations. The diplomats who had been lurking within them started walking about freely, enjoying the promise of summer in the bars and cafés they had previously been so keen to avoid with their store of eavesdroppers. The large German community, sufficient to sustain its own newspaper, *Der Deutsche in Schweden*, nervously stayed indoors and the German concerts that had been the high point of Swedish nightlife stuttered to a halt.

The American Legation enjoyed the greatest influx of visitors, its head frankly bemused by some of the new staff – businessmen and agents – he was required to entertain. The Soviet Legation was no exception, with a multitude of NKVD (KGB) men streaming through its doors day and night. Americans, French, Hungarians, Poles, Russians and Japanese were united in their realisation that Stockholm was about to become a well-stocked purveyor of unmissable German bargains, from atomic secrets to more mundane intelligence. They also realised the British Legation had been handling Walter Schellenberg and they were watching like hawks.

On 4 May Schellenberg waved from his Red Cross car as the convoy drove through Copenhagen. The happy crowds presumed he was part of the Red Cross team, and he obviously enjoyed escaping the fearful recognition he was accustomed to receive as an SS Brigadeführer. His new friend Count Folke Bernadotte, President of the Swedish Red Cross team, had laid on the transport. The month before, Bernadotte, Schellenberg and Himmler had organised the release of Swedish prisoners and Scandinavian Jews from prison.

Bernadotte was pleased to champion his new ally, for whom he felt great sympathy; he was sure the Swedish would wish to thank Schellenberg for his humanitarian deeds. A cousin of King Gustav, with great wealth and political influence, Bernadotte had every reason to feel confident that the German would receive the welcome Bernadotte believed was due to him.

At Copenhagen airport Schellenberg boarded his host's personal plane, taking off for Malmø, where he arrived at 7.15 a.m. the following day. Ten minutes later he took off in a Swedish military plane, landing at Stockholm's Bromma airport at 9.30 a.m. A Swedish diplomat escorted him to Tullgarn where discussions immediately commenced with Swedish Minister Von Post and the influential Swedish Foreign Secretary, Eric Bohemann.[2] They puzzled over Schellenberg's status as both Himmler's representative and government minister empowered by Dönitz to help organise the surrender of General Boehme and his 400,000 German troops in Norway, wondering if the Western powers would accept him as a mediator for Germany. The Swedish government had learned that General Eisenhower might be prepared to send a special delegation to Stockholm to participate in Schellenberg's negotiations, and were keen to be seen by the Allies to be playing an active role in peacemaking after years of neutrality. The proximity of the Soviet Union and the impending carve-up of Eastern Europe added to Sweden's sense of urgency about winning friends in the West and protection for their country's wealth.

Intimations of Eisenhower's interest may stem from an encounter the previous month in Germany. At 11 p.m. on 23 April Himmler had met with Bernadotte and Schellenberg at the Swedish consulate in Lübeck, and lectured them on the political and military situation:

> We Germans have to declare ourselves defeated by the Western powers and I beg you to transmit this to General Eisenhower through the Swedish government so that we may all be spared further unnecessary bloodshed. It is not possible for us Germans, and especially it is not possible for me, to capitulate to the Russians. Against them we will fight on until the front of the Western powers replaces the German fighting front.[3]

Bernadotte and Schellenberg helped Himmler compose a letter to Swedish Foreign Minister Christian Gunther, 'begging him to give his kind support to Himmler's communication' to Eisenhower.[4] The following day Bernadotte had flown to Stockholm, perhaps laying the groundwork for Himmler's plenipotentiary extraordinary to be seen by the Americans as a man they could deal with.

On 6 May Schellenberg arranged for the German Minister to Sweden, Hans Thompson, to go to the Norwegian border in a Swedish bomber plane provided courtesy of the government to discuss the surrender with General Boehme. Boehme was reluctant to recognise the powers Dönitz had vested in his new Minister Schellenberg before he left Germany. They attempted to get Dönitz to sort it out, but telephone lines were so bad that conversation was impossible. When Schellenberg later got through to Von Krosigk in Flensburg he found out that Germany had capitulated already and the British objected to any outside interference while Montgomery set about organising the surrender in Norway. Von Krosigk urged him not to proceed for fear that he might endanger the peace negotiations that were already underway in Germany. British reservations denied the Swedish government their opportunity to cement relations with the United States, relations that had become particularly strained over the past year because Sweden refused to be drawn into the war.

Over the next few days Schellenberg and Bernadotte paid several visits to Victor Mallet at the British Legation. It seems that Schellenberg's extensive dealings with the British and others in Stockholm, combined with his new status as Minister and the support he had received from the Swedish government, blinkered him from the change in his fortunes. Since he had lost his importance as a negotiator, Schellenberg's position was far less certain. Yet he found himself meeting Ministers, living in splendour, and free from the need for that constant glance over his shoulder for the Gestapo. It did not occur to him that any deal with the British might be imperilled by his thirst for a public role; he seemed impervious to the dangers he faced by seeking the limelight. Having been granted immunity from prosecution and having received a guarantee of security by the intelligence services – orchestrated by senior MI5 liaison officer Anthony Blunt via Ewan Butler – was one thing; to assume that such a deal could stand up to public scrutiny was to assume too much. The British could not be seen to endorse someone popularly regarded as a war criminal, especially one who seemed bent on continuing in public office.

When Schellenberg pulled up in Bernadotte's large open car outside the British Legation on the main road east out of Stockholm they were unable to drive through the entrance. Photographers waiting on the grassy knoll opposite the entrance had ample opportunity to capture for posterity the moment when Schellenberg and Bernadotte walked into the Legation.

According to Peter Tennant, as a result of these visits 'the cow's backside hit the proverbial rotaries'.[5] Fourteen telegrams were sent to London regarding the British Legation in Stockholm between 6 and 14 May, an unusually high number. It seems likely that Schellenberg's visits contributed to this flurry of telegrams, all of which are considered top secret and it looks certain that they will never be made available to the public.[6]

Watching British intelligence officers took great delight as the British government fell hard on Victor Mallet. Then posted in Paris, Tennant still kept close tabs on what went on at the Stockholm Legation through his successor, the new Press Attaché Jasper Leadbitter. Tennant was convinced that Mallet had been up to his neck in secret financial negotiations between the Wallenberg brothers, the Germans and the Swedish royal family, and hoped that 'for once this man would get his come-uppance'.[7] Peter Falk, still based at the Legation, took an interest because Schellenberg had run Karl-Heinz Krämer, the German agent Falk had been brought out to Sweden to combat. Since Ewan Butler's breakdown Falk and Tennant were both painfully aware that Schellenberg, Himmler and the British had contracted some deal for immunity from prosecution for war crimes. Butler was reporting to Anthony Blunt, to whom Falk was also sending the Soviet and British intelligence material he had gathered from Krämer, material that Blunt had been at pains to convince Falk was false. This coincidence gave Falk and Tennant the impression that a game was being played at the highest level from which they were both excluded.

Peter Falk recalled how Schellenberg's visits affected the Legation: 'It was so incongruous. A modestly dressed man, dressed as if he was a country squire in tweeds, creating such a negative atmosphere. He seemed to carry it with him.' Nobody wanted to be seen to associate with the German. All the same, Falk felt frustrated that he was not privy to the discussions and could not find out what was going on between Mallet, Schellenberg and Bernadotte. 'It left one feeling on the outside of it all, mildly irritated,' he commented.

Legation chief Victor Mallet had frozen at the sight of Schellenberg and Bernadotte. After his summons to see Churchill at Chequers, as a consequence of which he had to plead for his job, Mallet must have known that to entertain such visitors was to risk losing everything. Yet at least two other meetings occurred. Mallet confided in Peter Falk, that although he knew 'he wasn't supposed to meet Schellenberg after the last fiasco', he had been confused because Schellenberg seemed to have powerful backing to negotiate the surrender of troops in Norway. The German had assumed a 'status' which Mallet felt his influential friend 'Bernadotte seemed to have rather endorsed'.[8] This explanation accounts for neither the number of meetings once the surrender was out of Schellenberg's hands, nor why, according to Tennant, Schellenberg came to tell Swedish Foreign Minister Christian Gunther that he was going to be a Counsellor at the British Legation.[9] Himmler's Sonderbevollmächtigter believed that the agreement made through Butler guaranteed an extended sojourn in Sweden and that a distinguished career in intelligence still lay before him. This logic was to work for Schellenberg's *Ausland* SD protégé, Reinhard Gehlen, who set up an intelligence network in West Germany for the Americans after the war. Peter Tennant was horrified at this prospect. He sent two telegrams from Paris to London to inform the Foreign Office about their prospective German employee.[10] The reaction was fast and furious. In the early afternoon of 9 May Bernadotte received a message from the Legation ordering a halt to their visits.

Later that evening Bernadotte received another message ordering

Schellenberg to prepare to leave for Bromma airport the next day where an RAF Dakota would be waiting to fly him to London.[11] When Bernadotte's secretary rang the Legation for an explanation he was told that Schellenberg was urgently wanted for questioning. The SIS was clearly feeling anxious. As Bernadotte learned that transport would be arriving early the next morning to take his guest to the airport, Swedish papers broke the story of how their royal family was sheltering a war criminal. Furious, Bernadotte refused to let Schellenberg leave, claiming he was too 'mentally and physically exhausted' to travel. Finally it was becoming clear to Bernadotte and Schellenberg that they had misjudged his position. The British did not seem inclined to honour any deals or recognise his value as an intelligence resource. In the face of British displeasure, the Swedish government could not be depended upon to offer Schellenberg the security and status to which he and Bernadotte believed he was entitled. (Interestingly, it was believed in some circles that the Swedes had also offered Schellenberg immunity from prosecution).[12] After this stand-off a series of meetings began to decide the fate of Schellenberg and his entourage.

A British intelligence officer visited Bernadotte and Schellenberg on 11 May to discuss Schellenberg's future. Peter Falk first learnt of this visit a few days later when a French journalist following up an OSS tip-off asked him who this officer was. That same day, one of Falk's Swedish contacts also told him a meeting had taken place with an officer who had flown in on 11 May. Falk was puzzled; the Legation knew of no such visitor. He checked up on Mallet and Butler's whereabouts and found neither could have been involved. Falk drew another blank when he investigated passengers on British flights to Sweden, but then security was lax during those euphoric days at the close of war. However, there is compelling circumstantial evidence that this officer was Anthony Blunt.

Around the end of May one of the drivers at the British Legation, 'Morley' Phillips, a lover of promiscuous SIS officer Roger Hinks, was routinely questioned about visitors to Hinks' Stockholm flat. (Hinks was under surveillance due to colleagues' doubts about his loyalty.) Morley casually mentioned that weeks earlier he had spotted

Blunt, whom he knew from London, getting out of a civilian car on the quayside near the Grand Hotel.[13] Peter Tennant recalled this throw-away remark, passed on to him by Falk, some years later when he bumped into an old acquaintance from his days in Stockholm, Curt Juhlin-Dannefelt, at a party. Blunt came up in conversation and Dannefelt, who had since risen to become chief of Swedish Intelligence, mentioned that Swedish Intelligence knew Blunt had paid a fleeting visit to Stockholm at the war's close on business with the Swedish royal family. Dannefelt did not go into any further detail, and Tennant never linked Blunt's mysterious visit with Bernadotte or Schellenberg. Another close SIS associate and friend of Blunt, Sir Stuart Hampshire, admitted that nobody knew of his friend's whereabouts at this time. He could not confirm the widely held view that Blunt was in Europe cleaning up archives and the royal family's personal correspondence, remembering that 'Blunt had been particularly tight-lipped about this period'.[14] An unidentified source told Blunt's biographer that Blunt's explanation for his absence during this period was that he was 'escorting home a German who had worked for the British during the war and thought employment prospects were better in England than in Germany'. Maybe there was a grain of truth in this.

Whoever this officer was, he must have been involved in an extremely delicate negotiation. Swedish financier Jacob Wallenberg was close to both Bernadotte and Schellenberg. He thought that their main concern at that stage had been to establish the German's legal status in light of previous promises not just of sanctuary but the right to apply for Swedish citizenship. It is not possible to discover why the intelligence officers and services of the British Legation were not called in to assist. As Tennant put it, 'whoever represented British interests did so unusually unsupported and had the necessary authority to negotiate'.[15] Anthony Blunt's position in 1945 fits well with the qualities Tennant describes. Then a senior liaison officer in MI5's B division – which dealt with counterintelligence – in theory Blunt was working for Assistant Director Dick White. However, as White and others have admitted, in practice Blunt dominated his intelligence chief, Director Guy Liddell. Indeed, it has been said that they were lovers. Blunt enjoyed extraordinary liberties and Hampshire and others have stated that during this period Blunt was moving freely about Europe on unspecified duties.

The British Secret Services routinely left all top-grade information to be handled by a select group of men whose loyalty was considered unquestionable. Both Blunt and Philby belonged to this charmed circle. Blunt's work was not confined to B Division. He became Liddell's personal link with B1a, which ran foreign agents, and was allowed to take home Ultra transcripts of Abwehr and SD material that had been sent to Liddell. On critical occasions Blunt attended the JIC (Joint Intelligence Committee) that oversaw operations of all British intelligence services. He was perfectly positioned to pick up information about Himmler and Schellenberg. Philby was deputy chief of Section 9, which dealt with ciphers and aimed at countering Communist subversion. Frequent liaison with the Foreign Office, and his attendance at JIC meetings, placed Philby well to be aware of material emanating from Sweden or concerns about activities at the Stockholm Legation. Philby enjoyed similar autonomy in his anti-Communist role as he showed in his dealings with Dr Carl Marcus. Blunt would have had greater influence during the time of the troubles at the British Legation in Stockholm. Japanese spymaster General Makoto Onodera was selling a lot of high-quality Russian material to both Krämer and Schellenberg. It may be that Blunt was deliberately fielding this information from Krämer through Falk, and that emanating from Schellenberg through Butler, because he feared it might lead to his exposure as a Russian agent. If that had been the case, Blunt would probably have shared his concern with Philby.

During the time Schellenberg spent at Trosa many powerful Swedish friends visited him. Nevertheless, it was impossible to ignore the mounting antagonism in the press. The Swedish newspaper *Aftonbladet* published a series of articles about Schellenberg that criticised the Swedish government and royal family for sheltering him and hinted that they were to offer him citizenship. The government issued denials, but the tide of criticism could not be turned.

By 11 May the British demand for Schellenberg's removal coincided with pressure from the Swedish government as a result of media interest. Bernadotte and Schellenberg's minds were on the defensive, and needed to establish the latter's legal rights to sanctuary and Swedish citizenship.[16] Bernadotte proposed the Naval Academy in Stockholm harbour as the ideal and secure venue to carry out the questioning. On 12 May the British countered, reiterating their demand that Walter Schellenberg and all papers in his possession should be transferred to London immediately.

The following day Bernadotte hosted a conference of Swedish grandees. Another of Schellenberg's friends, Chief Swedish Intelligence Officer Lindquist, watched as Dr Nordwall and Dr Frickman of the Swedish Red Cross gave statements to back Bernadotte's testimony about Schellenberg's services to Swedish prisoners and Scandinavian Jews. Chief Justice Eckburg offered advice on Schellenberg's legal position were he to insist on remaining in Sweden. Eckburg was probably very well disposed towards the German; he had received regular visits towards the end of the war from Weissauer, Himmler's liaison officer, a Major in the Luftwaffe, and also knew Dr Wirsung, Himmler's adviser on legal niceties. After this conference the British Foreign Office were informed by Victor Mallet's office that Schellenberg was still too ill to travel and would remain in Sweden while he recovered and his position was clarified.

Continuing press interest strengthened the British position day by day. On 15 May Ewan Butler used SOE agent Johan Bøge to release a rumour through British Army Intelligence in Denmark that Himmler had decided not to come north to Sweden, but to make a breakthrough south to the Wolf's Lair. Swedish Intelligence also picked up this rumour, so it is likely, given Lindquist's relationship with Schellenberg, that this story would have reached Schellenberg's ears. This may have prompted Schellenberg's decision that day to entrust certain papers with Bernadotte's Stockholm solicitors, flouting the British request for all documents in his possession. These documents must have been his safeguard against any double-dealing by the Allies.

Holed up with his entourage at the Tullgarn palace in Trosa, Schellenberg and his secretary, Franz Göring, commenced writing an account of his wartime activities designed to help Schellenberg's

application for Swedish nationality. Later dubbed the Trosa memorandum, it claimed Schellenberg was anti-Hitler and had influenced
Himmler to seek peace and save the lives of Jews and prisoners.
Himmler comes across positively, a victim of circumstance ready to
be guided by his trusted deputy. It contained an eye-witness account
by his secretary Göring confirming Schellenberg's version of events.[17]
Schellenberg kept two copies, witnessed by Swedish Foreign Minister Gunther, and gave another to Bernadotte. He had become Schellenberg's honest broker, certifying Schellenberg's account of their
role in the saving of the Scandinavian Jews and prisoners and guarding
papers that Schellenberg felt it was in his interests to withhold from
the British. Bernadotte went on to use the Trosa memorandum to
deflect criticism of the Swedish government's role during the war,
publishing his own corroborative version of events a month later.

More intelligence services focused on Schellenberg's battle to prevent extradition. The US State Department started to criticise the
OSS for failing to take control of Schellenberg. The OSS started
talks with Brandin and Møller, the directors of the Swedish Match
Company, and on 26 May, Møller told them Schellenberg had
brought the Japanese into his talks with the British. This was news
to the OSS, and it seems the SIS were not involved as neither Falk
nor Tennant knew anything about it.[18]

Two secret meetings had already been held at the Japanese
Legation with Schellenberg before 31 May when another significant
meeting took place at Bernadotte's house in Dragongärden. Guests
included Schellenberg, Swedish Chief Justice Eckburg, Lindquist,
Chief of the Swedish Secret Service, Sir Victor Mallet and General
Makoto Onodera.[19] Whatever was discussed, it was so delicate that
British Foreign Secretary Anthony Eden suppressed all documentation relating to all discussions with the Japanese.[20] That Eden
documented these talks at all suggests they took place with some
official authority, as does Mallet's presence. Unfortunately, it will
be a long time before any light can be shed on what they discussed
as the files remain closed. It seems relevant to these meetings that
Peter Falk was convinced that the intelligence bourse run in Stockholm by Onodera throughout the war had been the source of

Krämer's Soviet intelligence about British Cabinet talks. Such high-calibre material, which indicated the existence of well-placed Soviet moles in the British establishment, could have been at the heart of the power Schellenberg held over Blunt and Philby.

American archives do not refer to these talks, yet shortly after Møller's revelation about Onodera's involvement, the OSS stepped up their involvement. After further talks, on 2 June Brandin and Møller approached Schellenberg with the suggestion that instead of London he should leave for American-controlled Frankfurt, where he could expect more generous treatment. After this proposal, American Military Attaché Colonel Raynes, Schellenberg and Lindquist met with Bernadotte at his house.[21] Bernadotte and his friends in the Swedish government could not prolong Schellenberg's sanctuary in Sweden any longer in the face of the public outcry spurred by press coverage. Schellenberg was increasingly alarmed by his peremptory summons to London. Despite the previous agreement with the British, he decided to take up the Americans' offer.

British and American Secret Services had been working together to question many key Nazi personnel. Once the agreement was made, the British should automatically have been notified. Yet although arrangements for his handover were confirmed on 8 June, Schellenberg continued to receive 'select visitors', including British, at Tullgarn without mentioning his impending departure. Bernadotte cheerfully played along with the deception. Unannounced, on the morning of 17 June Colonel Raynes, Bernadotte and Schellenberg left Stockholm with six small zinc-lined trunks filled with documents. An American Dakota flew them to Frankfurt am Main where they were met by the OSS. Bernadotte returned to Stockholm and the papers Schellenberg had left behind. Edmund King O/C escorted Schellenberg to the US Army Intelligence Centre HQ at Frankfurt. The man decried by the international press as a war criminal received a remarkably warm welcome, with a private room with a shower and instant room service that supplied excellent wine and real coffee – luxuries that were somewhat superfluous to the abstemious German.

The OSS snatch gave the Americans precious time to talk to Schellenberg before official British questioning occurred. This gave them a chance to try to discover what had gone on at the secret Anglo-Japanese talks in Stockholm, to evaluate what Schellenberg had to offer, and to find out why he was so important to the British. The extent of American awareness of British fears is revealed by the comment of an FBI officer who later dealt with Schellenberg at Frankfurt. He declared, 'This whole case is regarded by the Allied Counterintelligence Officers, and in particular by the British, as being the single most important case to come up in the history of espionage.'[22]

Colonel Raynes, military intelligence officers and an OSS officer, 'E.C.', commenced questioning immediately. Records are fairly vague, but Colonel 'R.R.', one of the first military intelligence officers to see Schellenberg, recalls watching Schellenberg explain the contents of zinc-lined boxes for two hours before they were removed for further analysis. Then the OSS started asking him about how the Nazis broke the Bern/Washington code in conjunction with deciphering experts who had been prepared to meet him since 10 June.[23] That codes should be the primary focus of their interest in Schellenberg suggests that the bulk of the documents that he had taken in his six zinc-lined trunks related to ciphers.

Anthony Blunt sent Kim Philby over to Germany once it was known that Schellenberg was in Frankfurt. Bernadotte met him at the British HQ at Bad Oeynhausen at the end of June and they had a confrontation that caused such bad feeling that they made their way to see Schellenberg separately. Bernadotte arrived first and could hardly contain his anger. The mess audience, including Colonel 'R.R.', learnt that the British were 'smarting' at their loss of Schellenberg. On learning this, the senior OSS executive, 'E.C.', decided on discretion and left a newly arrived FBI officer who was there to question Schellenberg on espionage in America, to take the flak from Philby.

'R.R.' clearly remembers the concern expressed by Schellenberg, and later Bernadotte, that the British might renege on the deal that they had struck to offer him immunity from prosecution.[24] Bernadotte also told the US military intelligence officers that the deal struck with the British was 'delicate and potentially embarrassing'.

It was obviously interesting to the OSS, who periodically excluded military intelligence personnel from the interrogation room.

A first-class row was building up between the British and Americans over the snatch. Today we cannot appreciate the charged atmosphere at Frankfurt. The OSS had only 'confidentially informed' the FBI that they held Schellenberg on 26 June once negotiations with the British about how to handle the prisoner were complete.[25] In a conciliatory gesture, the FBI's representative applied for permission to assist special case investigator Philby. The enthusiastic young officer commented in a report to his Director, John Edgar Hoover, that he had completed arrangements to sit in on Philby's interrogation of Schellenberg 'from the start'. Upon his arrival in Frankfurt, Philby had a brief meeting with the FBI officer and refused to let him join in. On 6 July the officer wrote again to Hoover, claiming he had changed his mind about seeing Schellenberg with Philby. He apologised that he was only able to question Schellenberg with an interpreter for a morning. It was strange that the FBI should take interest in a case so far outside their official remit: US national security. That anti-Soviet Hoover should wish to be personally informed underlines Schellenberg's value as a source of information about Soviet intelligence activities.

Philby enjoyed two days with Schellenberg more or less uninterrupted, time enough to establish exactly what the Americans had learnt and to re-establish the British understanding with Schellenberg. Then two more British Intelligence Officers arrived. Britain's Radio Security Service (RSS), whose job it had been to intercept enemy transmissions, had found out that the Americans were asking Schellenberg about German code-breaking. Sir Stuart Hampshire was dispatched, not realising that Philby had already been sent by Blunt. Hampshire and his fellow interrogator, a Mr Johnson, interviewed Schellenberg until 7 July, when he was flown to Camp 020 near London. This joint Allied decision to move him to a far harsher environment indicates British and American relations were back on track and the Americans had finished with him for the time being.

When Schellenberg arrived at Camp 020, Mr Johnson resumed questioning with another colleague, Mr Ferguson.[26] Although

Schellenberg was deprived of some of the perks offered at Bad Oeyn-hausen, walks on Richmond Common with Dick White marked him out from his fellow prisoners. White 'never ever knew quite what to make of Schellenberg'.[27] That White should visit Schellenberg at all suggests that a great amount of importance was attached to the prisoner. If senior RSS officer Hugh Trevor-Roper thought Schellenberg had little to say, as Hampshire claimed, why did he insist that Hampshire should question Schellenberg – for the second time – at a separate location in South Kensington?

Schellenberg's true value as a source of information for the Allies is confirmed by his interrogation by a combined Anglo-American team about the German perception of atomic warfare on 15 and 21 July. After this he was interrogated twice by British officers about Nazi successes in deciphering and brought to central London to be interviewed on more than one occasion by a commission comprised of a British chairman, a British specialist on deciphering and his American equivalent. Finally he was interrogated again about deciphering in general, the OKW code used by the German army and the SD research station intelligence codes.[28]

After several visits to the London Clinic, Schellenberg was diagnosed with kidney disease. His life became remarkably leisured. Increasingly, he was allowed escorted walks in Richmond Park, twice in the company of Dr Carl Marcus who had fled to the Allies months earlier. Marcus had obtained permission to ask Schellenberg's advice to help build up a network of agents in the British occupied zone of Germany.[29] Schellenberg was condescending when they met, as if their relative positions had not changed since the glory days of the Reich. He told Marcus he expected to be an intelligence supremo working for the Allies in post-war Germany and even warned him against co-operating too wholeheartedly with the British. By their second meeting, Schellenberg's questioning was almost over. Marcus asked Schellenberg how it had gone. Schellenberg replied airily, 'Oh, we were just shuffling our feet to smooth out the sand!'[30] Marcus decided not to seek any further help from Schellenberg.

As autumn drew in, Schellenberg seemed to be feeling fairly secure. He may have had good reason for believing this. The official

British questioning had not been aimed against Schellenberg as a potential war criminal but designed to find information that would crucify Kaltenbrunner. For example, an early progress report about his questioning on 28 July 1945 states,

> Up until now Schellenberg has been questioned mostly on matters relating to the Kaltenbrunner case, and the information obtained and included in the Progress Report is on a question and answer basis.
>
> Further subjects in preparation concerning the Schellenberg case [are] the organisation of Amt VI, the Mil Amt, Amt IV (the Gestapo), and information dealing with the notorious Dr Kersten, who among other things provided Schellenberg with information on Russia through his Chinese agent.[31]

It seems that Schellenberg's analysis of how the Amts worked was to be used to shift the burden of responsibility for war crimes on to Kaltenbrunner and Gestapo Chief Müller. Other records bear out this interpretation, suggesting a deal had been struck between Schellenberg and the Secret Service.

Storm clouds were gathering on the horizon. An early indication of US impatience with the soft British attitude to Schellenberg came from J. Edgar Hoover. Still keeping an eye on the prisoner who officially had little to do with FBI interests, on 17 August 1945 he couriered a toned-down report of the combined Allied interrogation of Schellenberg in Frankfurt to the SIS European desk. It was accompanied by a hand-written note that listed subjects of particular interest that had arisen. 'Japan' topped the list, even though only four out of 37 pages – and these buried in the middle of the report – dealt with Japan. This appears to have been a warning that they had learnt more from Schellenberg about dealings with the Japanese than the British either knew or would have wished. Hoover was signalling that top-level US interest in Schellenberg was ongoing and unlikely to abate.

After four months interviewing Himmler's favourite, an SS Brigadeführer popularly regarded as an arch war criminal, the British sent him to Nuremberg in mid-November as a witness for the case against Kaltenbrunner and Müller, not a defendant. The tone of the British final interrogation report was entirely sympathetic to Walter Schellenberg, suggesting a shambling and confused man who had been caught up in a situation over which he had no control. In conclusion, Squadron Leader Harrison stated, 'In striking a balance the scales hang considerably in his favour.' How could they justify such a benign interpretation? A foreword was added to the final report sent to Nuremberg. It was designed to help those, such as Anthony Marreco, who might be confused by Schellenberg's polished performance at the witness stand, to recognise that this was a sad and broken man.

The foreword explained that the poor Nazi Brigadeführer had visibly deteriorated during his interrogation, forcing them to follow the account he had written of his actions in the Trosa memorandum. Schellenberg was unable to write coherently and was so confused that he had muddled the interpreters. Information they had obtained earlier had been far clearer than his subsequent statements. 'In this connection it must be stressed that, taken by and large, Schellenberg has shown himself under interrogation to have little capacity for lucid exposition and to be confused in his written statements,' the file explained.[32] Hampshire defended this attitude, claiming Schellenberg 'lived in an unreal world' – he 'seemed to know little about what really went on in England, or how things were run'.[33] He found Schellenberg 'very unimpressive and a thug', preferring Kalten-brunner, who he regarded as 'a typical policeman – efficient and more intelligent'. It is puzzling how little this description of an unhelpful and enfeebled man matched up with the value placed on the witness, marked out by tabs on his Nuremberg file indicating special British interest.

According to British reports and the intelligence officers who handled him, Schellenberg was of no great consequence. Fortunately, the record of the American Nuremberg counsels' questioning of Walter Schellenberg is now available 'The general impression left by Schellenberg is of a man of remarkable intelligence,' they wrote. He was a man of 'insatiable ambition' who 'became disillusioned with [. . .] socially and intellectually inferior colleagues'. Once he was 'aware of the changes in Germany's fortunes [he had] paid in instalments for the journey home'.[34] Unfortunately, they did not expand on this oblique reference to Schellenberg's deal for immunity. However, it does illustrate the growing dissatisfaction of the US with Schellenberg's status as merely a witness to others' crimes. The British deliberately played down the German's ability, culpability and importance, prevarication that confirms the FBI officer's verdict that they considered it 'the single most important case to come up in the history of espionage'.

It was not until 4 December when the War Room in London received a communication suggesting that Schellenberg might be transferred to Washington for questioning 'unless there were objections', that the British began to realise the Americans were considering prosecuting Schellenberg.[35] No record exists of how they responded. The British could not raise objections if Schellenberg was of as limited use to them as they had made out. Nevertheless, Schellenberg remained in Nuremberg for most of the time, with occasional outings such as his trip to see the exhumation at Lüneburg. He was repeatedly interviewed about the minutiae of the most diverse subjects imaginable in response to a continuing stream of requests from Washington. Such filibustering tactics kept Schellenberg at the OCOWC Camp, inside the American zone, and it became obvious that the Americans, who virtually ran the show at Nuremberg, now effectively controlled him. The visit to Nuremberg the British had only intended to be temporary was going to last as long as the Americans wanted it to. The Americans were openly ignoring the 'British Interest' tag, questioning Schellenberg about issues that suggested his indictment for war crimes was inevitable.

According to CIA agent James Jesus Angleton and Peter Falk, the anglophile CIA adviser to Nuremberg, Frank Wisner was dealing with the affair in late 1947.[36] Wisner told Falk that both Schellenberg and Krämer had been 'loath to come up with the goods'. Both Germans were up to their necks in acquiring intelligence about the Soviets and British, but were reluctant to pass this on to the eager Americans.

Telegrams sent in mid-December 1947 between Dick White and Roger Hollis, chief of MI5's anti-Soviet F Section, reveal that the British Secret Services only learnt Schellenberg had been indicted after a routine request.[37] The situation was so fraught that the Americans did not tell the British what Schellenberg was charged with and the British did not feel able to ask. Communications state that they did not want a legal adviser at the trial, as they feared that they might be accused of torturing Schellenberg during his time in England. This seems odd. It seems more likely that they worried the offer of immunity might come out if the Americans felt they were showing too great an interest in Schellenberg. British nervousness was such that they insisted that no SIS witnesses should attend the trial. 'I would suggest that we await events and meet this [unspecified problem] as and when it arises, but in any event I think we should refuse to produce a witness,' they decided.[38]

The Americans' decision to indict a case of 'British Interest' was an unheard-of discourtesy with no obvious purpose. They cannot have taken this step unless it held out the promise of substantial gains, such as the release of further information, either from Schellenberg or the papers left with Bernadotte's solicitors.

A strange transformation in British attitudes to sentencing at Nuremberg came about around this time. The British Foreign Office started supporting Soviet complaints that sentencing at Nuremberg was far too lenient. They argued that the death penalty should be more widely enforced and that there should be no appeal against it – a penalty that, if found guilty, Schellenberg almost automatically faced. Since this stance was totally contrary to the previous Anglo-American attitude, it immediately merited cynical scrutiny from the CIA, who must have wondered whether this was targeted at one specific case. Britain's newly hardened attitude was promoted by a pliant British Military Governor, Air Marshal Sholto Douglas, who had succeeded Montgomery the year before.

Count Folke Bernadotte started visiting Schellenberg at Nuremberg under the guise of his role as President of the Swedish Red Cross. He met with Sholto Douglas and Sir William Strang of the Foreign Office on several occasions at the governor's headquarters, the beautiful, isolated Schloss Ostenwalse, where Anthony Blunt also became an occasional visitor.[39] However, there is no direct evidence linking Blunt with Bernadotte's meetings. By his own account, Sholto Douglas got on well with Bernadotte. It is tempting to believe that they talked about Schellenberg.

After Bernadotte's visits ceased, another press campaign began against his wartime role. This attack, led by a British historian attached to the secret services, implied Bernadotte was pro-Nazi. Bernadotte became so incensed that he wrote to the historian asking for an apology, which his wife says he never received.[40] This would suggest that the British still resented Bernadotte for continuing in his role as Schellenberg's broker, seeking to discredit the man whose solicitors were still in possession of Schellenberg's papers.

Bernadotte's reputation was badly damaged. Restitution seemed to be on offer when, on a later visit to London, William Strang of the Foreign Office suggested he would be the ideal person to take over in Palestine as the United Nations Representative. On 29 May 1948 Lord Cadogan nominated Bernadotte to the United Nations as the only candidate for the job – the most dangerous diplomatic post in the world. He got the post, and lasted just over four months before his assassination by the Stern gang on 17 September 1948. Schellenberg was left without a broker as he awaited sentencing, aware that his own defence was in tatters. The appalling wartime activities of an SS officer who had given crucial testimony in Schellenberg's favour had been exposed, thus discrediting all he had said. Schellenberg's humanitarian gestures to the Scandinavians and Jews were scrutinised and found to be a cynical exercise in self-preservation. Schellenberg, haughty and defiant in the dock, began to suffer from indigestion and claimed he was being poisoned.

On 10 August 1948, Alexander Hardy, Associate Trial Counsel, had produced the final brief on Schellenberg for US Brigadier General Telford Taylor, Chief Counsel for War Crimes. On 18 September, one day after Bernadotte's death, this was forwarded to FBI Chief Hoover at Hoover's request, reflecting continued interest in the Schellenberg case at the highest level. It was a damning indictment:

The evidence has established beyond reasonable doubt that the defendant is guilty under each count. Schellenberg not only kidnapped enemy and neutral nationals but in pursuance thereof murdered a Dutch officer in cold blood. Schellenberg participated in creating the Einsatzgruppen for the extermination of all resistance in occupied territories [. . .] In collaboration with these [Einsatzgruppen] he selected captured prisoners to be used for illegal purposes, in violation of the Geneva Convention, and murdered them after exploiting them [. . .] He bears a major responsibility for the program to exterminate the Jews and for the specific murder of 200 Jews shot in October 1941, and for the disposal of 8000 Jews from Serbia. He was not only aware of the criminal acts of the SS and SD, but participated in them as a principal.[41]

The death penalty seemed inevitable.

Before Schellenberg was sentenced a peculiar incident occurred in Rome that may have had some bearing on his fate. CIA agent James Angleton recalled that in October 1948 Anthony Blunt tried to interfere with the diplomatic mail of American diplomat Ralph Bunche, who was based in Rhodes, which was being sent to the CIA in Rome. Blunt was caught in the act with Roger Hinks and another British agent after a Belgian air freight official, Henri Miquelon, who was acting as their courier, betrayed them. They spent several hours in Italian police custody before the British obtained their release.

Bunche had been Bernadotte's deputy at the United Nations, succeeding him as Special Representative in Palestine. The material he was sending the CIA was the documents Schellenberg had left with Bernadotte's solicitors. A Swedish Intelligence source reveals that after Bernadotte's death they had acquired these papers, which contained details of Soviet moles. One of their officers flew to take the papers to Bunche in Rhodes before their ill-fated transfer to Rome. The same source explained that the courier, Miquelon, was in the pay of Mossad, the Israeli secret intelligence service, as well as of the Americans.

Sir William Stephenson learned of the Rome affair the following year. According to Foreign Office gossip Victor Mallet, then Ambassador in Rome after a spell in Madrid, had also been involved. Rumour had it that revered former Foreign Secretary Anthony Eden was compelled to make an unscheduled visit to Rome to smooth things over. When Mallet went to greet him, Eden had brushed him aside, loudly declaring, 'And who has been a naughty boy then – yet again.' Mallet's role in the incident has never been clarified. The only other person involved in the incident who had also been based in Stockholm was Roger Hinks. Hinks later died in his Rome flat during a visit from an SIS colleague.

A few days after Blunt's embarrassing arrest, American interest was heightened by an ill-conceived attempt to rubbish the material sent by Bunche. British MP Hector McNeil frequently acted as a conduit of information between the British Secret Services and Cabinet. On 15 October 1948 he dined in Paris with Cyrus Sulzberger, a senior American diplomat with known CIA connections who had had dealings with Bernadotte. McNeil was at pains to assure Sulzberger that the material the Americans had just acquired was deliberate Soviet disinformation aimed at the fabric of British society.[42]

Perhaps it is a coincidence that after acquiring these papers, in late November the CIA decided to resume questioning Schellenberg, thereby delaying sentence. This lasted until March 1949, when he was admitted to hospital for tests to determine the cause of his continued ill health. He was found to have suspected cancer of the liver and was still in hospital when the Americans decided to pronounce sentence on Case no. 11 Walter Schellenberg. Instead of the death penalty, on 14 April 1949 he was sentenced to six years' imprisonment *in absentia*. Both British counsels at Nuremberg, Sir Elwyn Jones and Anthony Marreco, were astonished. The leniency came from the American side, another reversal from their previous enthusiasm to upgrade Schellenberg from witness to a defendant for war crimes.[43] The British were not even notified of the judgment on their formerly 'special interest' case and they relied on a press cutting from *The Times* newspaper to complete their case file.[44]

Even after he had recovered, the Americans had more questions for Schellenberg. Milked dry, he was released in June 1951 to a hostile new world. He immediately sought sanctuary with an old friend, Swiss Intelligence Chief Roger Masson. Moved by the obvious deterioration in Schellenberg's health, Masson arranged to have him seen by a German surgeon, Professor Lang. Lang's report of terminal cancer came as a shock. Masson arranged to have Schellenberg treated at a nursing home in Romont, a town halfway between Lausanne and Freiburg.

The British interest in Schellenberg was only low-key when he was in American hands. Despite Masson's attempts to conceal Schellenberg's location, they had not lost his trail. The Foreign Office put in a strong objection to the Swiss government that Schellenberg was an illegal immigrant. He was forced to move on, settling on the shores of Lake Maggiore in Italy. The Italians took a more liberal view of the threat he posed and ignored British representations for his expulsion.[45] On 29 October 1951, Schellenberg asked for an audience with the Pope, which was hastily granted. The Americans drily recorded this fact in their files without comment, displaying no surprise that the ailing Nazi should retain power over such exalted people.

At the end of February 1952 Schellenberg gave his final interview from his large, secluded villa to journalist André Brissaud. 'His suit of beige tweed, although well cut, hung loose on him,' he wrote. 'I was struck by the colour of his face, a dark yellow verging on brown, and particularly by his extreme thinness, which pressed his skin against his prominent cheek bones, and by his hollow cheeks. Large rings emphasised the brilliance of his eyes. The lips were discoloured, obviously the man was ill – very ill.'[46] Schellenberg had terminal liver failure. Yet even during his last days, he complained bitterly to both Brissaud and the Italian police that he was under constant surveillance by the British Secret Service. He died on 31 March 1952, and was buried two days later in the public cemetery of Turin. Grave 1673 has no commemorative stone. The initial marble slab, marked simply 'Walter Schellenberg 1910–1952', was removed by persons unknown.

Shortly afterwards the FBI produced a report cautiously prefaced 'Walter Schellenberg purportedly dead!'.[47] British interest was still alive, now to be exposed as British fear. Their concerns centred on some 4,000 sheets of paper, Schellenberg's memoirs, which had been smuggled out by an American warder while he was still in captivity and sent to the Swiss publishing firm Albert Scherz. Terms had been agreed, but when Schellenberg visited the office after his release, he found the deal had been cancelled for reasons that were never made clear. When the publishers returned the manuscript it was clearly in disarray, and Schellenberg, in increasing ill health, was unable to approach another publisher before he died.

A German journalist re-edited the material for Schellenberg's widow and the resultant 3,000 pages that remained were hawked around Europe, coming to the attention of historian Heinrich Fraenkel in London. Fraenkel recalls a surprising visit from a celebrated British historian who wanted to view the material. This historian had repeatedly expressed his distrust of Schellenberg, and did so yet again quite vituperatively. Fraenkel could not understand why he should wish to see the material if it were considered to be rubbish, but honoured by the visit, Fraenkel handed it over. Much 'unnecessary material was removed from the script by the time it was returned to my care, a fact that I thought at the time quite a liberty', he commented.[48]

The same historian led the chorus of disapproval when a greatly condensed version of Schellenberg's memoirs was published by André Deutsch in 1956. As Professor Allan Bullock wrote in his foreword, the book was free from self-justification and rancour. The vociferous criticism of a decimated script that contained little relating to the British seems extreme. The book sought to diminish Schellenberg's wartime role, portraying Himmler as a victim of circumstance whom Schellenberg had tried to help. The book ends with the close of the war:

> On 9 May a last telephone conversation with Flensburg made it quite clear to me that any intervention [...] with regard to the internment of the German forces in Norway was not desired

by the British military authorities. For the time being my services were no longer required.[49]

This is as close as the book gets to criticising Britain. The confidence of the last line's implied suggestion that one day his assistance would be sought is the only obvious reason why the desire to discredit Schellenberg's every utterance was so strong even after his death.

The scandal of Blunt's interference with Bunche's diplomatic mail and Hector McNeil's clumsy attempt to dismiss the material coincided with a watershed in British relationships with the United States; it is open to question whether these episodes contributed to a shift in power between the Allies. James Angleton admitted that his 'anglophilic' perception of British Intelligence was badly shaken by the Rome incident. 'The Rome affair gave us due cause to have a longer look at him [Blunt],' he said. He found Blunt's efforts incompetent and 'worrying' and he could not understand why such a senior officer would become personally involved in such a desperate action if he did not have something personal at stake. Angleton thought the papers, which he claimed not to have seen, were mainly SD reports.[50]

It has been reported, first by Andrew Boyle in his 1979 book, *The Climate of Treason*, that Mossad informed Angleton that Kim Philby was a Soviet agent as early as 1947. Boyle concurs with Anthony Cave Brown's view that from 1947 Philby's treasonous behaviour was 'just becoming clear in high British and American intelligence'.[51] In the 1950s Wisner confided in Peter Falk that Mossad had given Angleton essential information about Philby's role as a Soviet agent. Angleton later confirmed that the Belgian courier Henri Miquelon worked for the British and the US secret services as well as Mossad. It is not known whether the Rome fiasco was directly connected to Mossad's discovery of Philby's activities, but the coincidence is suggestive.

In 1948, soon after the Rome fiasco, Madame Modrzhinskaya, head of the NKVD British department, wrote a memorandum analysing information received from Soviet moles in the British establishment. Her meticulous analysis concluded that by 1948 all

Soviet moles in Britain had to be considered compromised, a conclusion still believed by KGB men today. Her report was overruled by then ruling Politburo member Lavrenty Beria. What concerns had prompted her to write the memorandum in the first place? This suggests, at the very least, that some significant event had occurred. The Rome fiasco fits the bill perfectly. Perhaps Miquelon had sought to enlarge his income by selling information to yet another intelligence service, although plenty of people would have been in a position to pass on the information to the NKVD, directly or otherwise.

Contrary to popular belief, after Philby flew to Moscow in 1963 he was not made a KGB General, nor an adviser to KGB Chief and future President Yuri Andropov. In fact, once there he was not used in any active intelligence capacity. His debriefing lasted three years and then he became a propaganda icon, for domestic as much as for foreign consumption, living in a decidedly down-market Moscow apartment. Philby lived out his days a fugitive from his past, as disappointed, in his way, as Schellenberg.[52] As Heinrich Himmler had always known, once treason became public, no future role of any significance was possible.

Whatever other cards Himmler had held, the ones dealt by Schellenberg alone left a legacy of intrigue that was to plague Allied and Soviet Intelligence services. The reactions of the British and American Intelligence services offer, at long last, a fair indication of the strength of the hand Himmler had played to garner the extraordinary British offer of immunity from prosecution.

Schellenberg escaped the death penalty, whereas many Nazis were executed for lesser crimes. A bizarre tug of war took place between British and American Intelligence services over him that begs more questions than it is possible to answer. The British represented Schellenberg first as an innocent bystander and then a hardened criminal once he was out of their hands, revealing a level of anxiety about him that was based on much more than his unsavoury war record. Himmler's plenipotentiary extraordinary retained a power over the British Intelligence service that, at the very least, reflects a partial success for his master's meticulous forward planning for the SS's post-war survival.

Although cancer finished Schellenberg, public exposure did not extend to public execution. Unlike Schellenberg, as Himmler sat out his last days in Flensburg, he knew that he would be vilified as a war criminal and reluctantly prepared to go underground. 'They'll never find me,' Himmler boasted to Von Krosigk days before he sought anonymity – perhaps dressed up as Heinrich Hitzinger, perhaps somewhere else. It is a measure of the uncertainty surrounding Himmler's death that Kim Philby should set up the elaborate Operation Globetrotter in order to dispel doubts about the Reichsführer's continued survival.

Historians have accepted the story of Himmler's shabby suicide for almost six decades. His demise has merited a couple of paragraphs as a rule, in spite of a hundred-year ban on material relating to Himmler's death, an absence of post-mortem evidence, a paltry identification procedure, unacceptable photographic evidence and inconsistent and occasionally false accounts of his death. The architect of the Holocaust dwarfs all other historical figures in his monstrous crimes against humanity. Himmler's ambitions for the SS's survival and multiple plans for his own future call into question the complacency that colours our knowledge of his end. Insoluble doubts about the identity of the corpse at 31a Ülzenerstrasse leave us a numbing legacy, an unacceptable gap in the record that may never be filled.

APPENDIX

The contribution of
computer technology

Much has changed in the science of identification since the corpse of Heinrich Hitzinger/Himmler was dispatched to the crematorium. Instead of rough comparison of photographs and other such data, more refined methods are in common usage. Unfortunately, some of these methods have become popularised before they have become an exacting science.

Professor Peter Vanezis is a pathologist at the Human Identification Centre at Glasgow University. Vanezis' team has built up some 200 templates of men and women of different ages, builds and racial groups, but they admit they are at the beginning of a steep learning curve. They work with D Laser scans of the skull on to which they place a facial template, wrapped around the skull between 'virtual' pre-determined pegs that reflect various tissue depths. A computer allogram finally moulds the face in between the pegs to complete the hoped-for likeness.

This method is faster than the laborious clay modelling previously favoured. Nevertheless, the facial template does not always fit accurately; computers have their limitations and they need the skull as a matrix. It is still impossible to take a few oblique photographs from each side of a face and then build up an image of the rest of the skull and face. Even the 3D imaging company controlled by Glasgow University's Turing Institute, whose software has advanced beyond the laser, needs stereo pairs of simultaneous photographs of the whole face. Computer technology cannot help in the case of 'Heinrich Hitzinger'.

Due to his vast experience, Professor Vanezis' opinion is of considerable interest. He raised the possibility that storage of a body can produce bizarre distortional results due to pressure. However, 'Hitzinger's' corpse was left lying on the floor on its back for a very short time, no pressure of any kind being applied to any aspect of the face. Vanezis readily agreed that a disparity in the levels of the cheekbones is highly significant, especially when noted and commented upon by a pathologist during a post-mortem.

Whereas Vanezis has been building up a library of hard tissue data, another expert in the field has been concentrating on the more observable soft tissue features, so far neglected by forensic science because of their inexactitude. Alf Linney of the Medical Physics Department at University College London has built up a dossier of facial variations that he hopes will prove to be as useful in determining each person's identity as fingerprints. He takes 3D scans, measures set points such as the corners of the eyes and mouth and links these with lines that form specific angles, based on the hypothesis that these measurements will be unique to the individual. However, the oblique photos available of the corpse in question introduce unacceptable guesswork. Nevertheless, Linney's expert opinion is that a difference of more than 3mm in the height of a person's cheekbones would be immediately visible to the examiner. Linney feels that professionals examining a corpse could hardly be mistaken once they had gone to the trouble of detailing the asymmetry of the cheeks and the disparity of the nostrils. A pathology report that described a skewed face in such precise terms must be believed.

Notes

1 Reincarnation and Exorcism

1. Lord Elwyn-Jones, conv. with author.
2. Albert Speer, *Spandau: The Secret Diaries*, Collins, 1976, p. 12.
3. Anthony Marreco, letter and conv. with author.
4. Proc. Ntr 2307–47 and 2465–74.
5. Marreco, letter and conv. with author.
6. Ibid.
7. Elwyn-Jones, letter.
8. Speer, comm. and conv. with author.
9. Ralph Boursot, comm. with author.
10. Ibid.
11. Ibid.
12. Ibid.
13. Norman Rimmer, conv. with author.
14. Rimmer's recollection of conv. with Norman Whittaker.
15. Rimmer, comm. with author.
16. Whittaker's letter and testimony recalled by Rimmer.
17. Whittaker's testimony to Rimmer.
18. Ibid.
19. Ibid.
20. Ibid.
21. Ibid.
22. Ibid.
23. Ibid.
24. Ibid.
25. Whittaker did receive both his job with the War Crimes Commission and his MBE. Ottery and Weston were never sworn to secrecy, nor did they receive a medal for their work. Whittaker would have been furious had he known that CSM Austin also received an MBE before his death in 1972.
26. Extract, CSM Austin's testimony to historian Willi Frischauer. When the daughter of Dr Wells, who had certified Himmler dead, asked the BBC for a tape and transcript of Austin's broadcast she was informed that it had been lost many years ago. The BBC denied to me that it was lost, but failed to produce a copy. Sergeant Ray Weston was also annoyed by Austin's version of events, but his unsuccessful attempts to tell the media the truth invoked the wrath of army authorities.

2 SS 1

1. Auschwitz Trial Proceedings – Frankfurt 64–5; Roger Manvell and Heinrich Fraenkel, *Heinrich Himmler,*

Heinemann, London, 1965, Appendix B, pp. 252–3.

2. Ibid.

3. Ibid.

4. Isaiah Trunk, quoted in Adam Lebor, *Hitler's Secret Bankers – How Switzerland Profited from Nazi Genocide*, Simon & Schuster, London, 1997, p. 22.

5. BBC documentary, *The Nazis – A Warning from History*, 4 September 1999.

6. Ibid.; Christopher R. Browning, *Ordinary Men, Reserve Police Battalion 101 and the Final Solution in Poland*, HarperPerennial, New York, 1992, p. 55.

7. Ibid.

8. Peter White, et al., *Der Dienstkalender Heinrich Himmlers 1941–42*, Christians Verlag, Hamburg, 1999, December 1941 entry.

9. Walter Dornberger, *V2 – Der Schuss ins Weltall*, Bechtle Verlag, Esslingen, 1952, pp. 172–3; Manvell and Fraenkel, *Himmler*, pp. 168–70.

10. Heinz Guderian, *Panzer Leader*, Michael Joseph, London, 1952, p. 446.

11. Rudolf Semmler, *Goebbels – The Man Next to Hitler*, Westhouse, London, 1945, p. 179.

12. Roger Manvell and Heinrich Fraenkel, *The Canaris Conspiracy*, David McKay, New York, 1969, p. 195.

3 The Vengeful Chameleon

1. Central Archives, RFSA, Hoover Institute, 'Marga Concerzowo to Heinrich Himmler', 13 April 1928.

2. Alfred Andersch, *Der Vater eines Mörders*, Diogenes, Zurich, 1980, pp. 116–17.

3. Georg Hallgarten, 'Mein Mitschüler Heinrich Himmler', *Germania Judaica, Bulletin der Kölner Bibliothek zur Geschichte des Deutschen Judentums* 2. 1960/1, pp. 4–7.

4. Ibid.

5. Himmler's diaries, Central Archives, Hoover Institute, Stanford.

6. Ibid.

7. Central Archives, Microfilm 58, Hoover Institute, Stanford.

8. Ibid., Letter, 23 April 1923.

9. Ibid.

10. Ibid., Letter to Rössner, 12 March 1924.

11. Ibid.

12. Himmler's diaries, Central Archives, Hoover Institute, Stanford, entry of 17 June 1919.

13. Himmler's diaries, entry in December 1919. See also Manvell and Fraenkel, *Heinrich Himmler*, p. 9.

14. Werner Angress and Bradley F. Smith, 'Diaries of Himmler's Early Years', *Journal of Modern History*, vol. xxxi, December 1959, p. 217. I am indebted to Professor Werner Angress for copies and translation of original diary entry.

15. Himmler's diaries, 1922 entry. See also Manvell and Fraenkel, *Heinrich Himmler, Himmler*, p. 7.

16. Himmler's diaries, 1921 entry. See also Manvell and Fraenkel, *Himmler*, p. 9.

17. Himmler's diaries, 1921 entry. See also Manvell and Fraenkel, *Himmler*, p. 8.

18. Himmler's diaries, 1921 entry. See also Manvell and Fraenkel, *Himmler*, p. 7.

19. Himmler's diaries, 1921 entry. See also Manvell and Fraenkel, *Himmler*, p. 11.

20. Ibid.
21. Himmler's diaries, 1921 entry. See also Manvell and Fraenkel, *Himmler*, p. 6.
22. Himmler's diaries, 1921 entry. See also Manvell and Fraenkel, *Himmler*, p. 7.

4 The SS State

1. Manvell and Fraenkel, *Himmler*, p. 16.
2. Central Archives, Hoover Institute, undated RFSS Microfilm 161, Walter Darré, *Neuadel aus Blut und Boden*, Eher Verlag, Munich, 1934, part 2, p. 5.
3. Central Archives, Hoover Institute, RFSS Microfilm 155, 18 January 1943, *Die Schutzstaffel*.
4. Central Archives, Hoover Institute, Ludolf Haase, *Der Nationalsozialistische Orden*, undated Microfilm 98.
5. Ibid.
6. Konrad Heiden, *Die Geburt des Dritten Reiches*, Europa Verlag, Zurich, 1934, p. 27.
7. Bundesarchiv Koblenz, Microfilm 87.
8. Heiden, op. cit., p. 28.
9. International Military Tribunal, Nuremberg (IMT), 1948, vol. XXX, p. 226.
10. Fritz Tobias, *Der Reichstagbrand*, Groete'sche Verlag, Rastatt, 1962, p. 135.
11. Rudolf Diels, *Lucifer Ante Portas*, Deutsche Verlagsanstalt, Stuttgart, 1950, p. 412.
12. Albert Speer, *The Slave State*, Weidenfeld & Nicolson, 1981, p. 147.
13. Gerald Reitlinger, *The SS – Alibi of a Nation*, William Heinemann, London, 1956, p. 5.
14. Eugen Kogon, *Der SS Staat*, Verlag des Druckhauses, Berlin, 1947, p. 32.
15. Dr Carl Marcus, pers. comm.
16. Letter from Dr Richard Korherr to Himmler, 13 August 1943, in Korherr's private papers.
17. Letter from Richard Hildebrandt to Himmler, undated, in Korherr's private papers.

5 Peace

1. Martin Bernu and Maxim Mourand, *Friedensinitiativen Vachpolitik im Zweiten Weltkrieg*, Droste Verlag, Düsseldorf, 1972.
2. Jonathan Victor Marshall, unpublished MA thesis, *Bankers and the Search for a Separate Peace during World War II*, Cornell University, 1981, footnote to thesis.
3. CIA archives in author's possession.
4. Colonel Christie papers, Churchill College, Cambridge.
5. Sir Peter Tennant, unpublished manuscript and pers. comm.
6. Marshall, op. cit.
7. Swedish Intelligence source 'M', comm. with Peter Falk.
8. Marshall, op. cit.
9. Sir William Stephenson, pers. comm.
10. Letter, FBI Director J. Edgar Hoover to Berle, US State Department, FBI documents in possession of author.
11. Ibid.
12. Paper concerning the background of Princess Stefanie von Hohenlohe-Waldenburg, FBI document in author's possession.

13. A memorandum based on electronic surveillance of the encounter at the hotel, 30 November 1940, FBI document in author's possession.
14. Ibid.
15. Sir William Stephenson, pers. comm.
16. Marshall, op. cit.
17. Intercepted letter, Princess Stefanie von Hohenlohe-Waldenburg to Sir William Wiseman, 17 December 1940, and statement by Wiseman to FBI, FBI documents in author's possession.
18. Eight pages of transcript (incomplete) on meeting of Cyril F. Tiarks and Schacht, FBI documents in author's possession.
19. J. Cacciotti, comm. with author.
20. Lord Avon's papers, Aston University.
21. Documenti Diplomatici Italiani, 9th session, v-u Roma 1968, Lequio to Ciano 14 March 1941.
22. Kenneth de Courcy, unpublished letters, in author's possession.
23. Undated SD report on negotiations with Dulles, approx. spring 1943, in Bezymenski's papers, Moscow; letters from Hohenlohe to unnamed SS authority mid-February 1943, in Lev Bezymenski's papers.
24. Schellenberg papers, PRO.
25. Ibid.
26. James Angleton, pers. conv.
27. Marshall, op. cit.
28. Schellenberg papers, PRO.
29. Sir Peter Tennant, pers. comm.
30. Letter from Kranefuss to Brand, 3 August 1944, RFSS Microfilm 22.
31. Schellenberg papers.
32. Mario Rodriguez Aragon,

'Operation KN', Pueblo, 21 August 1958.
33. Sir Peter Tennant, pers. comm.
34. Anthony Cave Brown, Bodyguard of Lies, Star, London, 1977.
35. Sir Peter Tennant, pers. comm.
36. C. L. Sulzberger, A Long Row of Candles, Macmillan, London, 1969, p. 287.
37. Sir Peter Tennant, pers. comm.
38. Lord Avon's papers, Aston University.
39. Sir Anthony Eden cable to Victor Mallet, 23 December 1944, Lord Avon's papers.

6 The Stockholm Connection

1. Schellenberg papers, PRO.
2. Sir Peter Tennant, pers. comm.
3. Peter Falk, unpublished manuscript in author's possession.
4. Major Frederick Busch, 'Der Fall Krämer', Interrogation Report on Busch UFSETCI-FIR/67, National Archives, Washington. Also typewritten memoirs of Busch, in author's possession, p. 2. (Note: page numbers reflect sides of typescript and not original pagination sequence used by Busch.)
5. Peter Falk, pers. comm. and unpublished manuscript.
6. Peter Falk, pers. comm.
7. Ibid.
8. Ibid.
9. The appointment was discussed in three papers at the PRO, unfortunately withdrawn since my request to see them.
10. Dorothy Furse, pers. comm.
11. Harold Nicolson, pers. diary,

October 1943, and James Lees-Milne, *Nicolson – A biography*, vol. II, *1930–68*, Chatto & Windus, London, 1981.

12. Saarson, pers. conv. Peter Falk.

7 The Maison Rouge Meeting

1. Christian Lambolay, *Strasbourg Disparu, La Maison Rouge et L'Homme de Fer*, Contades, 1990, p. 15.
2. Ibid., p. 66.
3. Ibid., p. 69.
4. Ibid., p. 73.
5. Ibid., p. 69.
6. Ibid.
7. Ibid., p. 138.
8. Ibid., p. 64; conv. with Christine Jung.
9. Ibid., p. 64; conv. with Jung and Madame Baldet.
10. Ibid., p. 64.
11. Ibid., p. 69; conv. with Jung.
12. Marshall, op. cit.
13. Red House report, US National Archives, Washington, and British Public Record Office, released 1999, ref. BT 64/397/65656.
14. Ibid., British version.
15. Ibid.
16. Ibid., American version.
17. Ibid., British version.
18. Ibid.
19. Ibid.
20. Ibid.
21. Ibid.
22. Schellenberg papers, Washington, released to author 1989, questioning session 3.6.45, at Camp 020.
23. Albert Speer, conv. with author.
24. Dennis Rigden, *Kill the Führer*, Sutton, 1999, p. 76.

25. Ibid.
26. Ibid., p. 78.
27. Ibid.
28. Marshall, op. cit.
29. Ibid.
30. Ibid.
31. Sir Peter Tennant, pers. comm.
32. Ibid.
33. Marshall, op. cit. p. 6.
34. James Angleton, pers. conv.
35. Marshall, op. cit.
36. Ibid.
37. Ibid.
38. Sir Edward Playfair, pers. conv.
39. Jasper Leadbitter, pers. conv.
40. Sir Peter Tennant, pers. conv.
41. Ibid.
42. PRO FO 48073 N12503/40566/42, Jerram to Sevin 5.9.45.
43. Sir Peter Tennant pers. conv. and Sir Peter Tennant, *Touchlines of War*, University of Hull Press, 1988, p. 56.
44. Ibid., p. 58.
45. Heinz Pol, 'Nazis run world bank', *P.M.*, 11 May 1944.
46. Orvis Schmidt, 'Conversation in Switzerland with Dr McKittrick', *Morgenthau Diary*, pp. 329–33.
47. Marshall, op. cit.
48. Sir Edward Playfair, pers. conv.
49. Marshall, op. cit.
50. Red House report, British version.
51. Ibid.
52. Schellenberg papers, released to author 1989, point 17, p. 188 of summary as well as in detail in appendices.
53. Copy courtesy of Dr Scott Newton, Dean of History, Cardiff University.
54. Henry Morgenthau Jnr, *Germany Is Our Problem*.
55. Victor Klemperer, *Und so ist alles*

schwankend, *Tagebücher Juni bis Dezember 1945*, Aufbau-Taschenbuch-Verlag, Berlin, 1995, p. 361.
56. Sir Peter Tennant, pers. conv.
57. Red House report, American version.

8 Loose Ends

1. Andreas Biss, *Der Stopp der Endlösung, Kampf gegen Himmler und Eichmann in Budapest*, Seewald Verlag, Stuttgart, 1966, pp. 205–6.
2. McClellan statement, 6 February 1945, quoted in Lebor, op. cit., p. 274.
3. Biss, op. cit., p. 157.
4. Ibid., p. 163.
5. Lebor, op. cit., p. 263.
6. Biss, op. cit., p. 164.
7. IMT XI, p. 306.
8. Ibid.
9. Frau Hess, pers. conv.
10. IMT XI, p. 306; Jochen von Lang, *Der Adjutant, Karl Wolff*, Herbig, Munich, 1985.
11. Kurt Becher, Affidavit produced for Nuremberg hearing, case XI Doc NG2675.
12. K. Mocarki, *Gespräche mit dem Henker*, Droste Verlag, Düsseldorf, 1978.
13. Conv. with Peter Falk; Walter Schellenberg, *Schellenberg's Memoirs*, Odhams, London, 1953, pp. 433–5.
14. Howard and Secker, *A History of Israel*, Blackwell, London, 1971, p. 238.
15. Schellenberg papers, Washington, released to author 1989, pp. 33, 38, 55.
16. Ibid., p. 99.

17. Felix Kersten, *The Kersten Memoirs – 1940–45*, Macmillan, New York, 1957, p. 238.
18. *Ciano's Diaries*, pp. 39–43, edited by Malcolm Muggeridge, Heinemann, London, 1947.
19. Ibid.
20. Manvell and Fraenkel, *Himmler*, p. 159.
21. Ibid., p. 172.
22. Ibid.
23. Ibid., p. 195, and Reitlinger, op. cit., pp. 300–1.
24. Allen Dulles, *Germany's Underground*, Macmillan, New York, 1947, p. 163.
25. Schellenberg papers, Washington, p. 72.
26. Ibid., p. 72.
27. Ibid.
28. Ibid.
29. Manvell and Fraenkel, *Canaris*, p. 197.
30. Ibid., p. 224.
31. Rudolf Höss, *Memoirs in Captivity After the War – Commandant of Auschwitz*, Weidenfeld & Nicolson, London, 1959.
32. Albert Speer, pers. comm.; see also his *Inside the Third Reich*, Weidenfeld & Nicolson, London, 1970.
33. Letter from Berger to Himmler, July 1943, RFSS microfilm 56.
34. Letter from Berger to Himmler, March 1943, RFSS microfilm 56.
35. Albert Speer, pers. comm.; see also his *Inside the Third Reich*.
36. Ibid.
37. Ibid.
38. Ibid.
39. Ibid.
40. Ibid.

41. Schellenberg papers, Washington, pp. 53, 64, 94, 106.
42. Ibid., pp. 105–6.
43. Ibid., pp. 105–8.
44. Ibid., p. 108.
45. Ibid.
46. Hugh Thomas, *Doppelgängers*, Fourth Estate, London, 1995.

9 Preparations for Survival

1. Progress list of wanted war criminals, 4 pages, Eichmann Trial Documents, unedited papers. (Prepared March, amended December 1961.) Wiener Library, London.
2. Schellenberg papers, US Department of Army, Washington, released to author December 1989, p. 102.
3. Ibid.
4. Axel Springer, *Aus Sorge um Deutschland*, Springer Verlag, Hamburg, 1980. (Released when his eldest son Axel was found in Hamburg, having committed suicide.)
5. Schellenberg papers, PRO London, from V/48/F8 (Phelps) to WRC (Lt Burke), 2 January 1948 (ref. KV2/99 241d).
6. Ibid., KV2/99 240d.
7. Ibid., KV2/99. Questioning of Schellenberg by Captain Khan, 12 February 46.
8. Ibid., KV2/99, ref. 030/8/121.
9. 'Brown Book', courtesy of Dr Scott Newton, Dean of History, Cardiff University.
10. Exhibits to the report to the Attorney General, August 1983, Operation Selectionboard, p. 2.
11. Courtesy French Intelligence agent M.
12. Schellenberg papers, PRO K2/99. Questioning Schienke, Maria, ref. 030/8/121.
13. Ibid.
14. Ibid.
15. Ibid.
16. Schellenberg papers, US Department of Army, Washington, p. 117.
17. Ibid., p. 118.
18. Ibid., and investigations by author at Trosa.
19. Testimony of Sir Peter Tennant and Peter Falk, comm. with author.
20. Willi Frischauer, *Himmler*, Odhams Press, London, 1953, p. 256.
21. E. H. Cookridge, *Gehlen*, Hodder & Stoughton, London, 1971, p. 97.
22. Schellenberg papers, US Department of Army, Washington, p. 111.
23. Peter Cremer, personal comm. with author.
24. Letter from Luftwaffe to Baumbach, reproduced in P. W. Stahl, *"Geheingeschwader" KG200, Die Wahrheit nach über 30 Jahren*, Motorbuch Verlag, Stuttgart, 1977.
25. Manvell and Fraenkel, *Himmler*, p. 273.

10 The Arrest of Heinrich Hitzinger

1. Peter Cremer, pers. comm.
2. Nigel Hamilton, *'MONTY' Master of the Battlefield*, Hamish Hamilton, 1983, p. 523; P. Odgers, pers. comm.
3. Willi Frischauer, *Himmler*, Odhams Press, London, 1953, p. 254.
4. Heinz Höhne, *The Order of the Death's Head*, Secker & Warburg, London, 1970, p. 579.

5. Frischauer, op. cit., p. 256.

6. CROWCASS (Criminal Registry of War Criminals and Security Subjects) was run by Colonel Palfrey (British), and was an amalgam of the United Nations War Crimes List and 80,000 names in SHAEF's Personality Black List, described by Patrick Dean of the Foreign Office as misleading and unreadable (FO 371 51033).

7. Werner Grothmann and Heinz Macher, pers comm.

8. Airey Neave, pers. comm.

9. Paul Wolfgang, Göring, Brockhampton Press, 1999.

10. After the Battle magazine, No 14, p. 31.

11. Ibid.

12. Manvell and Fraenkel, op. cit., p. 274.

13. Ibid.

14. Ibid., p. 245.

15. Ibid., p. 244.

16. Ibid., p. 245.

17. Ibid., p. 246.

18. Ibid.

19. Ibid.

20. Ibid., p. 247.

21. After the Battle magazine, No 19, Report of Captain John Excell.

22. M. A. C. Osborne, pers. comm.

23. Ça Ira, Imperial War Museum.

24. Ibid.

25. Ibid.

26. S. Ganzer, 'Über einen eigenartigen hysterischen Dämmerzustand', Arch Psychiat., 30633, 1898.

27. Dr Wells, pers. comm., and Dr Wells' account to Oxford Medical Society, in author's possession.

28. Manvell and Fraenkel, Himmler, p. 247.

29. Dr Wells' account to Oxford Medical Society, op. cit.

30. Ibid.

31. Rimmer, pers. comm.

32. Dr Wells' account, op. cit.

33. Ibid.

34. Whittaker's diary, in possession of family.

35. Dr Wells' account, op. cit.

36. Colonel Browne, pers. comm.

37. Rimmer, pers. comm.

38. Whittaker's diary, op. cit.

39. Dr Wells' account, op. cit.

40. Ibid.

41. Friedrich Muller, The Price of Glory, 1960.

42. Dr Wells' family, pers. comm.

43. Whittaker's testimony to Rimmer.

44. Ibid.

45. Ibid.

46. Colonel Browne, pers. comm.

47. Dr Ian Morris, pers. comm.

48. Colonel Browne, pers. comm.

49. Mrs Attkins, pers. comm.

50. Colonel Browne, pers. comm.

51. Whittaker's diary and testimony to Rimmer.

52. Whittaker's diary and testimony to Rimmer.

53. Rimmer, pers. comm.

54. NARG 238 M 1270/R/26/466.

55. Rimmer, pers. comm.

56. Letter, Western European Department to author, 5 February 1981, in author's possession.

57. Manvell and Fraenkel, Himmler, p. 273.

58. Dr Wells, pers. conv.

59. Colonel Browne, pers. conv.

60. Colonel Osborne, pers. conv.

61. Brigadier J. S. K. Boyd, pers. comm.

62. Dr Morris, pers. conv.
63. Whittaker's diary, and *After the Battle*, No 14, p. 35.

11 Operation Globetrotter

1. Dr Carl Marcus, pers. conv. with author.
2. Dr Marcus, pers. conv. with author and Adrian Liddell Hart.
3. Ibid.
4. Klaus Barbie and the United States Government, Exhibits to the Attorney General, CI-SIR/63.
5. Dr Marcus, pers. comm.
6. Ibid.
7. Ibid.
8. Dr Marcus, pers. conv. with author and Adrian Liddell Hart.
9. Ibid.
10. Dr Marcus, comm. to Adrian Liddell Hart.
11. Dr Marcus, conv. with author and Adrian Liddell Hart.
12. Klaus Barbie and US Government, Exhibit CI-SIR/63.
13. Ibid.
14. Ibid., U/152583.
15. Dr Marcus, pers. conv. with author and Adrian Liddell Hart, and Barbie exhibit Y.10643.
16. Y.10643, 7 February 1947, Kirkpatrick Special Agent CI Corps, 97th CIC Detachment.
17. 1525831, 3 February 1947, Point 5 of report.
18. 652583, 8 March 1947, report of Captain Frazier.
19. File D 95246, 20 March 1947, report of John Dormer.
20. D 153208 CIC S3, 3 June 1947, Special Agent Charles R. Hayes.
21. Report of Dale M. Garvey, Exhibits to Attorney General.
22. Dr Marcus, pers. conv. with author and Adrian Liddell Hart.
23. Ibid.

12 Doubt

1. Whittaker's account to Rimmer.
2. Ibid.
3. Ibid.
4. Rimmer's testimony.
5. Ibid., and Corporal Bill Carrotte's account in the *Daily Mirror*, 6 May 1985.
6. Mrs Attkins, pers. conv., and Whittaker, testimony to Rimmer.
7. H. Fraenkel, pers. conv., and Willi Frischauer, op. cit., Prelude, p. 10.
8. Colonel Browne, pers. conv.
9. Ibid.
10. Ibid.
11. Dr Morris, pers. conv.
12. Colonel Browne, testimony to author.
13. Professor Keith Mant, pers. conv.
14. Dr Richard Bogle, pers. conv.
15. Koblenz Archives.
16. Speer, comm. with author.
17. Peter Padfield, *Himmler*, Macmillan, London, 1990.
18. Speer, conv. with author.
19. Dr Marcus, conv. with author.
20. Heinz Macher and Werner Grothmann, conv. with author.
21. Colonel Browne, testimony to author.
22. Colonel John McCowan, script donated to author.
23. Ibid.
24. Ibid.

25. Dr Morris, pers. conv.

26. D. W. Williams, pers. conv.

13 Sonderbevollmächtigter – the 'plenipotentiary extraordinary'

1. Captain Henry Denham, pers. conv.

2. Schellenberg papers.

3. *The Schellenberg Memoirs: A Record of the Nazi Secret Service*, ed. and trans. Louis Hagen, André Deutsch, London, 1956, pp. 449–50.

4. Schellenberg papers.

5. Sir Peter Tennant, pers. comm.

6. Strangely for the British Public Record Office, these telegrams were not identified in the catalogues by their subject but bunched together in a way that implied they covered the same topic. All were marked as unavailable to the public. These were referenced in the 1980s but have since been removed from the catalogues. This anomaly is confirmed by Dr Scott Newton.

7. Sir Peter Tennant, pers. conv. and unpublished manuscript.

8. Peter Falk, pers. comm.

9. Sir Peter Tennant, pers. comm.

10. Sir Peter Tennant, pers. comm. See also E. H. Cookridge, *Gehlen – Spy of the Century*, Hodder & Stoughton, London, 1971.

11. Schellenberg papers.

12. Josef Garlinski, *The Swiss Corridor*, Dent, London, 1981, p. 194.

13. Sir Peter Tennant and Peter Falk, pers. comm.

14. Sir Stuart Hampshire.

15. Sir Peter Tennant, pers. comm.

16. Sir Peter Tennant pers. comm. and Jacob Wallenberg, pers. conv.

17. Schellenberg papers.

18. Peter Falk and Sir Peter Tennant, pers. comm.

19. Sir Peter Tennant, pers. comm.

20. Among Lord Avon's papers at Aston University, the file on the 'Japanese Legation discussions' is closed until 2021. Three files lie in the British Public Record Office, also unavailable to the public and now no longer catalogued, marked 'Japanese Legation Talks, Stockholm', dated May 1945, and a telegram sent to London that month regarding the 'Japanese Legation, Stockholm', unavailable until 2021. The references to these files, also witnessed by Dr Scott Newton, no longer exist in the catalogues and will not be released to the public or researchers in the future.

21. Sir Peter Tennant, pers. comm.

22. Schellenberg papers (FBI version).

23. 'R.R.', American Military Intelligence officer, pers. comm.

24. 'R.R.', pers. conv.

25. Schellenberg papers.

26. Sir Stuart Hampshire, pers. conv.

27. Sir Dick White, pers. conv.

28. Schellenberg papers.

29. Dr Marcus, pers. comm.

30. Dr Marcus, pers. conv.

31. Schellenberg papers.

32. Foreword, Final Interrogation Report, Schellenberg papers – all versions.

33. Sir Stuart Hampshire, pers. conv.

34. Schellenberg papers, CIA and FBI versions.

35. Schellenberg papers, PRO version.

36. James Angleton, pers. conv.

37. Schellenberg papers, PRO

version, KV2/99 67897 T259
(9.12.47).
38. Schellenberg papers, PRO
version, KV2/99 67897 T263
(17.12.47).
39. Adrian Liddell Hart, pers. comm.
40. Bernadotte family, London, pers.
comm.
41. Schellenberg papers.
42. James Angleton, pers. conv.
43. Sir Elwyn Jones and Anthony
Marreco, pers. comm.
44. Schellenberg papers, PRO version
KV 2/99 264, *Times* cutting 21.5.49,
extract for file 600,561.

45. *The Schellenberg Memoirs*, op. cit.;
see also André Brissaud, *The Nazi
Secret Service*, Bodley Head, London,
1972, p. 17.
46. Brissaud, op. cit., p. 16.
47. Schellenberg papers, FBI version.
48. Heinrich Fraenkel, pers. comm.
49. *The Schellenberg Memoirs*, op. cit.
50. James Angleton, pers. conv.
51. Anthony Cave Brown, *Oil, God
and Gold*, Houghton Mifflin, Boston,
1999, p. 123.
52. Rufina Philby, *The Private Life of
Kim Philby – the Moscow Years*,
St Ermins Press, 1999, p. 278.

Index